AMERICA'S WAR IN SYRIA

AMERICA'S WAR IN SYRIA

Fighting with Kurdish Anti-ISIS Forces

BY
TILL "BAZ" PAASCHE, PHD
JOHN FOXX
SHAUN MURRAY

CASEMATE

Philadelphia & Oxford

Published in the United States of America and Great Britain in 2022 by
CASEMATE PUBLISHERS
1950 Lawrence Road, Havertown, PA 19083, USA
and
The Old Music Hall, 106–108 Cowley Road, Oxford OX4 1JE, UK

Hardcover Edition: ISBN 978-1-63624-152-4
Digital Edition: ISBN 978-1-63624-153-1

A CIP record for this book is available from the British Library

Printed and bound in the United Kingdom by TJ Books
Typeset in India by Lapiz Digital Services, Chennai.

For a complete list of Casemate titles, please contact:

CASEMATE PUBLISHERS (US)
Telephone (610) 853-9131
Fax (610) 853-9146
Email: casemate@casematepublishers.com
www.casematepublishers.com

CASEMATE PUBLISHERS (UK)
Telephone (01865) 241249
Email: casemate-uk@casematepublishers.co.uk
www.casematepublishers.co.uk

Contents

Introduction   1

Part I From Symbolic Airstrikes to First Coalitions:
June 2014–September 2015   7

Chapter 1 The Fall of Mosul: June–July 2014   9
Chapter 2 Shingal: August–November 2014   17
Chapter 3 Securing the Earth Berm I:
          December 2014–February 2015   21
Chapter 4 Securing the Earth Berm II: March 2015   35
Chapter 5 The First Wave of Aggressive Airstrikes:
          March–April 2015   45
Chapter 6 The First Major Offensive Against Daesh: May 2015   55
Chapter 7 Occupying Arab Lands: June 2015   63
Chapter 8 Daesh's Counter Offensive: July–September 2015   71

Part II The New Syrian Democratic Forces Go to War:
October 2015 to December 2016   77

Chapter 9 A New Alliance Is Formed:
          October 2015–January 2016   79
Chapter 10 Operation *Wrath of Khabur*: February–March 2016   101
Chapter 11 Between Operations: March–April 2016   121
Chapter 12 Crossing the Euphrates: May 2016   133
Chapter 13 The Meat Grinder: June 2016   145
Chapter 14 Rolling with the Operators: July–December 2016   167

Part III Defeating the Caliphate: An American Success Story:
January 2017–September 2019   175

Chapter 15 Rojava Becomes Formal: January–February 2017   177
Chapter 16 Operation *Wrath of Euphrates*: March–October 2017   189
Chapter 17 *Al-Jazeera Storm* and the American Exit Strategy:
                    September 2017–September 2019   195

Part IV Madness: October 2019–November 2020   201

Chapter 18 "America Has Blood on Its Hands": October 2019   203

Conclusion   211
Glossary   219
Endnotes   223
Index   235

"The S.D.F. is the best unconventional partner force we've ever had, anywhere."
—Brett McGurk, former coordinator of the war against ISIS

"The U.S.-led operation to defeat ISIS in Syria is the most successful unconventional military campaign in history."
—Elizabeth Dent for the Middle East Institute

Introduction

Sometime in June 2016, Baz found himself awake in a combat medic's perfect nightmare, hanging on the side of a civilian Bongo van, trying to follow a thin pink line on an otherwise empty GPS screen through the desert. On the back of the flatbed moaned about 10 civilians, or what was left of them. In a panicking stampede fueled by hunger and dehydration, the people had just tried to escape the besieged city of Manbij in northern Syria when they stumbled into a maze of improvised explosive devices (IEDs) the enemy had planted to fortify their stronghold. Alone amidst amputations, blood, dying children, and bodies turned to Jell-O from the blasts, Baz remembered John, the former U.S. Marine who had been stationed nearby after his Kurdish unit had been chewed up in another gigantic cluster-fuck the day before, involving the same IEDs, an ambush, and explosive rounds used against friendly forces. But we are getting ahead of ourselves.

"*Cek, cek*—left, left," Baz yelled in his broken Kurdish to an Arab driver who did not understand him. After more screaming and pointing through wind and dust, the van stopped in front of the shot-up house that the Kurdish unit had transformed into a forward operating base (FOB). Recognizing the commander of their medic team, Kurdish fighters and international volunteers huddled around the van.

"I need help!" Baz yelled at his fellows, who were now staring at the mayhem of mangled bodies on the flatbed. Whereas everyone else was frozen, John spun around and grabbed his chest rig. Without hesitation, he jumped right onto the back of the Bongo van. Immediately Baz barked, "*Zu zu habibi*—Go go my friend" to the driver, who floored it and made the tiny engine scream violently.

"Tell me what to do," was all John said. The perfect response to a severely imperfect situation. Unbelievable. Flying together through the desert in this moment of complete and utter despair forged a bond between the German leftist academic and the conservative U.S. Marine that perhaps only other combat veterans can comprehend. The universe had made them brothers-in-arms. Whether they liked it or not, they were now bound to each other and thus decided to make the most of it.[1]

Having seen and appreciated John's instant, instinctive response to the situation, Baz developed a deep respect for the U.S. Marine Corps, a respect other former Marines would soon confirm over and over again when they spearheaded the bloody urban assault we were all caught up in together. For John, this event had such a profound impact on his life that it initiated a chain of events that would ultimately lead to the idea of writing this book.

Baz and Shaun, meanwhile, had had their connecting moment in a small village outside Tel Tamir over a year earlier, in spring 2015. They had met in a guerilla camp somewhere in the Iraqi mountains from where they had been smuggled into Syria to join the YPG, the Kurdish People's Defense Units. After receiving some rather rudimentary training, Shaun, an Irishman with, according to *The New York Times*, "bright red hair and skin pale as the sky"[2] and Baz, the academic without any prior military experience, were deployed to the front lines in the defensive battle against the Islamic State (also called ISIS, IS or ISIL).

Back then, the YPG and their sister forces, the woman's defense units of the YPJ, were desperately trying to hold the lines against an enemy that had overwhelming firepower and momentum on their side. During those desperate days behind the earth berms the Kurdish forces had put up for cover, Baz and Shaun witnessed the opening air campaign by the U.S.-led Operation *Inherent Resolve*, a pivotal moment that marked the beginning of America's war against the Islamic State in Syria.

In early 2015, just before first light, when the eyes were getting heavy after a long night on guard, to Shaun and Baz, the four roaring engines of the AC-130 gunship were the most relieving sound imaginable.

Seeing the 40mm cannons rain death and destruction at the enemy was something words cannot describe. Only weeks earlier, ISIS had overrun a neighboring unit and beheaded several YPG/YPJ fighters. Now those enemies were dead, and soon the Kurdish forces Shaun and Baz were part of would advance over their still-smoldering bodies, pushing their surviving friends deep into the desert. With aggressive American airpower supporting the YPG/YPJ, the momentum had changed in matter of weeks. For the first time since the Fall of Mosul in the summer of 2014, anti-ISIS forces went on the offensive and carved a significant piece of territory from the Caliphate, the pseudo-state that Islamic State had announced.

However, while the operation looked spectacular on maps that could be held up during PR stunts, on the ground, it was rather boring. In fact, it was so unspectacular that fighters were becoming annoyed with the lack of action to the extent that YPG/YPJ command had to address all forces over the radio and explain that no fighting meant no dead, and that that was a good thing.

In hindsight, we conclude that this first wave of American air strikes and the loosely coordinated advance of Kurdish units into an empty stretch of desert was a test run. By spring 2015, ISIS had enraged the Western world, including President Barack Obama's liberal base, enough that an intervention was overdue. Yet, Obama had promised to end all military adventures in the Middle East, which ruled out a deployment of American combat troops. Obama thus needed a somewhat democratic militia to do the heavy lifting on the ground. The problem was that by then all democratic militias in Syria had been eaten up by the Islamists. With the Iraqi Army not operational and the Kurdish Peshmerga unwilling to advance, the Kurds in Syria and the YPG/YPJ remained Obama's only somewhat viable partner.

The problem was that the Kurds were connected with the leftist PKK, a listed terror organization that is in conflict with NATO partner Turkey. Born out of necessity and simply denying the very obvious links between the YPG/YPJ and the PKK, the American military began forming a careful coalition with the Kurdish movement for the better part of 2015. The Abdel Aziz and following Tel Abiat operations had been a tentative first date between the two unlikely partners: the Kurdish revolutionaries and Obama's military. During this first of four phases of America's war against Islamic State in Syria, the Kurdish homeland was liberated from ISIS.

The first and only time we all met in the field was on the eve of Operation *Sheddad* in March 2016, a date that coincided with the beginning of the second phase of America's war on ISIS. The meeting involved a secret briefing by the YPG's highest general and a bizarre piece of German intelligence. Less than 12 hours later, the YPG/YPJ would descend from the Abdel Aziz mountain ridge into the enemy's wasteland, and the dying would begin.

What makes the al-Shaddadi operation interesting in hindsight is not its comparatively small battle but that it was the first large operation for the new Kurdish-Arab-Christian coalition called the Syrian Democratic Forces, or SDF. Enabled by this wide coalition during the second phase, Daesh (the Arabic acronym for Islamic State, used as a derogatory term to challenge the legitimacy of Islamic State) heartland in the Arab desert could finally be assaulted. Whereas there had been no direct communication between the Kurdish forces on the ground and Operation *Inherent Resolve* in 2015, by spring 2016, Kurdish fighters were given the electronic means and trust to call in air strikes, including close air support by the loitering A-10 "Warthogs" that painted white circles in the skies over *Sheddad*.

The operation was also the moment when American and British special forces began appearing on the ground and French operators started blowing up enemy suicide bombers with their missiles. During this operation, trust was built between all involved. Together, the SDF and America, with support from France and the UK, successfully liberated an ISIS-held city and, consequently, by summer 2016, the young coalition felt confident enough to attack the Caliphate where it would really hurt.

The main battle of 2016 was for the major Daesh stronghold Manbij. Backed by AC-130 gunships, F18s, and U.S., British, and French special forces, SDF units, including John, participated in an amphibious assault across the Euphrates. With heavy American support that for the first time included large-scale deployments of special forces teams at the front lines, the SDF stormed toward Manbij, where they soon encountered fierce resistance. With mounting casualty numbers, the American operators began a close cooperation with Baz's new medic team.

★

Besides providing insightful analysis of America's role during the war, in this book we aim to introduce its allies on the ground and explain why they are in the fight. We show that, different to all other anti-ISIS forces, the YPG/YPJ, and later the SDF, were not just fighting *against* the Islamists but *for* an inherently democratic utopia. From this deep understanding of our allies and their sociopolitical agenda, an exit strategy worth its name, an exit strategy that is actually accepted by the people, will emerge almost organically. From an American military perspective, this means that American soldiers liberate instead of occupying a land they don't understand. As an American operator mumbled to Baz as they watched liberated people cheering the American soldiers, "this is a fucking nice feeling for a change."

We furthermore explain the way the Islamic State fought and why it was such an effective force. Adapting continuously to the escalating American involvement, ISIS remains a deadly opponent.

Going through the different phases of America's war shows how American foreign policy changed the battlefield from muddy, World War I-style trench warfare into a smooth, multiethnic, multireligious, pro-feminist killing machine that liberated thousands of square miles and tens of thousands of people from evil.

At the same time, we outline how America increasingly emancipated itself from Turkey's neo-Ottoman ambitions and threats and acknowledged what the Kurdish movement offered intellectually for America's sphere of influence abroad. In short, this book provides an explanation of why this military intervention was so successful.

★

This book is written from the perspective of the front lines and what we learned during the war against ISIS. We do not claim any objectivity. We went to fight fascists; there should not be anything objective about that. Given this grounded perspective, we reference the existing literature and reports carefully and only when unavoidable. When discussing events and battles at which none of us was present, we've drawn upon and refer to the many anonymous stories that circulated around the front lines. Although exaggerated over time, these narratives have become part of the local folklore. To the fighters pulling the trigger and securing the fronts, planting IEDs, or driving suicide trucks, they were reality. In a low-tech war, it is those stories that matter, not fact-checked reports targeting a Western audience. Trying to understand the conflict means listening to those tales. In many cases, the names of individuals and *taburs* (battalions within the YPG/YPJ) have been changed. Sometimes out of security concerns, but mostly because especially Baz is bad at remembering names.

Lastly, this manuscript will not reference websites detailing various body tolls, the financial costs of the war, the number of dropped bombs, or enemy positions destroyed. From our own experiences, we feel that existing databases are almost certainly inaccurate to a point of being useless. There are, for example, significant discrepancies between the official number of air strikes by the American-dominated Combined Joint Task Force—Operation *Inherent Resolve* (CJTF-OIR) and our experiences. We have seen streets littered with corpses that were eaten by dogs and later pushed into mass graves for hygiene reasons. They were not counted by anyone. Instead, we argue that those anonymous numbers are part of the problem. They help politicians and experts dissociate from the war. It seems that to decision-makers, conflicts have become statistics and bullet points. Dead humans are reduced to anonymous numbers, the next column showing how much it had cost to kill them. But anyone who has seen war does not need numbers to know its costs.

PART I

FROM SYMBOLIC AIRSTRIKES TO FIRST COALITIONS: JUNE 2014–SEPTEMBER 2015

CHAPTER I

The Fall of Mosul: June–July 2014

This story begins in June 2014 with the Fall of Mosul, an event that not only marked the symbolic beginning of what would become known as the Caliphate, but also where our personal journey through the region starts. At the time, Baz was working as an assistant professor at the University of Soran in the autonomous Kurdistan Region of Iraq. The area's uniquely complex territorial layers and the tragic story of the Kurds, a people and nation without a state, is what had drawn Baz there in the first place.

Instead of denoting a specific country, Kurdistan simply describes the Kurds' historic homelands. Geographically, the Kurds are distributed between parts of Turkey, Iran, Iraq, and Syria. In each of the four states, the Kurdish minority has been subjected to genocide, oppression, and humiliation. Given, until now, their minor geopolitical importance, the Kurds have been one of the region's underdogs whose allies, including the United States, have continuously betrayed them, leading to more genocide. Departing from this policy, as a result of the 2003 invasion of Iraq, the Kurds have been granted autonomy status.

What makes the Kurds relevant for American foreign policy in the Middle East are four characteristics that seem to apply for all geopolitically important Kurdish factions. First, despite being predominantly Sunni Muslims, the Kurds have no problem with having Islamists amongst their ranks. Even the Kurdish Islamist Party is not what one might think; Baz was able to have a heated debate with their members without incurring any personal risk. Second, for various historical reasons, many Kurds have a deeply rooted understanding of democracy that includes the rights of minorities, not just the rule of the strongest, as has been the norm in their four hosting nations. Third, when America has sided with them, they have always proven themselves a loyal partner. Since the 2003 invasion, for instance, not a single American soldier has died in the Kurdistan Region in Iraq in combat. Instead, U.S. Special Forces and Kurdish Peshmerga have an excellent track record of taking out Islamist strongholds in the Kurdish Region. Fourth, the mountains in the Kurdistan Region in Iraq have massive, partially as-yet unexplored oil reserves.[1]

Of course, this all sounds too good to be true. The first catch is the notorious inter-Kurdish rivalry. During any short interval when their people as a whole don't face an existential threat, Kurdish factions turn on each other. The other catch is that when a nation aligns itself with Kurds, either Turkey, the central government in Iraq, Iran, or the Syrian Regime become angry, and that outcome does not usually fit America's agenda.

With regard to the first catch, in the case of Iraq, the internal split runs between the two major Kurdish parties: the Kurdistan Democratic Party (KDP), run by the powerful Barzani tribe, and the Patriotic Union of Kurdistan (PUK), run by the influential Talabani family. Both parties occupy their own major city. In the case of the KDP, that is Erbil. The PUK has their stronghold in Sulaymaniyah. Both parties have their own Peshmerga forces numbering hundreds of thousands of fighters. The last time they fought each other was during the Kurdish Civil War in the 1990s, but many in the region feel that the next inter-Kurdish conflict is already brewing in Shingal—the Kurdish name for the infamous Iraqi city of Sinjar.

The KDP and the PUK, as well as some of the smaller parties, form the Kurdistan Regional Government, which meets in the Parliament in Erbil. However, the power of the Parliament should not be overstated. The Kurdistan Region remains a somewhat authoritarian tribal society in which the disgruntled are oppressed by informants and a mighty internal security service.

Yet the Kurds, in particular Barzani's KDP, are America's last allies in Iraq. With the Shia-dominated government in Baghdad listening to the mullahs in Iran, not Washington, and many Sunni Arabs having turned to the Islamists, the Kurds remained the only Iraqi success story America can boast after the long and vicious wars going back to 1991. Thus, the carefully blossoming elements of democracy, such as the shiny Parliament in Erbil, are often inflated as symbols of Iraqi democracy in order to fit the narrative that hides the obvious: that the whole Iraq War was a disaster.

To Washington, losing the Kurdish areas in Iraq would mean having lost the entire country. Even President Obama, who wanted to avoid a war by all means, could not let that happen when faced by ISIS. People in the Kurdish Region knew that. To many, it was clear that American intervention had to come eventually. The question was, how many dead would be needed for Obama's support base to accept another military "adventure" in Iraq?

★

At the beginning of summer 2014, Baz was in the process of setting up a comparatively cushy academic career. Then came ISIS, and everything spiraled out of control. As soon as Mosul fell and ISIS continued their fascist blitz further south, Baz teamed up with some journalists. Together, they drove past the reinforcements for the advancing Kurdish Peshmerga to the newly forming front lines. The closer Baz came to Mosul, the more uniforms and Humvees, previously provided by the American government, he saw along the road, where they had been left by the panicking American-trained Iraqi Army. Baz took photos of all of it, powerful symbols of the disastrous American foreign policy in the country. In Mosul, large stockpiles of American military material, including armored fighting vehicles, ammunition, and assault rifles, fell to ISIS.

When Daesh closed in on Mosul and the Iraqi Army began their hasty withdrawal, the Peshmerga of the autonomous Kurdistan Region and the advancing Islamists raced each other to fill the security vacuum that was created. While Daesh got Mosul, the Peshmerga took the oil-rich Kirkuk. The countryside in between was an ever-changing network of checkpoints, the ownership of which would change frequently. Those who got lost in this maze could literally lose their head over the situation.

When Baz and the journalists arrived at the last Peshmerga checkpoint before the Caliphate, a bizarre scene unfolded: carnival in the desert.

It looked like every Peshmerga general and their staff was there to have a glimpse of Daesh, the enemy that had the politically interested world holding its breath. Amidst a group of other clerics, a Sunni imam (a religious leader) was yelling at the Sunni Islamists and into a hundred microphones. Meanwhile, young Kurdish Peshmerga who were trying to look like U.S. Navy SEALs in knock-off 5.11 gear and bearing Airsoft scopes that were welded atop AK dust covers were posing for the elite of the international press. "Look like Rambo. Ahh yes, that's good."

About 400 yards away, outside the effective range of an AK, the next checkpoint emerged like an apocalyptic mirage from the desert heat. Flying over the guard hut was the black flag of the Islamists. Between the two checkpoints were hundreds of civilians' cars, fleeing the Caliphate through the still open borders and into the recently extended autonomous Kurdistan Region. Right then and there, it looked like any other busy desert border. Everyone was just hanging out in the open, smoking cigarettes, trying to look cool. Watching them through the binos, the Daeshis at their checkpoint were doing very much the same. Even the civilians looked somewhat relaxed. In fact, the photographers were growing frantic trying to find the money shot of desperate children that day. Later, a French TV journalist put on a helmet and body armor just for his report. He actually asked people to leave the background of their shot; apparently, they looked too casual, and that did not fit the footage people at home expected from Mosul.

During the following days and weeks, Baz drove around the front lines, interviewing confident generals or politicians and, given the quiet along their entire front, increasingly cocky Kurdish soldiers. Except for a few skirmishes at night, the new border between the Caliphate and the Iraqi part of Kurdistan remained inactive. Yet it was not suspiciously quiet, with everyone expecting an imminent attack; it was just quiet.

At the time, commentators, including Baz, speculated that the Kurds might emerge as the actual winners of the conflict. Filling the security vacuum the fleeing Iraqi Army had left, the Peshmerga extended their autonomous region to include territory that they had fought over for decades, and that was privy to their possible independence. Without going too much into the constitutional mess America's pre-emptive withdrawal in 2011 had left, the desert bordering the official and undisputed territory of the autonomous Kurdistan Region was in fact very much disputed. Different parts of the region that included Mosul, Kirkuk, and everything in between was claimed by the central government in Baghdad as well as by the Kurds. Although Article 140 of the new Iraqi Constitution clearly outlines steps to solve the problem, it is unlikely to be implemented. Since the central government would most likely lose the area to the Kurds, Baghdad has no interest in actually dealing with the problem.[2] Thus, Article 140 was (and is) ignored by Baghdad as well as Obama, who wanted a quick exit.

With the Fall of Mosul and the retreat of the Iraqi Army, the Kurdish Peshmerga simply implemented Article 140 and took those territories they had demanded since the existence of the state of Iraq. In late June 2014, with Kirkuk under the control of the Peshmerga, the Kurds were perfectly fine with the situation. They'd never wanted Mosul, an important Arab city. They wanted Kirkuk, which was indeed historically Kurdish (even Saddam Hussein acknowledged that fact when he settled Arabs in Kirkuk to change the demographics). The fact that underneath Kirkuk lies one of the largest onshore oil fields made the issue even more complicated.

The Kurds also counted on the Americans to have their back against Daesh, and banked on the fact that the enemy would surely not be foolish enough to draw the U.S. Air Force into the conflict. Out of their target's sight, Daesh would stage dozens of high mobility multipurpose wheeled vehicles ("Humvees") and suicide vehicle-borne improvised explosive devices (SVBIEDs[3]) and attack surprised Iraqi outposts with an overwhelming force. During that time, Daesh applied what Confederate General Stonewall Jackson would in the 19th century have called "defeat in detail." Although the Islamists had surprisingly limited numbers, they used speed and mobility to quickly pull together a force that would momentarily outnumber and outgun the overstretched static defenders in their ad hoc FOBs.

First, SVBIEDs would detonate themselves amidst the checkpoints or defenses, thus creating a moment of deadly confusion. Guns blazing, a broad attack formation of brand-new American Humvees, commandeered by holy warriors, would ride into the chaos and kill everyone. The enemy turned themselves into a suicidal tsunami of steel and .50cal rounds. Besides an air force that would collect intelligence and continuously bomb the staging areas for those assaults, there was little to stop this phenomenon.

This way, Daesh advanced through Iraq with rapid speed. Wherever they encountered resistance, they committed mass killings on a horrific scale. The fear they spread was part of their strategy. With stories of these killings circulating, people stopped revolting against the new rulers. Scared into submission, Daesh needed no occupying force, just a network of informants and the Hisbah, the religious police who would enforce the rules of the Caliphate. The threat of the ISIS fighters returning and the complete distrust in the abilities of their own military, the Iraqi Army, was enough to keep the civilians quiet while a surprisingly small band of apocalyptic fighters continued their breathtaking campaign.

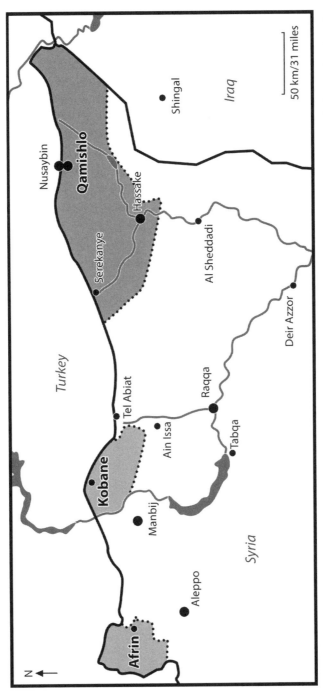

Map 1: January 2014: Three autonomous *cantons* — Afrin, Kobane, and Cizire — in Syria. The *cantons* overlap with the predominantly Kurdish areas in Syria.

CHAPTER 2

Shingal: August–November 2014

Unchecked by the international community, in early August 2014, ISIS columns attacked Sinjar, or in Kurdish Shingal, the homeland of the Yazidi people. The Yazidis are a religious minority, long predating all three monotheistic religions of Christianity, Islam, and Judaism. Ethnically, the Yazidis are a part of the Kurdish community. However, even if they are moderate or secular, culturally, the Kurdish majority grew up in a Muslim society. With their ancient religion, the Yazidis were thus always kept at the fringes of that community. To many Muslims, they were falsely known as devil-worshippers.

What unfolded next around Shingal was a genocide so brutal and absolute, so organized and cold, that it surprised even fellow Islamists. In particular, the slave markets trading captured Yazidi women and their systematic rape by their captors (in Daesh's belief system, a religious necessity to induce Judgment Day) disturbed the humanist part of the world. Everyone who watched the tragedy unravel knew that these were not some local militiamen gone mad but a new kind of evil, something that made Saddam Hussein and Osama bin Laden suddenly look like reasonable folk.

Unfortunately for the Yazidis on the ground, Obama had won an election with the promise to end the war in Iraq and later Afghanistan (and by implication not to start new ones); therefore, the commander in chief was reluctant to intervene, meaning Daesh was able to get away with genocide. Thousands of men were lined up, shot, and buried in mass graves and the women enslaved while the remaining free Yazidis died of dehydration on top of their holy mountain in the scorching summer heat.

Finally, in early August 2014, Obama ordered air strikes.[1] The justification for the first round of rather symbolic bombs was not the mass slaughter of the Yazidis but a reported Daesh assault against Erbil. Apparently, American lives were suddenly in danger and a military intervention was unavoidable. Coincidentally, Baz had talked to one of the generals, an old Peshmerga who had fought Saddam Hussein in the Kurdish mountains and was now in charge of defending Erbil, just a few weeks earlier. Having gotten some insight into the defense of the city, the Peshmerga there seemed to know what they were doing.

To believe that some artillery piece and a convoy[2] that the American bombs took out in the first wave of bombings were a threat to the city seemed far-fetched. However, in the end, the supposed Daesh attack served its purpose. While in Erbil, people were drinking latte macchiatos outside the United States consulate, the rhetoric was that American citizens were at risk of being beheaded by Daesh. By inflating the threat, the United States administration finally felt they needed to bomb the enemy, but by then, the damage had been done.

As to why, or even if, Daesh turned on Erbil remains a mystery. Years later, Arab officers in the Iraqi Army would tell Baz that the old genocidal Ba'athist elite that formed part of Daesh's leadership at the time simply hated the Kurds so much that they could not resist killing them. From all the answers floating around, this one is the least crazy. However, once the U.S. Air Force got involved, Daesh turned on the Kurdistan Region, all gloves off. The inexperienced Peshmerga soon lost several cities as well as the vital Mosul Dam.

Meanwhile, the tragedy in Sinjar continued to escalate. Tens of thousands of desperate civilians were stranded on a surrounded mountain in the unforgiving heat, and the very old and very young began dying. The following outlines how the tragedy came about but also how it continued from then on. While none of us was present personally, this account is the summary of what the involved people told us.

Having survived dozens of genocides before, the Yazidis had a relatively strong presence in the Iraqi Army and, given the unfolding situation, the freedom to take their weapons home. When the Iraqi Army withdrew, the Yazidi fighters were not too concerned since they had the means to defend themselves. What's more, their supposed Kurdish brethren, the Peshmerga, had moved into their area to fill the security vacuum the Iraqi forces had left.

Promising to protect them, the Peshmerga forces loyal to the powerful Barzani tribe confiscated the Yazidis' weaponry. When the enemy came, the Peshmerga ran as well, taking all weaponry with them. Why the Peshmerga fled remains a mystery, although there are plenty of colorful conspiracy theories. Maybe it was just another story of scared young men who spread panic like wildfire amongst their ranks. Either way, alone and outgunned, the genocide of the Yazidis unfolded.

The only one who assessed the situation correctly and tried to take action was the PKK, a Kurdish guerilla movement fighting for their rights in Turkey, whose military high command saw the existential threat the Islamists posed for the Yazidis. Unwelcomed by either the Iraqi Army or their Kurdish Peshmerga brethren, the PKK units had to infiltrate the Shingal region, where they prepared for the inevitable.

When the attack came in early August, it was those PKK fighters and various improvised Yazidi militias who stalled the Daesh attack long enough to enable many civilians to flee onto the single mountain in the otherwise flat desert: Mount Shingal. Those fighters who survived the initial battle managed to continuously stall the Daesh Humvees against all odds. Thus it was the PKK, alleged terrorists, who gave their lives on the slopes of the mountain for a people they did not know, whose language they did not understand, and whose cause was not theirs.

Some would argue that the PKK simply wanted to take over Shingal in order to extend their influence, but such abstract geopolitical visions don't make people fight the way these young men and women did. It was a deep belief in humanism and democracy that made them hold the line in a battle that could only end in their deaths.

Only a few months later, John and Shaun would fight at the same front as the PKK in Sinjar and realize that this belief in a just world was not simply propaganda, but the reason why many PKK fighters would endure the muddy and miserably cold trench warfare around the mountain. In our view, the PKK fighters who died on the mountain deserve for their story to be told.[3]

Back in August 2014, however, the Yazidis and the few remaining PKK fighters were barely surviving, while the international community had finally managed to drop a couple of bombs and a few water bottles on the mountain. And while politicians were telling each other how tragic this whole Shingal business was, it was the YPG/YPJ who opened a corridor through the Daesh lines. Fighting for survival, outnumbered, and outgunned themselves, the YPG/YPJ had the will to do the right thing when no one else would. Risking an international incident, they crossed from Syria into Iraq to help the people simply because the Yazidis asked. It is no coincidence that the YPG, but especially the YPJ, had many Yazidi volunteers among its ranks after Shingal.

With all of its bizarreness and at times dark humor, this war now began to really intrigue Baz, and soon he felt comfortable enough to cross the Syrian border into the Kurdish areas called Rojava for a second time, to see what the YPG/YPJ were really about.

CHAPTER 3

Securing the Earth Berm I: December 2014–February 2015

Meanwhile, in America, John was looking for ways to get in on some of the quickly escalating action in the Middle East. Fallujah, Tikrit, and Mosul; these were all places in which Marines had fought. The fact that the Islamists controlled them again drove the ex-Marine into a fury.

On 9/11, John was 11 years old. A few years later, he watched on TV as Marines kicked in doors during Operation *Phantom Fury* as part of the Iraq War. Being from a dysfunctional family John prefers not to talk about, he tricked his parents into signing Delayed Entry Program forms that enabled him to quasi-join the United States Marine Corps (USMC) at the age of 17. He had simply had enough of home and wanted to join the elitist brotherhood, his chosen family. Unfortunately for John, by the time he was ready to deploy, President Obama had announced the American withdrawal from Iraq and Afghanistan. There would be no combat deployment. Like so many U.S. Marines before him, John got cock-blocked by politics, a fact that left a massive, almost shameful void.

In 2012, still fresh out of the Marine Corps, John was attending college in San Diego, CA, and learning to translate his Marine Corps discipline and strength into civilian life. Knowing how to handle a gun, he did the obvious and eventually started his own security company. By building a team made up of friends from the Marine Corps, John turned a small set of specialized skills into a career in sunny Southern California. Yet the sense of unfulfillment caused by the missing combat deployment kept nagging him in the back of his mind. As everyone who has ever met John has heard him say, "Just two generations. I was just two generations of Marines too late." Over the years, he eventually realized that money and meeting celebrities would never fill this void.

Spending his free time drinking whiskey and cursing his late birth, John monitored different conflicts around the world. During the conflict in Libya in 2011, he tried to chat up the documentary filmmaker and journalist Matthew VanDyke. When the Free Syrian Army (FSA) was making the news in the escalating Syrian civil war, John booked tickets to Istanbul, Turkey. With a buddy of his, they planned to find their way to the Syrian border and try to join the FSA from there. However, when his friend got cold feet, John had to cancel his trip as well.

Once Mosul had fallen, John was online day and night, trying to get an in with anyone fighting Daesh. He was already packing to fly to Erbil with plans to try to join the Kurdish Peshmerga in Iraq when he came across an article about Jordan Matson, the American who had joined the YPG in Syria. "Bam, that was it." John got in touch with Jordan on Facebook. Jordan connected him with an anonymous Facebook profile and, a couple of weeks later, in December 2014, John was smuggled into Syria by the PKK.

John flew into Iraqi Kurdistan to fight Daesh in Syrian Kurdistan, but even though they faced the same existential threat, the different Kurdish factions hated each other so much that they kept sabotaging their operations—a fact that many Kurdish people we talked to on the streets did not appreciate. This meant that instead of taking a casual drive across the only border post between Syria and Iraq that was run by Kurds, his journey involved safe houses, smuggle routes, and guerilla camps. Having stumbled into the quagmire of inner Kurdish rivalry that would eventually get Shaun thrown into a KDP prison in 2016, John had to try to make sense of it all in December 2014. He knew about the division of the Kurdistan Region in Iraq between the KDP and the PUK and that the PUK had a better rapport with the Kurds in Syria. This was why he had landed in PUK territory. But as to why the KDP kept the border to the YPG/YPJ closed, John only began to understand this in the PKK's guerilla camp.

Both the PKK and the YPG/YPJ are part of a movement that draws on founder of the PKK Abdullah Öcalan's ideas on federalism, democracy, and freedom. In brief, historically, the PKK fights for Kurdish rights in the Kurdish parts of Turkey. Due to the firepower of the Turkish military, the leftist guerilla movement has bases in Syria, Iraq, and Iran to which they can retreat and remain for the most part unmolested by the Turkish Air Force. Members of the movement refer to themselves as *hevals*, usually translated as "friends." However, the term has complex connotations, including the leftist "comrade," the military "brother," and in the case of *hevala*, the female version, the idea of a fighting sisterhood. *Heval* or *hevala* had by now become a prefix to the name of all members of the movement. Referring to a member of the movement without using the prefix *heval/hevala* is therefore a serious insult and should be avoided at all times.

With the PKK having bases in Syria and representing Kurdish resistance, the chronically oppressed Kurds there became intrigued by Öcalan's writings. In 2004, the movement reached a critical mass and, in 2012, when the Syrian Regime had to withdraw from the Kurdish areas to protect the Syrian "rump state"[1] around Damascus, the *hevals* filled the security vacuum and implemented the idea of "Rojava" in parts of northern Syria. Rojava refers to a political theory defined by direct democracy, anti-racism, and radical gender equality; it supports a form of anti-nationalism that ignores borders in favor of a free society.

With the poorly equipped YPG/YPJ just forming, stories from that time tell of four fighters sharing one AK with only two magazines. They carried the rest of their rounds loose in their pockets. Others were armed with cheap double-barrel shotguns. In its heyday, the YPG/YPJ literally consisted of civilians rising up to fill the security void the withdrawing Syrian Regime had left. They had been hairdressers or welders the day before; now they were at improvised checkpoints with rudimentary roadblocks, heating themselves around bonfires in empty oil drums.

Daesh, who hated the atheist movement, saw Rojava as a low-hanging fruit. The genocide in Shingal having gone well from their perspective; now, they wanted more. What they did not expect was the fighting spirit of the Kurdish underdog in Syria. At the time, Rojava was not a connected territory but rather three isolated areas of Afrin, Kobane, and Cizire all along the Syria-Turkey border. The *hevals* refer to these areas as "*cantons*," drawing associations with the *cantons* in the Swiss federal system. Both Kobane and Cizire *cantons* were under heavy attack from different Islamist groups. With the Islamists having the superior weapons from Mosul, a desperate war for Kurdish survival ensued. Disappointed by their progress, the Islamists began sending in more reinforcements, which led to the dramatic escalation of the battle for Kobane in late 2014.

Meanwhile, in a safe house, John had met Erik Kostandinos "Kosta" Scurfield, a British Royal Marine whom John had coincidentally read about a few weeks prior. The online news article talked about a Royal Marine who was training with the U.S. Marine Corps in the Mojave Desert. When the training exercise was complete, the Royal Marine Battalion took a short vacation, or "libbo," in Las Vegas, Nevada. It was during this short time in Las Vegas that Kosta had made his first attempt to travel to Syria to join the Kurdish fight.

Kosta had joined the Royal Marines to protect civilians in precisely the kinds of situations the Yazidis and Kurds were now in. However, because he felt that his country had made no attempt to intervene, he chose to take matters into his own hands. These plans were thwarted when Kosta was stopped by officers with Immigration and Customs Enforcement before he could board the plane, and he ended up making headlines that would catch John's eye soon after. Although Kosta's name was not released in the article, John was impressed by the move and had circulated the article amongst his Marine buddies. When he met Kosta in person, the two bonded immediately, despite being very different. Where John would listen to his war porn audiobooks and heavy metal, Kosta would read about Malcolm X, Sophie Scholl, or Muhammad Ali. Where John wanted to fight against the bad guys, Kosta wanted to defend the good ones. He wasn't a leftist but he was seeking justice in this truly unjust world. Being critical of Western imperialism, Kosta felt that the West's meddling in the region had facilitated the growth of ISIS. Yet, Britain and America let Daesh commit genocide. This disturbed Kosta so much that he formally separated from the Royal Marines and travelled to Kurdistan. Now, he sat in a guerilla camp with his conservative American brother, debated politics, laughed, and drank all-important *chai*—black tea with a lot of sugar that is traditionally served in small, tulip-shaped glasses.

Enjoying a glass of *chai* together is an ancient tradition in the Middle East that communicates hospitality and precedes every important conversation or negotiation. In return, not offering a guest a *chai* is deemed a very serious insult. It's important stuff.

★

In the meantime, Baz was on his second trip to Rojava in Syria. His first visit in March 2014 having been an intellectual gold mine for a political geographer, this second visit in October 2014 would touch Baz to the core and leave him with no other choice than to join the YPG.

Sitting in the tent of a Yazidi family who had just escaped Mount Shingal through the corridor the YPG/YPJ had opened at Newroz refugee camp, Baz drank *chai* and listened to their story. The husband spoke of the night they had been attacked by a wave of bloodthirsty maniacs in American war machines. A tale of disappointment, desperation, and betrayal. Of unnecessary death in a lost battle. Of AK rounds against up-armored Humvees. They showed Baz a video they had recorded on a phone. A grainy night sky lit up by muzzle flashes and traces.[2] The man's wife had been shot in the leg. Their infant son had also been shot and did not survive. He lay forgotten on the desolate Mount Shingal. They spoke of marauding Daesh gangs who combed through the mountain, some looking for valuables, some for girls, others for the right men to kill. The family considered themselves lucky since the gang they encountered had only been looking for Shia Muslims and had let them go. When the story inevitably came to the raped women, few had words. Some would just bang their fists against their heads and breathe heavily because screaming out loud was not part of their culture.

It was at this moment that Baz understood on an emotional level who Daesh really were: fascists. To him, Shingal, where black-cloaked men sorted people into those who were worthy of life and those who weren't, was the ramp to the Auschwitz of his lifetime. Understanding the nature of the Islamic State on this level suddenly connected his present with one of the essential questions of his adolescent life in Germany: What would you have done when the fascists took over?

At the age of 16, in response to fascist pogroms in Rostock-Lichtenhagen in Germany in 1992 and the brutal murders by neo-Nazis in Mölln and Solingen in 1992 and 1993—towns that were not far from the city where he grew up—Baz had visited the remains of the concentration camp Auschwitz. As a German who tried to learn from history, he was inevitably led to the question of what he would have done in 1933, when the Nazis came into power in Germany—a question he could never really shake off.

Now the fascists were just a few miles away, boasting about having commited genocide, and an entire region was asking the world, "Why will no one help us?" There it was, the question that had confronted him since his teens. What do you do now that fascists are just on the other side of the nearby earth berms? To Baz, not joining the YPG would have implied that he would have bowed to the Third Reich. It meant that he would have looked at the floor when the Gestapo came knocking and he would have told them about a "suspicious" neighbor because they insisted on a name. Probably by overtheorizing his heritage and life, Baz had maneuvered himself into an intellectual corner that meant he had no other choice than to go to war. To Baz, anything else would have rendered his intellectual life mere empty words. And yet at that point, he was just a jazzed-up geography teacher, a leftist conscientious objector. The only time he had fired an actual rifle was on a gun range in Cambodia, shooting at coconuts.

★

Very much on edge and without a clue about what they were getting into, John and Kosta, the two battle buddies, arrived at the front lines in Rojava, Syria, in a village called Arja (near Jaza, halfway between Qamishlo and Shingal) in late December 2014. Fortunately for them, all eight foreign volunteers had been put into the same unit. The other *americani*, the Kurdish term for all foreign fighters, made sure they got squared away as best as possible and gave them the tour of the front line. What the two saw was a medieval-looking earth berm with a network of fighting positions that connected a series of villages in an unbroken line between the border with Iraq in the east and Serekanye, a city at the Turkish border in the very west. Such earth berms in Syria formed the de facto borders in the fragmented landscape the war had created. Everyone protected their territory with a berm and World War I-style trenches.

This particular berm was the first and last line of defense, and was utterly overstretched.

All villages south of it were occupied by Daesh, who had their own defensive installations. In that section of the front, the lucky side would occupy one of the few strategic positions in the otherwise flat desert, including a network of hills (*tells*), one of the massive grain silos, or a school building. In John and Kosta's case, the enemy were the lucky ones and occupied a nearby *tell*, on which they had a DShK, nicknamed a "Dushka" (a 12.7mm machine gun, the Russian equivalent to the .50cal)—a gun that would harass them every night and day.

Having just left the still comfortably warm San Diego, in this fucked-up desert, John was "freezing his tits off." It was miserable. A lot of nothing, so the wind could really make uncomfortably cold weather feel unbearable. The villages were all deserted and had not been maintained for months. There was mud everywhere. Everything was always wet. Filthy stray cats and dogs slept on the rotting mattresses in the fighting positions made of sandbags, earth walls, and rocks during the day. During the nights, the *hevals* lay on the mattresses and could feel the bugs crawl over their bodies. Every night, they would take direct fire from the hill and try to return fire on an enemy they never saw. All that was visible were the red tracer rounds of the machine guns and muzzle flashes. They were tired all the time, and the only joys out of the day were unlimited Arden cigarettes, irreverent military humor, and the small chance that Daesh would be dumb enough to cross the berm. It was almost like Vietnam but without the exotic plants.

However, that was not really what fucked with John. He was used to "eating a shit sandwich" from the Marine Corps. What fucked with him was the way this war was being fought. It was almost like the YPG/YPJ, as well as Daesh, would do everything different than what he had learned. None of them was aggressive. During the day, they would only have one fighter on guard, staring at the no man's land with sleepy eyes. At night, they would all be out on the berm and in the fighting positions, waiting for an enemy that never came.

The reason for this was that the battle for Kobane was raging at the same time, so both the YPG/YPJ and the enemy were focused on that. As a result, their entire front line was quiet. In a way, that was good, because when the YPG/YPJ front-line units saw the enemy, they almost certainly died. Even in these sporadic attacks, though, the enemy could still assemble a superior force, unmolested by American fighter jets, and send in a wave of suicide bombers to overrun the position.

Realistically, then, the defenders' role was to send out a warning and try to stall the advancing Islamists for as long as possible. Mobile *taburs*, the YPG/YPJ's main fighting units, that were deployed strategically behind the front lines would then come in and plug the hole in the berm. According to the circulating stories derived from the original defenders, most would be decapitated and those who weren't were taken so the enemy could do unspeakable things to them.

This war was miserable and dirty. There was no satisfaction to be derived from fighting. It just involved grinding away at the defenders. Morale, an essential word in YPG/YPJ culture, was hard to maintain. To make matters worse, since Rojava was under almost constant economic boycott from all sides, there was not enough food. The *americani* in particular were sick, hungry, or both, and they had all the time in the world to talk about their misery. Yet boosting morale was one of Kosta's strong points; he always put the team before himself and would find ways to lighten the four Westerners' moods.

However, with time, John began to understand how this war worked. The *hevals* he fought with did not get pumped up for a year and then deployed for a foreseeable time to blow shit up and go home again. These guys were here for the long run. They had been doing this for years and would do it until they died, probably before they reached the age of 23. For many, this *was* their home. They had nothing but the clothes on their backs, their AK, a simple chest rig containing just four magazines, and a few tools that they had found along the way that fitted into a pocket. They did not even have backpacks. The Kurds did not believe in backpacks or any personal property at all for that matter. It just slows you down when fighting a guerilla war.

When small ambush teams went out to harass the enemy or place IEDs along their supply lines, John and Kosta had to stay back. At the time, the *tabur* commanders were not used to the international volunteers and were quite rightly worried that a dead international fighter could ruin their career within the movement. Frustrated and at the end of their wits over this, John and Kosta's small group requested to go to the Shingal front line. They had seen a few news reports about the fighting taking place in the infamous city—a place where hundreds of Yazidi girls were kidnapped and held hostage as sex slaves or forced to become brides for Daesh members.

Before this request could be put into motion, however, John broke his arm doing something so politically incorrect that it shall remain a secret in order to avoid unnecessary controversy. Thus, when the group suddenly got the green light to go to Shingal, the commanders told John that he had to stay back. John, though, thought, "Fuck that." The stubborn Marine threw his gear into the back of the Hilux, jumped into the cab, and began ripping off his cast.

Soon the group was racing east and pounding cans of Black Panther, the Syrian equivalent to Rockstar Energy Drink. While they crossed back into Iraq and thus into a geopolitical labyrinth of alliances and factions, AC/DC's "Thunderstruck" blasted from the stereo. However, all the symbolism and absurdity of the situation was lost on them because right then and there, they were Marines going to war. John began to reflect on this moment. All of his training and all of his knowledge was about to be tested. After this, he would either be a proven Marine or a bitch. There was no middle ground.

They soon arrived on Mount Shingal and found their way to Shingal City, the largest settlement in the area. Looking at it from the high ground of the mountain, the whole city was completely and utterly fucked up by war, and this was even before America rolled out their more comprehensive air campaign. When John and his friends had a look around the front lines, they could not believe it at first. It was almost like the set of a movie: completely abandoned, a Daesh flag here, a Daesh flag there, and occasional logistics trucks driving in the distance to resupply the enemy.

The *hevals* occupied the first two rows of houses into the city, which were situated on a cliffside. After those two rows, there was a large drop in the terrain, and the city continued about 10 feet below. The enemy held the city below the cliff, including the strategic school buildings and the massive grain silo. However, Daesh, ingenious as they were, had turned the tactical disadvantage into an advantage and dug a large tunnel system underneath the city. During the siege, they moved fighters and material through these underground streets, so when the United States began their air campaign, Daesh had their own urban Ho Chi Minh Trail. Behind the *hevals* further up the mountain were Peshmerga units who, despite better equipment, heavy weapons, and larger numbers, preferred to hang back in the second front line.

It was still depressingly cold and muddy when John and his friends found their way along their own network of tunnels and paths through broken walls that ran parallel to the front line. Every once in a while, there were fighting positions in the wall, on roofs, or in the mud berms. The houses that were the least damaged hosted small teams of *hevals*. Slowly, the *americani* began noticing that some of the *hevals* were not like the others. They were not YPG/YPJ, but instead belonged to various militias, including Yazidi self-defense groups and the PKK. These fighters were not like the kids at the quiet front line of Arja but were experienced guerillas. The fact that they were older and still alive meant that they were good at what they were doing. These men and women were the real deal, the kind of warriors a Marine could learn from. Trying to make the best of the situation, the *americani* began making a cold and muddy house habitable. Scavenging in the shelled remains of the neighborhood, they found a very improvised set of furniture.

At that time, in January 2015, Kobane was still hogging Daesh's as well as YPG/YPJ's attention, so the days were quiet unless a Daesh sniper popped up from one of their many tunnels to remind you to keep your head down. By the time the Kurds and John returned fire on the possible sniper position, the bastard was long gone. Think whack-a-mole with lunatics wearing suicide belts. As John said, "That shit wears you down."

Once or twice a day, an American jet came by and dropped a bomb. However, the air strikes were more a show of force and, at that point, did not impact much on the battlefield. To the anti-ISIS alliance on the mountain, they just broke up the routine.

During the night, the Peshmerga behind them would exchange heavy machine gun and mortar fire with the enemy. The PKK, Yazidi forces, the YPG/YPJ, and John lay in their positions between the mayhem, watching the tracers light up the skies, waiting for the attack that, once again, John never saw. Whenever the *hevals* went on one of their missions behind enemy lines, the *americani* had to stay back.

Eventually, John realized that there would be no large offensive in Shingal for a long time. According to the rumors, the different Kurdish factions and Americans were in negotiations about how the liberation should go down. Having done much of the heavy lifting, the PKK wanted to liberate the city. They had the support of the PUK Peshmerga. Of course, that infuriated the KDP Peshmerga. Technically, this was their territory and, having run away before, they wanted to use the opportunity to make up for the shame that was sticking to them. The whole time, the Americans pondered whether or not they wanted to start a proper war in the first place. So far, Obama was getting away with a few air strikes in Iraq and Syria to appease the media and their partners, but the air campaign was not coordinated with offensive operations or decisive enough to seriously soften the enemy.

With time to kill, Kosta began reflecting on his own role in the conflict and came to a similar conclusion to the one that Baz would reach about half a year later. Did this war really need another rifleman, or was there a way to bring more to the conflict? When the *tabur* had a gunshot casualty, the most obvious lack of expertise within the YPG/YPJ presented itself to Kosta. When the *hevals* wanted to throw a casualty on the back of a Hilux with only a scarf wrapped around the leg, he stepped in, tightened a tourniquet around the limb, and evacuated the wounded American volunteer via a stretcher the group of *americani* had put together only a few days prior using an old U.S. Army cot from the Iraq invasion and a spare rope. Kosta therefore understood that what this militia clearly needed was medics, as well as more contemporary medical knowledge amongst the ranks.

In the Royal Marines, Kosta had received above-average medical training. Although not a combat medic by trade, he was sensitized to the issue and soon acknowledged that he was the highest-qualified medic in this entire sector of the front line. Over the next weeks, Kosta therefore told John about his idea of setting up a medical team within the YPG/YPJ and the need for comprehensive combat lifesaver training.

At the same time, John learned that his business back home in California was being jeopardized, and he had to make the decision to sacrifice the business or continue waiting for an offensive in Shingal. John chose to tap out and regroup. For him, this first trip was only about orientation and he would be back soon. By contrast, given the sacrifice he had had to make in order to get there, Kosta wanted to stay a bit longer.

Once he had left, John did not have much contact with Kosta—as was normal during that time. The YPG did not permit cell phones; the only way for a foreign volunteer to have access to the internet or communication was when the group was back in the rear and a commander allowed them to use an internet cafe out in one of the local towns. Thus, John knew that the fact that no communication was possible meant that Kosta was at the front lines, doing what he had gone there to do. Then, on March 4, 2015, John awoke to a few Facebook messages from a mutual friend. Kosta had been fatally injured during the battle for Tel Hamis on March 2, 2015.

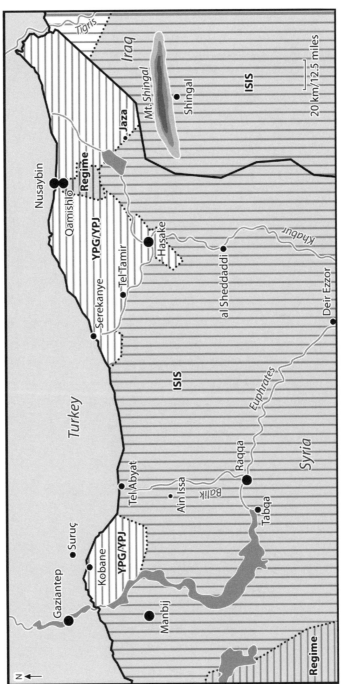

Map 2: Front lines in September 2014 around the Kobane and Cizire *cantons.*

CHAPTER 4

Securing the Earth Berm II: March 2015

Meanwhile, Shaun was getting out of the British Army and gearing up for his own aggressive humanitarian deployment to Rojava. Born in London to an Irish family in 1991, his early childhood had coincided with the tail end of the Troubles, the sectarian civil war in Northern Ireland. With the city still being occasionally terrorized by dissident Irish separatists carrying out a low-level bombing campaign, Shaun began a quest for identity and belonging that would ultimately lead him to the trenches of northern Syria.

During the 1970s, 80s and 90s, the IRA (Irish Republican Army) targeted London with terror campaigns that, despite relatively low casualty rates, spread fear. Fighting for a unified Ireland, the IRA wanted to bring the war home to the British and show Londoners what it was like to live in a war zone.

Growing up in Finsbury Park, a multiethnic neighborhood in London, Shaun was not picked on as a "Fenian" or "Paddy" (both derogatory terms for the Irish). Being just one of dozens of ethnic or religious minorities in the area, his Irishness was never an issue. However, his understanding of his identity changed as he first listened to the news, where after the occasional bombing, he heard phrases such as: "the Real Irish Republican Army claims responsibility for …." Thus to a young Shaun, his supposed Irishness was not about heritage or patriotism. Instead, it was transmitted to him via news footage. It seemed to be about brutal men in camouflage jackets and balaclavas, holding guns and patrolling in fields.

Around the same time, Shaun realized that, outside the neighborhood's particular social bubble, he was not English, either. A pale, freckled kid called Murray by some, became one of "them," one of the terrorists. And yet during visits to Ireland, he was the "cousin from England." Growing up confused, neither identifying with patriotism nor sectarianism, the slightly awkward kid hit puberty.

Watching *Independence Day* or news clips of U.S. Special Forces on night raids in Afghanistan, Shaun's naive and searching mind began to admire the achievement of freedom and liberal democracy and the struggles it took to get there. However, given his background, these achievements were not linked to particular nation-states but rather to a Western community with a set of shared values. Yet this world had a center: America, the self-proclaimed last remaining superpower.

Since the UK saw him as Irish, he had no emotional connection to the place; to him, the UK was just where he lived. Increasingly, Shaun replaced his missing identity with the idea of a Western humanist community. His world had no racial or religious undertones; it was purely about ethics, values, and the Western way of living. It was a naive understanding forged by an interest in the news, Hollywood blockbusters, and an underlying sense of displacement within a complex world.

When he watched 9/11, he was 10, and when the wars in Afghanistan and Iraq unfolded, just like the Bush Jr. administration at the time, he could not understand why the Iraqis didn't cheer America for bringing them their version of freedom. Why were the people in their villages not cheering for the new democracy? He believed that it was Saddam Hussein, the brute, who had suppressed the people who stood between them and human development. With the moustached and beret-wearing dictator gone, the people would naturally embrace freedom and democracy.

Whilst mulling over those issues and surfing the news websites, young Shaun began daydreaming about defending this concept of civilization and freedom, about patrolling the poppy fields of Afghanistan, or charging in on a convoy through Baghdad. These daydreams were not necessarily about crazy combat and heroism but rather about contributing to something bigger than himself. To live the theory, the idea that finally explained everything. At a point when most others wake up and shake off theirs, his daydreams and theories coalesced into his identity.

With both Afghanistan and Iraq clearly having gone sideways, Shaun increasingly "radicalized." In a way, Shaun became the perfect soldier for the "end of history,"[1] the time period in the early 1990s of liberal interventions and the victory of America's freedom and democracy over the crumbling Soviet Union. Capitalism had won, and from now on, the entire world was free to become like the West. Nation by nation, tyrants would fall; there would be no more war, no more starvation, and soon, everyone would enjoy the same freedom and opportunities. Shaun needed to fight for Bibi Aisha, the horribly mutilated girl on the *TIME* cover in 2010.[2] He believed in the abstract new conflicts and was willing to give his life to provide villagers he didn't know with a freedom they did not want.

Different from John, the epitome of a U.S. Marine, or Baz, who would become known as the big angry German, Shaun did not necessarily fit the cliché of a warrior you might get from consuming the Hollywood version of war. Consequently, family and friends were rather surprised when in 2011 he joined the 1st Battalion of the Royal Irish Regiment, a British Army unit.

People often asked Shaun why he joined the British Army instead of the Irish Defence Forces. He explained that his decision was not about a nation, it was to partake solely in intervention that would build Western democracy and liberalism from the ashes of oppression. The Irish were not fighting those kinds of wars, the British were. To him, the decision was anything but complicated.

Scared of becoming the weakest link in the unit, Shaun arrived at the barracks in top shape and passed his basic training with flying colors. In hindsight, this initiation was essential for him. By becoming a soldier in a war that was bigger than all of us, he had found a home. However, unlike John, enlisting was not about creating a chosen family. Shaun had grown up in a loving environment. His idea of home was about identity. It was about finding a reason to fight, to die, and thus to live a meaningful live.

Then the usual happened: policies changed, deployments got canceled at the very last minute, and yet another generation of soldiers sat in their barracks cursing their bad luck. Ready to kill and die in the fight against evil forces, Shaun was furious and disappointed to be constrained by politics and the poisoned legacies left behind from the War on Terror. Sobered by the reality of the military, his days in the army began to drag on. Just like John, he started following the various conflicts and developments emerging from the short-lived Arab Spring of the early 2010s. Having hit a dead end with the Brits, the idea of fighting with someone else for our freedoms started blossoming. His new identity as a soldier began merging with the feeling of inadequacy and shame about missing his combat deployment and not having played part in something bigger.

When Daesh was not yet Daesh but just the Islamic State in Iraq, his roommate in the barracks had shown Shaun a video of the Islamists attacking Iraqi Army positions in broad daylight, driving around Anbar Province in Iraq like they owned the place. Just like in Afghanistan, America had simply left, and the savagery was back with a vengeance. That was not good. When he watched Mosul and Sinjar fall, he made his decision. As soon as he walked out of the Clive Barracks a civilian in early 2015, Shaun began gathering supplies, swapped a few notes on Facebook, and left for Rojava.

★

In March 2015, Baz and Shaun met in a transit camp in Iraq. John had come through the same camp just over a month before. Smuggled along similar paths, the two made it to the newly created academy for international volunteers in Rojava. During the very rudimentary 10-day military training, Shaun and Baz bonded. Since the training was utterly useless (the highlight was firing seven AK rounds each at the gun range), Baz learned the very basics of warfare from Shaun—skills that are essential in order to start fighting Daesh.

However, although Shaun knew how to fight thanks to his time with the British Army, he lacked a deep understanding of the region and the militia he was going to join. He soon learned that developing a basic cultural literacy, comprehending the history of the people he wanted to fight for, and gaining an in-depth knowledge of regional dynamics would be essential to navigate this war. He understood that military experience with a NATO force might not necessarily be a benefit. This war was being fought very differently to the ones they had taught him about back home. Some of the missing knowledge he needed was supplied by Baz, who introduced him to regional politics.

The two also bonded with Jefferson, a Brazilian who had obtained American citizenship by joining the U.S. Army Infantry. Back home, he lived in a van in the Bay Area, concocting schemes to get quick and easy money. While Jefferson was not a criminal per se, nothing he did was strictly really legal, either. He lived in a constantly contested gray zone, somehow getting away with things by being familiar with far-fetched loopholes in the local bylaws or having the odd insider tip on some race he heard from someone who knew someone.

Jefferson was incredibly street smart. His skill was to be the person to whom insiders would tell inside information for no apparent reason and without wanting anything in return. He was smooth and savvy and had thus never been to jail. One of Jefferson's trademarks is that he always speaks the truth. No filters at all. In the mountain camp, for example, he would stare at Baz, chuckle, and say, "Despite your PhD, you are the dumbest of all of us. You made good money and had something good going, and yet you are here." He is the guy you imagine crawling around the Amazon with an old 45 to hunt down illegal loggers. Together, Shaun, Baz, and Jefferson combined an interesting set of skills that gave them a decent chance of surviving this war. Following their guts, they decided to stick together.

To Baz, the most meaningful event from the training was meeting Hevala Azadi, a young Kurdish woman who was giving some of the Westerners in the camp their Kurdish *noms de guerre*. Prior to his departure, Baz had come up with the name "Baz, the Falcon." The name works in Arabic and Kurdish. In both cultures, falcons are adored—not necessarily for their brute force and power but for their stealth and patience. Yet falcons can kill so swiftly that the victim is dead before it can see the attack coming. Falcons are smart hunters, and for Baz's very own version of an intellectual warrior, it was a fitting name. Then, almost as soon as Baz walked into the camp, Hevala Azadi looked at him and said, "Ahh, from now on, you are Heval Baz." None of us is particularly spiritual, but to Baz, that definitely felt like a good start. She also gave Shaun his *nom de guerre*, "Sherzad, the Master of War," though the name embarrassed him, and he could never say it with a straight face. "It sounds like a comic book superhero."

Graduating unceremoniously from the academy, Shaun, Baz, and Jefferson went up to Kracho, a massive *tell* in the desert overlooking a network of ancient oil drills and sipping pipelines. Out of oil barrels they were handed their weapons: brand-new Russian AKs, still greased up the way they had left the factory. The manufacturing date stamped into the rifles was 1965. When asked where the weapons had come from, the commander answered, "You know, Heval Baz, as soon as there is war, someone will sell weapons from somewhere. That's just how it is."

When Shaun and Baz turned around with their AKs, they discovered Jefferson standing there holding an M16, a weapon so rare and precious that usually only commanders and designated marksmen—or women— would have one. Yet someone had given him one simply because he asked for it. That's how Jefferson's world could be. On the receiver, the rifle had the American government's stamp. When new, it had been a United States military-issued weapon. On the butt was a blue sticker with white markings in Arabic that was put on when the United States handed their weapon stockpiles over to the Iraqi Security Forces (ISF). Then, possibly in Mosul, Daesh had captured the rifle and taken it to Syria, where it had been used to fight the Kurds. Somewhere during this process, the Daesh fighter had been killed, and now a slightly crazy ex-U.S. Army Brazilian-American volunteer would use it to fight Daesh. That's fucked up. American foreign policy in a nutshell—or better, a rifle.

All tooled up, the three friends jumped onto a pickup heading for Tel Tamir while most other international volunteers left for the supposedly more active Hasake front. The reason for this was that Shaun and Jefferson had heard from a guy who seemed to have his shit together that there was a big operation coming up. The rumored staging area for the first ever offensive against the Caliphate was Tel Tamir, a currently quiet front line.

After a couple of days, Shaun, Baz, and Jefferson arrived at Tel Erfan, a logistics hub in a ruined former lake resort that had had its peak in the 1970s. The whole place was notoriously dirty and incredibly depressing.

The young commander seemed more like a substitute teacher whose unruly classroom had gotten out of hand. The unit he had been left in charge of spent most of its time swatting away flies and drinking *chai*.

At almost every base, Shaun, Jefferson, and Baz had seen fighters clearly under the age of 19, thus, technically, child soldiers. In fact, throughout our time in the YPG/YPJ, we were in *taburs* that were made up of about 30 percent underage fighters. Shocked at the time, Shaun asked Baz why there were so many. Having been puzzled by that fact himself, Baz had asked the YPG as well as members of different civilian organizations that same question in 2014. At first, all of them insisted that no one under the age of 15 was at the front lines—a fact that all of us can confirm from our experiences. The reason there were 15-, 16-, or 17-year-olds at the front was simple: there was no one else to enlist. Defending Rojava had been such a fierce, ongoing battle that many of the 20-year-olds had already become *şehîds* (the term for "martyr" that is used before the name of every fallen member as a mark of respect). Most *taburs* had almost no fighters older than 23.

If the older teenagers hadn't armed themselves, Rojava might have fallen. While this was by no means an ideal situation for any teenager, it is an unfortunate consequence when fighting for the survival of your ethnic group. In the same way that teenagers fought in the American War of Independence and the Civil War to defend their families, teenagers in Rojava fought.

The base in Tel Erfan was next to a massive water dam overlooking the valley between Tel Tamir, Hasake, and the Abdel Aziz mountains. The entire area below the base was occupied by the enemy. At the very edge of the high ground, the YPG/YPJ had built a 30-foot-high medieval-looking defense tower with 5-feet-thick concrete walls. The tower itself had no entrance and was only accessible through a long tunnel that had IEDs on the wall. In case the position was ever overrun, the defenders could blow up the tunnel and turn the tower into their Alamo position. The whole scenario had a distinctly apocalyptic vibe to it.

Stuck at this bizarre base for an unforeseeable future, the three friends spent the days having pointless debates about absolutely nothing. Jefferson had a great sense for people's convictions, passions, and weak spots.

When bored, he would dispute one of those convictions just for fun. This was always followed by an endless discussion that got so heated that sometimes even Jefferson would forget that it was just a joke.

The communal meal at the base was like playing Russian roulette with your stomach. You had to eat but the chances of getting a very nasty stomach bug were about one in six. This was eaten in a part of the base in which there was a TV that was constantly running. Every single time a romantic scene came on, a room full of heavily armed Middle Eastern teenagers would giggle. Meanwhile, Shaun tried to negotiate the base commander into submission so they could go to the actual front. It was like a very fucked-up Groundhog Day in a truly bizarre desert outpost.

Then, one afternoon while staring at the ceiling, a sudden thump jerked the friends up from their mattresses. The walls vibrated with the sharp WHACK of a blast somewhere not too far away. Outside, *hevals* were shouting. Something was happening. People were running to get a vantage point to watch the valley, from where plumes of black smoke were billowing. Suddenly, the sky was filled with roaring jets. It was May 2015 and, for the first time, America was about to bring the war to the enemy.

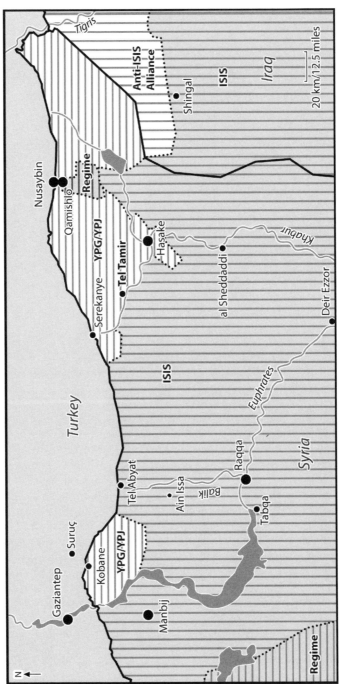

Map 3: Front lines in May 2015 around the Kobane and Cizire *cantons*.

CHAPTER 5

The First Wave of Aggressive Airstrikes: March–April 2015

Until this point, the American military intervention had been limited to a few uncoordinated air strikes around Erbil or Shingal, where John had watched them. Only for short and absolutely unavoidable operations, such as the recapture of the vital Mosul Dam, did the air strikes become more aggressive. In Syria, air strikes were therefore limited to the prevention of the fall of Kobane, a strategic Kurdish city at the Turkish border.

By October 2014, the entire Kobane *canton*, one of the three parts of Rojava that used to include Kobane's countryside along the eastern banks of the Euphrates, had been reduced to two city blocks. Cornered between the deadly Islamists and the hostile Turkish border, the remaining *hevals* were desperately fighting for every square foot of freedom. With their positions being shelled by American weapons Daesh had captured in Mosul, the Kurdish forces ran out of territory to retreat to.

According to the stories, the *hevals* were wishing each other farewell, sharing their remaining cigarettes, and swapping a symbolic last bullet with their friends. A bullet for the moment you needed one the most: to evade capture. When it was almost over and the Islamists were already celebrating their victory, an American jet dropped a 500-pound bomb into the mad melee, killing hundreds of enemies.

Another important story that came out of this battle was the martyrdom of Şehîd Arin Mirkan. Her unit had been cornered, and they were running out of ammo. Some say she strapped grenades to her body and charged into the Daesh lines. Others say she carried an anti-tank mine or a captured suicide vest. The death toll varies, from her killing 10 ISIS fighters to 40, but these details don't matter. This story is about Rojava and its woman fighters, who sacrifice their lives for life, not death. Different to the Islamists, bombers, the YPJ do not martyr for hate but love for their *hevals*, so in the future, women and girls can live an equal life. While it is likely that aspects of these stories have been exaggerated with time, the broader strokes of the narrative are accurate. They are parables for a war between good and evil. Light and darkness. Love and hate.

Back to Tal Erfan, where Shaun and Baz witnessed the end of the symbolic American policy. In March 2015, America had decided to go back to war, and its air force had shown up in large numbers. From one second to another, the valley exploded while jets went thundering by. All over the place, pillars of smoke were rising from the bombed Daesh position.

Refueled by tankers high above Rojava, American jets continued their assault until they'd used up all their bombs and new planes came to replace them. Watching the valley burn, sipping his hot *chai*, Shaun suddenly stated, "For that view alone, the journey was worth it." How true. Without realizing it back then, Shaun and Baz had the best seats from which to watch the very beginning of the first phase of America's war against Daesh. These were not a couple of symbolic or mission-specific air strikes but an air campaign that was supposed to soften the enemy before a ground assault. To everyone watching the bombardment on the ground, it was clear that this was a game changer. From now on, the war in northeast Syria would look very different.

For the people and fighters of Rojava, these bombs meant hope: hope of surviving the day and hope that maybe there wouldn't be another genocide, at least for now. For many of them, the intervention did not come too late; they were just grateful that it came at all. The fighters around Baz and Shaun could not believe what they were seeing: the U.S. Air Force committing and fighting on their side. Immediately, fighters referred to the bombing planes as "Heval Obama." Interestingly, all over Rojava, *hevals* had the same response, and from this moment on until the end of his presidency, "Heval Obama" would be the term used for any friendly jets. This term of respect means something in the deserts and mountains of the Middle East.

Yet, the Kurdish revolutionaries who were now singing the praises of their new American *heval* had every reason to be surprised to see the United States on their side. The YPG/YPJ and their affiliate political parties around the PYD (Partiya Yekîtiya Demokrat, or Democratic Union Party) are part of same Kurdish movement as the PKK. Since the PKK fights for Kurdish rights in Turkey, one of America's NATO partners, the United States, as we've mentioned, lists the PKK as a terror organization—one of two main actors in a conflict that has cost an estimated 40,000 lives since the early 1980s.[1]

At times, the conflict between the Turkish military and the PKK was a full-on war that raged in wide parts of southeast Turkey. In fact, many of the weapons Turkey used against the PKK were American-made, meaning that in the past, American F16s had bombed, not supported, the *hevals*. That the United States would actually fight on their side was thus an unlikely scenario. What the *hevals* at the muddy front lines did not know about was the growing public pressure that was mounting on Obama to intervene in the war against ISIS.

With the Western world slowly comprehending the gravity and scale of the genocide against the Yazidis, public opinion had changed and, suddenly, Obama's liberal base accepted the need for a humanitarian intervention. However, having been elected on the presumption to end all wars in the Middle East, an American troop deployment was ruled out. Obama needed an ally on the ground whom he could support with air strikes and weapons.

On the comprehensive list of every possible candidate for an alliance, the YPG/YPJ were at the very bottom. To start from the top of that list, Iraq's army was not operational and needed some serious restructuring before they would be able to reclaim their country. The Kurdish Peshmerga were content with the territory they now occupied. They did not care too much about Mosul, an Arab city. Also, any further advance into Iraqi territory would have been highly unconstitutional. Taking Kirkuk, something that had at least some constitutional grounds, would create enough tension once Daesh was gone. In short, the Peshmerga were also not an alternative for any offensive operations against Daesh. The third actor that was emerging in Iraq, the pro-Iranian Shia militias, were not an option, either—but rather a massive future problem.

In Syria, the pro-Iranian government and the pro-Iranian Hezbollah (a large and powerful Shia militia from Lebanon) were also not viable options. Furthermore, all effective democratic antigovernment fighting forces had gone by 2015. With the United States and others having waited too long, the powerful Islamists had either killed or assimilated all formerly democratic fighters. This really only left one-and-a-half more options for America: the leftist YPG/YPJ or some poorly defined moderate Islamists. America went for the Islamists.

In our imaginations, this decision was made by aged Cold War veterans in badly fitting suits with their sleeves rolled up who still occupy senior positions. From the wooden wall of a dark corner office, an old, yellowish J. Edgar Hoover portrait glared at them through the lingering cigar smoke just to remind them who the real enemy was: the commies. The result? America sided with known Islamists rather than supporting a group that had once called itself Marxist-Leninist. Implemented by agents who probably thought John le Carré novels were too slow, the whole operation was a colossal disaster for the agency.[1] The fuck–up peaked when the tube–launched, optically-tracked, wire-guided (TOW) missile that the CIA delivered to those moderate Islamists ended up in the hands of Daesh. To explain a little more, the TOW is an anti-tank guided missile (ATGM). Given that armored SVBIEDs are one of the enemy's deadliest weapons, light and mobile surface-to-surface missiles that can take out SVBIEDs are a game changer. For reasons unknown, the CIA had repeated the same textbook mistake they'd made with antiaircraft missiles and the anti-Russian insurgents in Afghanistan in the mid–1980s.

The upshot was that during the Manbij operation later in 2016, Daesh used ATGMs against YPG/YPJ and SDF forces. American medics from Baz's team treated some of the survivors. Although we will never find out whether those were the missiles that came from the CIA, it would be so dark and funny if they were—a fitting story for the Middle East.

Then, in in early 2015, with the YPG/YPJ now their absolute last option, Obama and the American military finally accepted their fate and began talking to the revolutionaries. They have not regretted it since. And yet aside from confirming the air strikes, the official position of Obama's State Department was one of ignorance. The YPG/YPJ's role in the operations was downplayed. According to Washington, the Kurds were just one part of a much broader anti-ISIS alliance, including Arabs.[2] America's wording was an attempt to appease Turkey, but it did not reflect the picture on the ground, where local Arab allies appeared to be mere political proxies and Kurdish forces dominated the campaign. It wasn't until much later that American forces exclusively trusted the Kurds when it came to support and air strikes.

While publicly the United States was as indifferent as possible, in the early stages, they could not possibly ignore the reality that the YPG was the best option. Rising tensions with Turkey perhaps forced the Obama administration to publicly announce the deployment of 50 U.S. Special Forces to Syria to avoid giving Turks plausible deniability in any clashes or attacks that might endanger American troops, even though it was known by guys on the ground, including us, that American troops were already there.

★

After a few days, Shaun's approach bore fruit. Having annoyed the commander enough with his constant requests to go to the front lines, some random guy showed up with a Toyota Hilux to take Shaun, Jefferson, Baz, and some others to their front-line unit. Everyone climbed inside or on top before the driver embarked on a suicidal race around the front line. With Kurdish rebel tunes booming on the sound system, the *heval* explained that the vehicle had to be faster than the Daesh snipers' reactions. He got lost somewhere in between the front lines, so he drove around the ghost city of Tel Tamir, looking for someone to ask for the way. He found some local *Asayîş*—a hybrid of police and internal security agency—who invited the group in for *chai*. (*Asayîş* are the ones at the checkpoints and those who bear the brunt of SVBIED attacks. Indeed, the *Asayîş* were probably the most underappreciated actor in Rojava in terms of security and stability.) The driver was sure that he would find the way now and, after some more sweet tea, the mad race continued.

Then, just as had happened to John before, the car suddenly dropped the three friends in the middle of nowhere. Standing in a deserted-looking *gund* (village) somewhere at the front lines near Tel Tamir, the friends were lost and on edge. Then, a garden door opened, and a sleepy *heval* welcomed the startled group in. Inside, YPG fighters were sleeping on mattresses or playing chess. In the kitchen, two *hevals* were preparing dinner. While Baz talked about geography with one, Shaun had to explain why he was not a member of the Irish Republican Army. Jefferson, meanwhile, was floating around, trying to find more of the precious 5.56 rounds for his M16.

As it turned out, they had landed in a sniper unit. However, since there were not enough sniper rifles and the front line was overstretched, the *tabur* had been converted to a regular front-line unit. After *chai*, the *hevals* took Shaun, Baz, and Jefferson on a tour that was very similar to the one John had been given a few months before, about 62 miles east of this location. This front line was quiet. The enemy were still focusing their military efforts elsewhere, and they would not launch any major offensives to expand anytime soon. This was the sort of place where future holy warriors performed *ribat*, part of Daesh's military training, on the fringes of their Caliphate. Sometimes, however, experienced Daesh fighters would travel the front lines and attack complacent *taburs*.

The village the snipers occupied had been part of the Christian community around the Khabur River and Tel Tamir. Only a month before, Daesh had taken 200 members of this Christian community hostage. The settlement numbered about 40 homes around a church with a wire-framed crucifix on the roof. There was a tall water tower pockmarked with bullet holes at one end of the village and flying on top was a tattered Rojava flag. Each house had a small compound wall and a little garden, and there were lanes running between them that were just wide enough for a car. Looking around the village, it looked like a tight-knit community had lived here for perhaps several generations. It seemed like it had once been a pleasant place to live, with scattered family photo albums recalling better days of smiling faces at local gatherings and weddings. The houses were mostly trashed and looted, and graffiti from ISIS daubed the walls. Every home was still fully furnished with wardrobes full of clothes. The Christian community must have left at very short notice. Yet, it was evident that they had seen it coming: visa applications for Australia and New Zealand littered the floor in many of the homes.

Shaun, Baz, and Jefferson were shown the same long earth berm John had guarded in similar fighting positions, made of sandbags, earth, and rotting mattresses. In the no man's land ran a little creek with high grass and IEDs on each side. The enemy occupied the village about 220 yards south of the position. With Daesh and the Kurds still focused on the Kobane front line, the way the war was being fought had not changed. It was still miserable, only the weather was a little better and there was less mud. During the day, no one fought, and only a couple of *hevals* were on guard while the others tried to sleep. One of the guard positions was in an isolated building at the outskirts of the village. This was out of earshot of the rest of the *taburs*, and there were no radios. Random shooting was so commonplace that if the guards there fired their weapon, the unit would simply ignore it at first. In case of an attack, it would have required a couple of magazines fired in full auto just to get someone else's attention. The enemy knew where the daytime positions were and would regularly use them for target practice.

To boost morale back at the front-line village, one day, the YPJ filled one of the pools in a house right at the front line with water and started to splash around in it. The sound of free women laughing floated across the mined no man's land until the angry jihadi neighbors heard them. They answered with religious slurs and automatic fire.

When it got dark, both sides warmed themselves up for the long night, firing their heavy machine guns at each other. When the *tabur* left for their nighttime positions, Jefferson's latest catchphrase was, "Tonight, we are going to die. Tonight, they will come for us." As soon as darkness set in, everyone came out onto the berms, listening into the quiet and for the enemy to creep up. The only noteworthy difference from John's story was that Shaun and Baz had two *tells* on their side. One of these had former water treatment plants on top that now hosted heavy machine guns. On the smaller one were positioned the *tabur's* remaining snipers.

Within days, Shaun, Baz, and Jefferson's lives in the village became normal. They were constantly fighting their neighbors in the next village, but there was no decisive battle. The snipers got to know by sight most of the enemy fighters as they continuously watched the village through their scopes. Within weeks, getting shot at whilst going to get a *chai* had become nothing more than an inconvenience. There was no wider picture or geopolitics. Isolated in the desert, it was just about two villages, about 10 people on each side who spent all day fantasizing about each other's deaths. In all honesty, it is scary how fast the human mind can adapt to the apocalypse.

So far, this particular Daesh village had not been bombed, but that changed after a few nerve-racking, long, and quiet nights when suddenly, two AC-130 gunships showed up.[3] When the gunships were right above the front line, they ejected a volley of red flares, forming bright, glowing angel wings as if to tell the *hevals* that from now on, everything would be OK.

Continuously circling over the front lines, the AC-130s immediately pounded Daesh positions with long salvos of their cannons. Given the time delay between the visual explosion and its sound, a bizarre, asynchronous spectacle unfolded in the pitch-black desert. On every perfectly round, almost white, explosion, the thumping sound of the cannon and the bang of the impact would follow. Wherever the enemy tried to move, they were taken out immediately. Yazidi fighters in the YPG unit listened in on the enemies' unencrypted radio chatter. Every time the enemy talked about another brother "having gone to paradise," they smiled, satisfied. With the gunships around, the entire YPG/YPJ front got a break.

Far more effective than its 40mm cannons was the gunships' psychological effect on the enemy. Up to this point, the night had been theirs. Daesh had used its cover to launch surprise assaults, sneaking up, planting IEDs, and then disappearing back into darkness. From one night to another, that changed. What had previously hidden them now made them show up on the AC-130's thermal and night vision cameras. Thus unable to move, the Daesh fighters were trapped in their positions. At night, the AC-130 was basically a flying panopticon. Their message to the enemy was, "At least on this front line, your days of advancing are over."

During the day, American jets and drones continued to bomb all convoys, staging areas, and known ISIS positions. The Kurdish unit tried to sleep while F18s were bombing their opponents on the other side of the creek. Coming in low over friendly territory, the American jets would pull up over the *heval*'s heads and release their bombs. Every explosion shook the former children's room where Baz and Shaun were squatting in an abandoned house, rocking them to sleep. This incredibly aggressive air campaign continued day and night for another week, keeping the pressure on the enemy at all times. Daesh had not only lost their momentum, they were also unable to regroup, even to move. Instead, they were caught in bunkers that were slowly being chewed away by American bombs.

CHAPTER 6

The First Major Offensive Against Daesh: May 2015

In early May, the atmosphere around the Tel Tamir front line changed. First, the fighting between the heavy machine guns intensified beyond the usual bored exchange. Almost to show that they were still alive after another day of heavy bombing, at the break of dawn, the enemy would suddenly open up on the YPG/YPJ positions. Suddenly, all *taburs* had to prepare for an operation. Fighters stripped and cleaned their weapons before lubricating them with diesel. The drivers filled buckets with a mixture of mud and water and smeared it all over the white Toyota pickup trucks, including the headlights and windows, coating it in a sand-colored paste that dulled the reflective shine from the sun and camouflaged it against the terrain.

A YPG logistics truck came by and dropped off fried chicken. Within seconds, the mood changed throughout the unit. The women of the YPJ, about a third of the unit, who would usually have their own area in the little village, came over for the large communal feast. After *chai*, music was played, and fighters began dancing. There was adrenaline and excitement in the air. As a *heval* explained to Shaun, Jefferson, and Baz, good food meant that the unit would go on an operation very soon. While this was explained to them, someone told Baz, Shaun, and Jefferson to grab their bags and jump on a pickup.

Having been transferred to a different *tabur*, they would participate in one of the first offensive operations against the still growing Caliphate. It was also one of the inaugural operations in the young alliance between the YPG/YPJ and America. What the three friends participated in was a unique experiment, combining the YPG/YPJ's PKK-inspired guerilla tactics and modern airpower. However, on the ground, it was just miserably cold and boring.

As soon as night had fallen and the AC-130s had moved into position, Baz's *tabur* and about two or three other YPG/YPJ *taburs* sped past the enemies' burning defenses into the dark, sometimes over roads, sometimes over dirt tracks, and often across the desert grain fields. Every once in a while, the *tabur* would jump off their trucks to secure a compound, village, or junction. The next moment, the unit would begin advancing again. In between, the gunships took out Daesh positions.

When the sun came up the next morning, the *tabur* was in a village already halfway between Tel Tamir, their point of departure, and the Abdel Aziz mountain range, the operation's goal. The enemy's defenses had broken down, and the small guerilla units advanced fast. Throughout the day, the *tabur* continued their advance with the trucks following in one another's tire tracks to avoid mines. Teams occupied crossroads or a cluster of houses and hung around for a while before being sent elsewhere to plug a gap in the defensive lines there. All of these ground movements were carried out with constant air cover. In some cases, teams would disembark and wait for an armored personnel carrier (APC). About six fighters would cram inside the old Russian APC and advance onto a larger village. In a very World War II-like maneuvre, a gaggle of *hevals* would walk behind the beast and use it as cover during their advance under fire.

At one point during the advance, Shaun, Baz, and a couple of *hevalas* from the YPJ had been tasked with securing a dusty village when a band of about 50 Arab fighters rolled in. Some of them wore suicide belts; some of them were black Tuareg fighters from northern Africa who had washed up in Syria; one of them had a large sword on his back. All of them had big beards and angry eyes. This was the first time either of the friends had met the Arab fighters in their coalition—the ones America supported with weapons and ammo instead of the YPG/YPJ because, apparently, we were the terrorists.

Some of these Arab allies had once fought for al-Nusra, aka al-Qaida, and when they saw the two white guys seemingly alone in the desert with no Hilux, for a brief moment, there was tension in the air. Weapons were held closer and feet shuffled in order to find a good stance. Just before it came to a Mexican standoff in the Syrian desert between former Islamists-turned-friends, an academic, and an Irishman, the YPJ's commander stepped in and ordered the tribal fighters to leave, which they did. The former al-Qaida affiliates, people who had fought for their version of an Islamic State in which a harsh version of Sharia law would have ruled, took orders from a woman when they had the advantage on their side. This was because they knew the YPJ and had no intention of breaking the peace of their fragile alliance.

In late May, the valley between Tel Tamir and the Abdel Aziz mountains was filled with black smoke. The crops were burning all around. While some of this was collateral damage from stray rounds and air strikes, the scale of the blaze indicated ISIS had made a poor attempt at trying to screen themselves from the aircraft. The YPG/YPJ advance stopped suddenly after just a couple of days, and the *tabur* was split up to be deployed at the new front line, ready to defend against a possible counterattack.

In reality, for Shaun, Jefferson, and Baz, this meant being stuck in the middle of nowhere in a tiny compound with some grumpy old Arab couple. It was getting hot, there was not enough food, and a huge snake lived in the shitter. No one had seen any fighting. It was bad, and Shaun got a nasty stomach bug that only the snake enjoyed. Yet this village was part of a long frontier of improvised FOBs. Although it felt unspectacular at the time, this was Rojava's new frontier. The enemy was out of Tel Tamir, a strategic city, and most importantly, with the Islamists retreating, people could return.

At some point, a shot rang into the early night. A *heval* yelled "Daesh, Daesh!" and kept firing rounds into the desert. The team or *takem* put out all fires and formed a 360-degree protection, the commander called someone on the radio who called someone else, and a coalition jet appeared over the village within five minutes. Eventually, it turned out that the teenager on guard had shot himself in the foot to get away from the fighting. Apparently, he had just returned from recovering after a very similar event. Yet it was trivial experiences such as this that switched the

YPG/YPJ from feeling vulnerable to invincible. The jets made everyone relax a little. The revolution now had an air force.

Presumably from the rotting, flea-ridden mattresses, Shaun, Baz, and Jefferson contracted a strange kind of very itchy skin disease, so they were sent to a house for recovering injured fighters until the rash had gone, which took about a week. For Shaun, the stomach bug, rash, and everything else were getting to be too much. He needed a break and so he tapped out. He wanted to recover in Erbil and take it from there.

Although boring on the ground, from a more strategic perspective, this first large joint operation must have looked impressive. While the Americans took out all known targets, on the ground, the YPG/YPJ rapidly advanced deep into the enemy's territory. Wherever Kurdish units encountered Daesh fighters they could not deal with themselves, they called in an air strike or a truck with a heavy machine gun. If the enemy had fortified a village with bunkers and the offensive encountered some more serious resistance, the village was surrounded by units pushing up from the rear. Meanwhile, the two or three *taburs* who led the assault would continue to leapfrog forward. The key to the operation was to keep the momentum. The enemy was running. They had opened their lines and were disorganized. While the YPG/YPJ kept up the insane speed, American jets picked off retreating Daesh fighters.

Essential for this kind of warfare were the Kurdish assault or mobile units, the *taburs*. A *tabur* is the largest fighting unit and consists of 30 to 40 fighters divided into three teams of *takems*. Usually, two *takems* were YPG and the third was YPJ, each containing about 12 fighters. Each *takem* was broken down into two teams for the smallest fighting unit, with five to six fighters each.

When advancing with a battle group of four *taburs*, 12 *takems* would roll in their own Hilux. Flying through the desert, from the high ground, the front-line commanders (and later, U.S. Special Forces) could direct these *takems* to secure junctions (*gunds*) where critical roads intersected, or *tells*. Within seconds after the arrival of the Hilux, a *takem* of 12 fighters would secure the perimeter with nine AKs, one shoulder-held grenade launcher (RPG), and two belt-fed machine guns. While the position was secured, other *takems* leapfrogged forward, securing the next strategic position. The first *takem* would mount up within a minute or less and advance in a feverish routine.

Besides the dug-in IEDs, the biggest threat to the advancing units were SVBIEDs. In the absence of ATGMs, the YPG/YPJ used up-armored front-loaders. Traveling just behind the advancing *taburs*, the iron beasts the YPG mechanics had wielded in their workshops would be called up to the front lines, and as soon as the advance held, berms were put across the roads of the new border with the Caliphate and around the front line of *takems*, blocking all SVBIEDs. When the battle groups continued, these berms would be cleared for the advancing *taburs*. Since their armored SVBIEDs were unable to cross these berms, ISIS hated the front-loaders, which were usually operated by local Arabs. Many of the drivers whom we met had been shot several times.

Pinned down by American air strikes, the static defenders were overrun in no time. As soon as a YPG/YPJ unit contacted the enemy, America dropped some very large bombs or sent an A-10 to *brrrrrr* them. This was an American-Kurdish blitzkrieg, and Jefferson, Shaun, and Baz were in the midst of it, drinking *chai* and trying not to step on a mine.

Each *tabur* moved simultaneously in just three Toyota Hilux Double Cab trucks, which meant that there were about seven or more fighters in full battle rattle in the cab and five or more on the back of each car. In order to allow for this speed and mobility, all a YPG/YPJ *tabur* carried was ammo, about 10,000 cigarettes, and *chai*. Everything else was scavenged in the places the *tabur* secured. Besides sleeping quarters, cooking utensils, and entertainment, this could include food the enemy had left behind. To test if something was poisoned, a piece would be fed to one of the dogs that always roamed around. If the dog was still alive after 10 minutes, the *hevals* would have a hot meal that night. During offensives or in cases when a front line got cut off by tactical counterattacks, it was common that the little logistics trucks driving around food could not make it for some time. When this happened, a *tabur* would simply run on a nicotine-caffeine-sugar high for days.

YPG/YPJ *taburs*, often made up of local teenagers, thus fought in the most spartan way possible, embracing guerilla warfare to the maximum. From the moment the order to move came in on the radio, it took an average YPG/YPJ *tabur* about 10 minutes to be on their way, leaving their temporary base behind.

★

Between late May and early June 2015, this new front line along the northern slopes of the Abdel Aziz range had been secured by a coalition of various Kurdish and Arab support units called border guards, and the fighting *taburs* got the call to move out again. Ten minutes later, the *taburs* were on the move, racing east. Apparently, the operation would continue. The YPG/YPJ had pushed deep into the enemy's territory; now the Kurdish-American alliance wanted to attack Daesh's wide-open eastern flank. While the *taburs* were moving east, radio chatter confirmed the rumors: Kobane units were also on the offensive, pushing west. Squeezing the enemy from both *cantons* could only mean one thing: the YPG/YPJ would attack Tel Abiat, a strategic border town with Turkey and one of Daesh's logistic hubs in the region.

Although the operation made sense from a strategic level, to the Kurds, it meant much more. It meant that the two isolated *cantons*, Kobane and Cizire, would try to connect. This strengthened the Kurds strategically and would give their revolution a chance to survive. Supporting this next step of the operation was also a signal America sent to the Kurds as well as their NATO partner, Turkey, which was furious about the alleged PKK offensive along their southern border. Moving forward, the USA would no longer bow to Turkey's protest, but would prioritize the war against ISIS with their new partners. In other words, the operation signaled that the United States would have the YPG/YPJ's back. Still moving east through the empty desert, the *hevals* from the *tabur* understood this message very well and began cheering when the news came in over the radio.

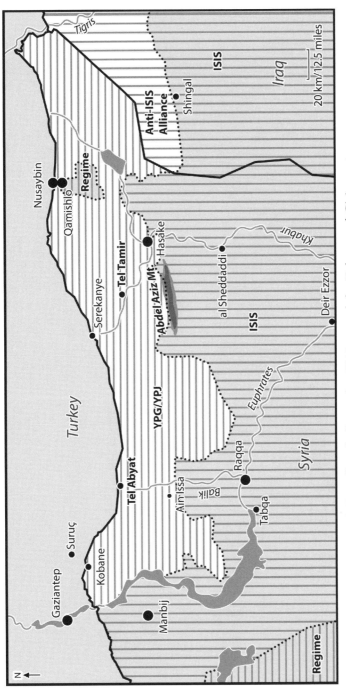

Map 4: Front lines in September 2015 around the Kobane and Cizire *cantons*.

CHAPTER 7

Occupying Arab Lands: June 2015

In June 2015, the *tabur* arrived at the staging area for the big push eastward toward Kobane. From there, different *taburs* embarked on a mad race for Tel Abiat and to be the first in the city. The assault included several battle groups that were closing in on Tel Abiat from different directions. Two *taburs* and possibly one of the two old Russian armored personnel carrier (BMPs) would spearhead each battle group. Then followed the command element with the front-line commanders and the "Dushka" trucks that could support the assaulters. Behind the front-line commander followed more *taburs* to either support the assault, or local *Asayîş* units to secure the villages and establish a network of checkpoints.

This way, the YPG/YPJ closed in on the fertile lands along the Balikh River. In the desert, water means life; people settle around it. Where before the desert had been widely empty, now the advancing *taburs* encountered an increasing number of civilians. However, these civilians were predominantly Arabs, not Kurds. Whereas the Cizire and Kobane *cantons* were predominantly Kurdish, the area in between was Arab. From an American-Kurdish perspective, opening a corridor through Arab lands that connected the two separated Kurdish areas was a necessary compromise in order to establish a strategic base from which to fight the Caliphate.

On the ground along the Balikh River south of Tel Abiat, the *hevals* noticed a difference from their past experience, when people had cheered them. Now, civilians were spitting in front of the YPG/YPJ trucks, glaring at the fighters. The YPG/YPJ were seen as invading and occupying, not liberating. Indeed, many of the Arabs in the area had profited from Daesh. After decades of neglect at the hands of the Alawis, a pro-Shia regime in Damascus, many Sunni civilians in that area saw Sunni Islamists as liberators. They were happy with Daesh and despised the atheist Kurdish revolutionaries.

Without any intelligence on the situation, a small team of five fighters would jump into the ancient BMP and speed toward an enemy village. In the center of the village, the *hevals* would jump out of the beast, search, and secure the place. Usually, the villages would consist of brown mud huts in a brown desert with scared mothers huddling over their children while a German and a Brazilian-American kicked in their doors with their safeties off. This whole operation started to feel bad.

One day, Baz and four other fighters were sent in the BMP to secure one more village. As soon as the team had jumped out of the tank, they knew that this had been a Daesh stronghold. The houses were nicely painted and there were green lawns, indicating access to precious diesel for water pumps. This suggested a close collaboration with the Islamists. Furthermore, all civilians had stayed behind, including the men who were now pretending to ignore the tank and armed fighters. However, when the BMP left, the civilians began yelling at the team of five now stuck in the village.

Next, from the direction of the enemy, men in their 20s on motorbikes appeared on a nearby hill and watched the village. Warning shots were fired and, suddenly, there was a prebattle tension in the air. Everyone knew that something bad was going to happen very soon, including the civilians, who melted away. The YPG/YPJ team that included Baz secured the first building next to the road that led toward Daesh territory. Then, a white Toyota Hilux appeared behind a corner about 100 yards away. At the same time, two of the *tabur*'s trucks rolled in from a different direction. Baz and a second *heval* on the roof tried to warn their commander about the car, but their commander thought they were referring to their own trucks. With the white Hilux from enemy territory still closing in, there was a moment of confusion.

When the Hilux was less than 25 yards away, the YPG's *takem* commander and second in rank clued in and signaled the truck to stop.

When the *takem* commander walked toward the Hilux, he looked inside, stopped, and sprinted back to safety, yelling "*Lede, lede!*—fire, fire!" The enemy had come to kill the YPG/YPJ team, but the *hevals* had already set an ambush.

In that village somewhere south of Suluc, the *tabur* was then tasked with establishing defensive positions and securing the sector until other units could move up and take over the defense of the new front line. Indeed, the village was in the very area the human rights watchdog Amnesty International mentioned in a report[1] that accused the YPG/YPJ of war crimes, in particular, forceful displacement and destruction of Arab villages. While in a way all of this is true, on the ground, it felt somewhat different to what the report suggested.

During the summer of 2015, the valley of the Balikh River was a lawless, ungoverned space populated by guerilla units holding a poorly defined front line. The enemy would attack in civilian clothes, and many civilians provided intel on YPG/YPJ positions. No one knew what was going on since the YPG/YPJ had to try to coordinate a massive military operation with just some cheap walkie-talkies. *Taburs* were cut off from supplies and their front-line commanders all the time. Enemy SVBIEDs drove around looking for targets. YPG/YPJ positions were randomly mortared. Of course, the civilians were being moved away from the fighting. Some call this forceful displacement, others common sense. The truth is probably halfway in between.

Regarding the issue of starvation, and with all due respect to Amnesty International, in the summer of 2015, the whole of Rojava did not have enough food. That included YPG/YPJ, the Kurdish, and unfortunately, Arab civilians, too. The reason for the lack of food, however, was not the YPG/YPJ but the economic embargo being imposed by all sides, including Turkey, the autonomous Kurdistan Region in Iraq, and the Syrian Regime.

The second war crime the report highlighted was the destruction of Arab villages. Baz can confirm that is true. The entire village in which the *tabur* was based was ransacked by *hevals* from that unit. The inside of every single house was trashed. Indeed, some of the young *hevals* went to the effort of ripping out every page of every Arabic book. It was the language of the oppressor, and instead of just burning the books, they wanted the satisfaction of destroying them bit by bit. They also cut the cord of every single electronic device. They ate the edible animals and killed the rest anyway. What Baz witnessed in the village was a deadly cocktail of armed young men full of racial hatred and a lust for revenge.

Kurdish fighters, representing the formerly repressed, now had Arabs, their former oppressors, begging for their lives. It was war in its most primitive and horrifying form. After a couple of days in the village, there was not a single functioning or useful item left. When Baz saw a stomped-on bottle of medicine for a baby, he lost his shit.

Citing the movement's ideas on humanism and respect, Baz brought his concerns to the *tabur*'s commander, who just nodded in a tired and somewhat absent way. His answer was, "War, Heval Baz. It's war." Fuck that. To Baz, Amnesty International, and the Geneva Conventions, it was a war crime, and the perpetrators should be held responsible. Steaming with self-righteousness, Baz and other international volunteers grabbed their bags to hitch a ride out of there.

Reflecting on the situation years later, Baz's assessment became more nuanced. At the time, the YPG/YPJ could not organize their own forces on the battlefield. The militia simply did not have the means of communication for an organized operation behind the front lines. At least in the case of the destruction Baz witnessed, there was no organized attempt to change the demographics of the future corridor in favor of the Kurds (in other words, to push Arabs out of their homes in order to make this area Kurdish).

To Baz, the explanation for what had happened was much simpler. The destruction of the village was committed by kids who had fought in a nasty war for way too long. Many of their friends had died at the hands of Daesh. Growing up Kurdish in the Middle East, they had learned to hate Arabs. So yes, these kids did commit a war crime. When they were bored and angry, they destroyed a Daesh village in a war that had escalated.

However, what they did not commit—in contrast to pretty much everyone else in Syria—were mass killings, torture, or any form of sex-ualized violence and abuse. Instead, the movement allowed international observers into these disputed areas south of Tel Abiat. There are not many factions in the Middle East that would even consider such transparency. According to Rojava's idea of restorative justice, all of the *hevals* who had been involved in the destruction were required go back to the village, apologize to their Arab elders after sharing *chai*, and help restore it with the budget they received from the movement. While we know that such reconciliation occurred in some places, we do not know if that was the case in the described village.

At the time, though, Baz was less reflective. He had not experienced for himself what the enemy was really like. So far, he had just been driving around the desert with a bunch of kids, drinking *chai*, and smoking too many Ardens. Baz did not yet know that blind rage. He was still an intellectual. The war had to be right and just. Otherwise, he had no reason for being there.

Thus, still fuming, Baz and other international volunteers arrived at an improvised logistics hub just behind the front line, where they ran into a bunch of white dudes in civilian clothes with no badges but bearing Gucci weapons and all sorts of nifty gear. They were not international volunteers. In fact, they were French special forces unsuccesfully trying to stay anonymous.

With the French special forces came what would become known as the "Internet Van," a white van that always had internet and was used by the militia's media team as well as the special forces. It was clear to everyone that France had begun coordinating air strikes and wanted to see what the YPG/YPJ were like from up close. It was also rumored that many of the jets bombing ISIS were not American or British, but French. However, none of us could confirm that. It was June 2015, three months before the official beginning of *Opération Chammal* (Operation *Sandstorm*), France's military operation against the Islamic State in Iraq and Syria. In January 2015, ISIS had attacked Paris. Now, France was bringing the war to ISIS.[2]

From an American perspective, the operation was still going extremely well. Covered by air strikes, the highly mobile units advanced with rapid speed. So far, there were very few casualties on their side, no civilians had died in the bombings, and the enemy had put up virtually no resistance.

It was almost too good to be true. Yet the alliance was fragile, with little actual communication between the Kurds and American forces. America felt a bit like a third entity on the battlefield with no physical connection between the forces on the ground and the Combined Joint Task Force—Operation *Inherent Resolve*, or CJTF-OIR. Thus, the special forces were a welcome sight for many *hevals*, since they signaled that the relationship might be intensified in the future.

Whilst Baz and the others were watching the special forces guys, a truck containing some German-Turkish Maoists pulled up. Some crazy communists had just founded an international unit and were looking for more volunteers. Baz asked if the unit would destroy villages. Looking shocked, the Maoist *heval* denied it, so Baz and Jefferson jumped on the truck. In war, priorities change quickly. As long as these dudes from their weird leftist sect were cool with civilians and went to the front lines, they were good enough.

The new outfit only had one *takem* of about 12 fighters, split into two teams. The *heval* in charge was not fit to lead a unit. Maybe back home he was a nice guy, but out there, he should never have been in a position of power. He was a political compromise between the different Turkish communist groups involved in the unit. At first, that did not matter. With American jets bombing all known enemy positions just ahead of advancing Kurdish units, the offensive still went well and, within the *takem*, team commander Heval Mazlum was the one actually in charge.

Heval Mazlum was one of these guys who were made for war, and he knew it. Without war, he would have probably had an OK life, but in war, he excelled. He was one of the few people in whom war brings out the best; it makes them go beyond the norm. He started with Hezbollah when he was 11. Now he was much older. Sometime in his 20s, he'd become a communist, so he continued to fight with them. Having developed a reputation as a fierce warrior, Heval Mazlum knew all the relevant people and negotiated his *takem* to spearhead one of the advancing battle groups.

Under his leadership, in a rush, the *takem* of international fighters secured one village after another, each time waiting until reinforcements arrived and then continuing the advance. However, speeding through the desert, they encountered not a single enemy. Suddenly, they were in Tel Abiat, and the enemy had gone. The large grain silo had already been adorned with the obligatory huge YPG flag. In the streets, convoys of YPG/YPJ fighters were celebrating. Daesh had given the surrounded city up and retreated via Turkey.

For the YPG/YPJ, this was a historic moment. Everywhere in the city, *hevals* were celebrating, shouting *"Rojava kalas*—Rojava is finished." At this stage, the predominantly Kurdish areas were under YPG/YPJ control; the Kobane and Cizire *cantons* were connected and secured through an alliance with the mighty America. To some *hevals*, the war was over. Rojava was free. *Kalas*, or finished, they could go home soon and fight Turkey again. What a bizarre reason to celebrate, but whatever. The operation was officially declared over, and the majority of American jets disappeared. Attached to Tabur Şehîd Azadi, the communist *takem* including Baz and Jefferson was now deployed south of Tel Abiat.

★

Similar to John, who had experienced life in the U.S. military, Shaun was still uncomfortable with YPG's fighting style. Compared to his training in the British Army, the YPG/YPJ had no resources, very limited training, and did pretty much everything differently to his training. He felt that this war was being fought somewhat recklessly, and while he was generally OK with dying, he did not want to throw his life away.

Hanging out in Erbil, after a few days, Shaun realized that he needed a proper break from the region and flew to Berlin for some much-needed R&R. He partied for two weeks and visited the Gestapo Museum in between. After this booze-infused intermezzo, Shaun felt ready for war again and flew back to Erbil. His plan was to join the Iraqi-Kurdish Peshmerga. From what he could see, they had better gear, helmets, matching uniforms, and a rank structure. In short, they looked more like the British Army, a force he understood.

After he had linked up with other former Rojava vets who had joined the Peshmerga, he quickly changed his mind. Apparently, the Peshmerga did not do much fighting. Instead, they pulled endless boring guard shifts behind berms. Although Shaun did not yet understand the historical and constitutional reasons for it, it was clear to him that the Peshmerga would not do much more advancing. They were content with what they had, and the enemy did not have the resources to launch any large-scale attacks against them anymore. If he wanted to fight Daesh, he had to go back to the *hevals* across the border.

Trying to get comfortable with the idea of returning to the YPG, he picked up a teaching gig at one of the many international schools in Erbil, where he taught English to the grandchildren of some of Iraq's highest-ranking politicians. Dealing with the spoiled kids of Iraq's super-rich elite made Shaun reflect on his time in Rojava. Over there, politicians did not have either licit or illicit access to such wealth. Rojava's politicians lived in regular apartments, eating simple food unless they had to provide a meal for honored guests. Witnessing the contrast in Erbil, a comparatively Westernized city, Shaun found a new respect for the *hevals*.

At the same time, he realized that the cultural differences that had presented a challenge to him existed in Erbil as well. Here, they were just masked by the new shopping malls and multiplex cinemas. Once he held his first salary, a brown envelope filled with brand-new 100-dollar notes, in his hand, he decided to go back to Rojava.

Just like John, he promised himself not to constantly insist on being right. This was not his war; he was just a visitor to an ancient conflict. If he wanted to succeed, he needed to take a step back and relax. He reminded himself he was here voluntarily and could leave at any time. This was a privilege other *hevals* did not have, so he would suck it up. Shaun acknowledged the complexity of the conflict and his very limited understanding of the place. During his second tour, he would begin to float with the current instead of swimming against it the entire time. He had to think more like the guerillas, not regular British infantry.

CHAPTER 8

Daesh's Counter Offensive: July–September 2015

The corridor through Arab land connecting Kobane *canton* with Cizire *canton* that had just been opened needed to be secured against counter-attacks. Celebrating their easy victory, *taburs* went to serve their boring stint at the berms. Whereas the *taburs* had previously rushed through the villages to get to the empty city, they now had to go back to secure the area. While the units were slowly moving back south, they walked into a landscape of IEDs the enemy had left for them. Wherever a *tabur* went, there were IEDs. Still drunk on their supposedly easy victory, inexperienced units became complacent and were torn to bits by mines and booby traps.

One morning, Baz smoked a cigarette with Heval Mazlum and asked the experienced fighter how to survive a war. His answer was "luck." Later that day, Heval Mazlum, Jefferson, and others left for a small operation to clear some villages and compounds.

In the late afternoon, Baz and the rest of his unit heard a massive explosion. Judging by the dirty black pillar of smoke that rose from behind a nearby hill, it was too big to be an air strike, plus low-grade explosives had been used. Seconds later, the radio chatter confirmed what everyone already knew. The team had been hit with an IED. Half an hour later, the trucks returned. When Jefferson jumped out, he shook his head. "Heval Mazlum is dead."

It emerged that, following the orders of a front-line commander, the *hevals* had searched a few villages and were done for the day. Yet the ambitious commander had wanted to search one more village, ignoring the warnings of a local. Heval Mazlum had told Jefferson that he had a bad feeling. Managing to leave the rest of his team behind, only Heval Mazlum went to follow the order. The next moment, he and the *hevals* from another unit disappeared in a ball of fire. As became apparent later, Daesh had connected several Russian anti-tank mines underneath the village. Triggered by a sophisticated IED, the entire village and everyone in it simply evaporated. Luck. It's all about luck.

With Şehîd Mazlum gone, Tabur Şehîd Azadi's commander and the commander of the international *takem* were suddenly actually in charge, and the situation began to unravel. Within a week, half of the YPG/YPJ *tabur* and the attached international *takem* were either dead or severely wounded. The situation escalated when Tabur Şehîd Azadi and the international *takem* were attacked with an SVBIED. A barricade had been placed too close to the badly set-up FOB. The enemy had seen the weakness in the defenses and used it. Letting complacency spread like cancer, many *hevals* had been sitting behind the barricade to catch a cool evening breeze when a civilian car had driven up. The driver had looked like he wanted to ask for the way. Then the car exploded. According to Baz, who was protected in a walled courtyard, the car's chassis formed into a huge piece of shrapnel that sliced its way through the *hevals*. The entire force of the SVBIED's blast was directed forward toward its target. Daesh had turned suicide bombers into a sophisticated weapon that almost equaled air strikes in terms of casualties inflicted and morale damaged.

In the immediate aftermath of the bomb, Baz went up on a roof, securing the perimeter in case the enemy sent in gunmen. When he looked over his shoulder into the courtyard, he saw young Heval Akif in a fireman's hold between two friends. Hanging there unconscious, his entire front was burned black. His uniform was black, his face was black, and his hair was black. The only color in all the black were red tears of blood running from his eyes all the way down his cheeks.

Over the years, in Baz's head, this snapshot of the injured Heval Akif has turned into a dark painting of hopelessness and despair, an image that leaves him so emotionally overwhelmed that he feels the need to scream so his head doesn't explode. Thrown on the back of a Hilux and driven for two hours to the closest hospital, somehow, Heval Akif survived.

According to a popular conspiracy theory that tries to explain the easy victory, Daesh sold Tel Abiat to the Kurds. We, however, think that Daesh's retreat had just been a ruse in a larger plot. In the summer of 2015, Daesh were not prepared for the American-Kurdish alliance. With Tel Abiat not ready to withhold the combined force, the enemy was realistic. Instead of throwing their lives away in a battle they were sure to lose, they retreated into Turkey, where they outflanked the YPG/YPJ. Somewhere around Jarablus and Manbij they re-entered Syria and waited for the American jets to disappear and for the YPG/YPJ to become complacent. Once this had happened, Daesh returned to the Balikh River valley and fought back in the form of an insurgency.

On a very small scale, the front along the corridor had many similarities with the failed American invasion of Iraq in 2003. Evading a direct battle they could not win in the countryside, Daesh waged a guerilla war against the YPG/YPJ, causing constant casualties in faceless attacks, messing with the invaders' morale. Many in the YPG/YPJ were guerilla fighters themselves and were overwhelmed with controlling a hostile population. They were used to fighting for and with the people against the invaders. Here in the Balikh valley in the summer of 2015, all of this had changed. It was messy and against everything the movement stood for. In a short period of time and with very limited means of communication, Daesh had adapted to the changes on the battlefield and, in particular, American airpower in a way that undermined the YPG/YPJ's own ethical code and thus the morale of the *hevals*. Tel Abiat was not an easy victory and demonstrated just how clever Daesh were. Rojava would not be finished until the Caliphate was gone. There could be no peace with those neighbors. This meant that the war would not only continue, it would get much worse. The *hevals*, including Baz, realized that.

★

For obvious reasons, that place now had bad juju, so Jefferson and Baz hitched a ride to a different front line. They ended up in Hasake, a major city of strategic importance. Until the beginning of Ramadan, the holy month, in June 2015, the limits of Caliphate had ended south of

Hasake. Trying to compensate for the recently lost Tel Abiat, Daesh thus launched a Ramadan offensive against the Regime there. At the time, the Syrian Regime held large parts of the city. However, it was not prepared against such an offensive and pulled out of various neighborhoods ahead of Daesh's assault. Wherever the Regime created a security vacuum by leaving, the YPG/YPJ and Daesh raced each other to fill it.

Having just experienced the might of American airpower around Tel Abiat and the nearby Abdel Aziz mountains, in Hasake, Daesh made sure not to attack the YPG/YPJ and draw America into this particular battle. Instead, the Sunni Islamists turned on the Shia fundamentalists from the Lebanese Hezbollah who had arrived to fight on behalf of the Syrian Alawi Regime. Occasionally, presumably Russian jets would bomb Daesh on behalf of the Syrian Regime, but we never got confirmation of the origin of those bombers. What we do know is that they had a distinct triangular shape and came in from Regime-controlled territory.

The *tabur* Jefferson and Baz joined occupied two large school buildings, the preferred base for anyone fighting on the ground in Syria. As some of the *hevals* would explain later, the Syrian Regime had built the country's schools in a specific way in case of an uprising. All schools therefore had solid walls and were at least two stories high. They were always sited at strategic locations, such as junctions, the entrance of a city, or on high ground. The rule in this war was whoever controls the schools controls the settlement. Essentially, urban warfare in northeastern Syria was a war over school buildings, places of education for a future generation.

This particular school in Hasake was next to the highway coming into the city from the south, overlooking a large, open field. Whoever controlled the school thus controlled a large neighborhood and the vast field between the city and the villages. The next village Daesh was in was about 800 yards south of the school, across the field. In the neighborhood southwest of the school was the front line with Hezbollah. During the day, the *hevals* would roam the deserted city, trying to find a functioning shower or food.

During those days, Baz and Jefferson got to know Heval Armanc and Heval Bawer, two Kurdish fighters who together epitomized the best of the movement. Heval Bawer was disciplined and well versed in the theory of democratic confederalism. In his early 20s, he was hospitable and reflective—attributes that both Baz and Jefferson knew would get him killed very soon. Heval Bawer cared too much in order to survive a war like this. Heval Armanc was funny and good for morale. When Baz had first met him, Heval Armanc had climbed up on the roof of the school's entrance and cut off an Assad banner with a large combat knife. Although his commander was concerned about the politics behind Heval Armanc's stunt, other *hevals* were cheering him. He was a fearless fighter.

During the clear nights, when Baz was on guard on the roof of the four-story high school in Hasake, he watched Daesh and Hezbollah, the two most extreme factions of Sunni and Shia Islam, fight each other during their holy month. The many individual gunshots mounted to a cacophony of death that had nothing tactical or strategic about it. It was hundreds of weapons being fired in an act of blind rage, trying to annihilate the archenemy and secure themselves a spot in their sect's paradise. In between, the sound of Regime helicopters intensified the soundtrack dramatically when they dropped their barrel bombs in the Daesh quarter. Trying to chase the helicopters away, several Daesh machine gunners fired their weapons in the air. In the dark night, their tracers drew red circles into the skies. Responding to the barrel bombs, Daesh sent in waves of SVBIEDs that raced toward the Hezbollah positions, where they would detonate themselves. On both sides, religious fanatics were literally trying to die so they could break the fast with the prophet. What Baz watched during those night shifts was not normal fighting. It was insanity.

At more than 120 degrees Fahrenheit, the days were unbearably hot, filled with flies and boredom. With nothing but time, Baz roamed around the school, where he found a picture one of the children must have painted just before the Daesh offensive started. In the rather disturbing drawing, everyone was dead or bleeding. A young girl was bleeding from the head while a sniper aimed at her. Planes dropped bombs on civilians who were bleeding. An old man with a crutch was bleeding from his hip, walking in a puddle of blood. Next to him was a child. In the top-left corner were an ambulance and two medics. From their stretcher, blood ran into another pool of blood. In the bottom-left corner were two cheerful women, holding a Syrian flag. As if to make a statement, the red triangle in the Regime's flag morphed into, guess what, one of the blood pools. It was an honest reflection of how the children in Syria saw men like Baz. It was very sobering. He had come here to do good, but was he really doing that, or was he just another fighter in an endless war?

Although looking at the drawing during those feverishly hot days in Hasake was almost painful, Baz kept staring at it in fascination. Clearly, Syria had enough people running around with AKs shooting other people. Still seeing Heval Akif's burned body in his mind, the need was obvious. What this war did *not* have enough of was people trying to save lives, not take them. During this epiphany, Baz knew that he had to become a combat medic, or at least something close to that. Having lost about 15 pounds in body weight in the last five months, he was ready to tap out anyway. With a clear plan in his head, he therefore went back to Germany and signed up for an emergency medical technician (EMT) course. Similar to John and Shaun, this first tour was more of an orientation. The real deployment was still to come.

PART II

THE NEW SYRIAN DEMOCRATIC FORCES GO TO WAR: OCTOBER 2015 TO DECEMBER 2016

CHAPTER 9

A New Alliance Is Formed: October 2015–January 2016

In early October 2015, a new alliance was formed in Hasake: the Syrian Democratic Forces, or SDF. In their very brief English press release,[1] the SDF was explained as a multireligious and multiethnic force that would fight for democracy in Syria. However, in a war characterized by an ever-changing network of thousands of militias and alliances, this new force did not receive too much attention at first. Instead, many, including us, thought of it as a rhetorical exercise and diplomatic PR stunt initiated by the Americans.

Throughout the first phase of the American intervention in Syria, the official discourse of the White House and State Department was the denial of the obvious: the YPG/YPJ were not the PKK; the YPG/YPJ were just one of many anti-ISIS groups in Syria who were supported with air strikes; the YPG/YPJ did not receive ammunition, just Arab groups affiliated with the YPG/YPJ; and the YPG/YPJ were not key partners.[2] The reason for this position was Turkey. To keep the peace with their NATO partner, America had to downplay their support for Turkey's enemy: the PKK and their affiliates the YPG/YPJ. However, anyone who had spent just a couple of days in Rojava knew that, in reality, this was utter nonsense.

During the first phase of America's involvement when it dealt with the YPG/YPJ, probably more than 50 percent of their fighting units were made up of PKK ranks. For stateless people, solidarity is essential in order to survive in a hostile region. Without the PKK, there would not have been enough weapons, ammo, and experienced trigger pullers.

Without the PKK, the people of Rojava would have shared the fate of the Yazidis in Shingal. In fact, none of us was ever a particular fan of the PKK; however, their role in this phase of the war is undeniable. Accusing the YPG/YPJ of being affiliated with PKK on the eve of their genocide was never a valid point, but rather the rhetoric of poorly informed partisan politics. Without the PKK, in 2014 and 2015, tens of thousands of civilians would have died, or been displaced or enslaved.

However, during this second phase of American involvement, the SDF solved the whole PKK-YPG/YPJ issue for the Americans. Instead of having to refer to a loose and nameless anti-ISIS entity somewhere in the desert or the PKK, the Obama administration now had an actual neutral reference point: the SDF. Suddenly, the YPG/YPJ were recognized as being just two out of 15 other militias, including Christian forces and many Arab tribal warriors.

Then, a little later, in December 2015, the Syrian Democratic Council (SDC) was created. Where the new SDF are the de facto defense forces, the SDC is its political counterpart. Where Rojava used to be predominantly Kurdish (although all leadership positions reflected both genders and diverse ethnic and religious groups), in the SDC, the proportion of Arabs increased. Both the SDF and the SDC combined to constitute the first step in a long process of moving beyond a Kurdish democracy project toward a regional one. Both were born from democratic confederalism because nobdy else in the region pushed for similar federalism and a decentralization of armed forces. And both were soon to become the official reference point for American success in Syria. Indeed, during this second phase of American involvement against ISIS in Syria, the Obama administration soon forgot about the YPG/YPJ and began praising the glorious SDF, a multireligious, multiethnic alliance capable of defeating Daesh.[3]

While all of this is most certainly true, the benefit for Obama of introducing the SDF was a positive by-product of the alliance and not the actual reasoning behind the new force. In reality, the assumption that Arab tribes, ancient Christian communities, and Kurdish groups who have all been fighting for their existence for hundreds, if not thousands, of years would all jump and gather around a table as soon as America whistled is the kind of arrogant, Western-centric thinking that got everyone into the present mess in the first place.

What the new SDF was really about was Rojava. When Baz had visited northern Syria as a geography teacher, he had had the opportunity to debate the idea of Rojava with one of the three heads of the Cizire *canton's* assembly in Amude. In late 2014, while the YPG/YPJ were still fighting for survival, Baz had asked one of its representatives where the actual borders of Rojava were. The answer by the co-chair of the assembly was, "Rojava has no borders; it is an idea of freedom, equality, and democracy."

"But how does YPG/YPJ protect an idea? They need to have borders they can protect, a territory they secure. Armed fighters need to have a physical line in the sand they are ordered to hold," Baz probed.

"YPG/YPJ protects the people who want to live free and democratic," was the answer.

"I don't understand this. Without a defined territory, how can Rojava become a state, then?"

"Hahaha! Heval, Rojava does not want to become a state. Rojava evolved beyond borders and nationalism. That's why it is about true freedom."

The idea of Rojava is based on democratic confederalism, a political theory written with the blood and tears of a stateless people: the Kurds. At its core, democratic confederalism identified the nation-state as the root cause for the people's suffering. Almost every single ethnic and religious group in the region had, at some point, been victim to the new concept of the nation-state. Instead of bringing peace and stability, the Western notion of statehood as introduced to the Middle East in the early 20th century created nothing but brutal regimes, police states, and biographies governed by fear.

Consequently, democratic confederalism aims to make the nation-state meaningless. It is the political evolution beyond statehood. Instead of a nation-state, the theory advocates a federal landscape in which each religion and ethnic group can live their lives the way they want, free of any hostile or ethnically or religiously different regime interference. The theory is about freedom and autonomous self-administration, not nationality and territory. The freedom of Sunnis, Shias, Christians, atheists, Yazidis, Kurds, Arabs, Turkmen, Assyrians, Chaldeans, youth, and women. The only concessions expected from all participating groups are gender equality and adherence to a set of very basic freedoms, including the right to education, the right to a fair trial, and so forth.

In the past, Daesh had offered the notoriously discriminated-against Sunni Arab tribes in Syria a similar deal: they would reign over their lands again. They promised the Sunni tribes status and prestige, something they had forgotten under the pro-Shia Assad clan. Daesh promised to end the disenfranchisement of the tribes. In return, they had to join the apocalyptic cult and abide by a set of crazy rules that impacted all levels of life. Somewhere along the way, Daesh even managed to replace love with rape.

The SDF offered the same tribes not only the opportunity to truly rule their land with their own militias but also to enjoy life whilst living it. The SDF offered the tribes actual freedom in their lands: to govern their own affairs in an ancient tribal manner. This was the best deal the tribes had been offered in decades. The whole hearts-and-minds approach of Western militaries is not about taking off your boots before meeting with elders, soft heads instead of helmets, or drinking *chai* during patrols. It is about alliances like the SDF.

Democratic confederalism is the political theory behind Rojava, and Rojava is protected by the SDF. Thus, the SDF fight for an idea of free people, not a territory. Only four months earlier, the YPG/YPJ had occupied Arab lands in the Balikh River valley south of Tel Abiat. A military necessity had therefore forced Rojava into a compromise with their own political theory, and its fighters had paid dearly for that mistake. For a brief moment, Rojava had abandoned the moral high ground and did what everyone else did. They'd conquered and occupied. Consequently, they'd faced a hostile population. Immediately, the enemy had used this weakness and turned it to their advantage. Moving amongst a friendly population, Daesh waged a small-scale insurgency the YPG/YPJ were not prepared for in any way. In the past, they had been the ones doing the guerilla fighting. There, it was the other way around.

With the arrival of the new SDF forces, which included groups from the Tel Abiat region, this problem had been solved. Arabs from the Balikh River area would now secure their homes while Kurdish units would pull out gradually. When founding the SDF, the Balikh River area changed from an occupied territory into a free autonomous region where folk could mind their own business; meanwhile, the Kurds just zapped through on the highway. Instead of being assimilated into a predominantly Kurdish *canton*, the people around Tel Abiat thus became their own administrative unit and governed their lives directly. This was a good deal and, once their own leaders had explained it to their people, they actually liked it.

On the ground, it meant that where Baz had been spat at in the summer of 2015, in the summer of 2016, the same people smiled when his *tabur* came by. What's more, with the creation of the SDF, Baz finally understood the idea of Rojava. It wasn't about the geographically Kurdish areas in Syria. It wasn't about territory, either, but the people who decided to be free. Until now, Rojava had been about the three Kurdish *cantons* (Cizire, Kobane, and Afrin). Now, it included the wide desert and Raqqa, Daesh's capital city.

It is worth noting here that although democratic confederalism aims to overcome the nation-state as an institution that governs everyday lives, the theory does not argue for the abolishment of statehood. Fighting for the end of all states is an unrealistic utopia. Democratic confederalism is not about a political utopia but a lived democratic society. So, instead of fighting the state as an institution, democratic confederalism opts to ignore it. For this reason, the SDF does not threaten the territorial integrity of Syria. They do not want independence and a state of their own. What the SDF does want is autonomy: a radical federalism. They want to be left alone within the existing borders of Syria. If the Assad clan rules Damascus, it is of little concern to Rojava. Here, this difference between autonomy and independence is not academic wordplay but essential for understanding. Autonomy is an achievable goal. Under the right circumstances, even dictators can grant it without losing face. Independence simply wasn't achievable. Neither Turkey nor Syria would concede any of their territory. Before it came to that, both states chose to defend their territorial integrity with yet more genocide.

The new alliance also enabled the YPG/YPJ to emancipate themselves from the PKK. With the formation of the SDF, the YPG/YPJ no longer needed PKK fighters for their immediate military advice or weaponry in order to survive. With the SDF in place, the YPG/YPJ could find their own voice and fighting culture. Thus, the PKK began their partial withdrawal from Rojava. When so-called experts claim that the names YPG/YPJ and PKK could be used interchangeably, they, again, apply a rather Western-centric perspective. The Kurds are not the homogenous group one might think when looking at it from the West. Concepts such as pride, respect, and dignity play an essential role in Middle Eastern power games.

Fighters from Syria who fought in Syria did not like it when Kurdish commanders from Turkey bossed them around. Fighters from Rojava did not always trust commanders from Turkey but were ready to follow their own people into death. Many Syrian Kurds would have even preferred an Arab commander from their region over another Kurd from the PKK. This point matters as it can win battles or be the extra motivation to stay awake during endless nighttime guard shifts when the enemy is crawling around with long knives.

Despite commonly held beliefs, along the front lines, there was always a difference between the PKK members from Turkey and the Syrian YPG/YPJ. The Syrian *hevals* often thought the PKK were arrogant whereas the PKK frequently viewed the Syrians as dumb villagers, or *gundis*. Many PKK fighters also did not want to be there. They did not care about Rojava or Daesh and wanted to fight Turkey back at home (we constantly overheard conversations during which young fighters asked to return to Turkey). Thanks to the SDF, some of these tensions were lifted when the PKK began pulling out many of their fighters.

Indeed, over time, the SDF slowly changed its sartorial style from mountain guerilla-chic to a desert rebel fighter look. In 2015, we remember how the PKK fighters who came in from the mountains were appalled when they had to change from their comfortable, identity-giving PKK uniforms into the poor-quality pyjamas in YPG cammo. With the PKK's withdrawal and the success of the SDF, the guerilla pants and original red army AKs were out. Copying their Arab allies, even Kurdish fighters started wearing skinny combat pants, fashionable sneakers, and hoodies.

At the same time, generations of international volunteers left their gear behind for their friends when they departed the war. So, slowly, a

Western special forces style emerged. Plate carriers and badges bearing the YPG or YPJ logo that international volunteers bought at the bazaars became status symbols on the uniforms of this spartan militia. The fashionable rifle became the American M16 instead of the AK the *hevals* had previously loved. In addition to airsoft scopes, plastic M320 grenade launchers were now seen. Commanders suddenly carried Glocks instead of Makarovs. We interpreted this as a sign of increasing trust between the Americans and the SDF as well as the SDF's internal alliance between the Kurds and Arabs.

★

When Shaun left Erbil and was smuggled back into Rojava in October 2015, he was not aware of any of this. Given the renewed conflict between the PKK and Turkey, his second trip through the Kurdish mountain camps in Iraq had been a sobering experience. The old transit camp had been bombed, and many of the *hevals* we had met there had died. With the Turkish F16s above, there was no more volleyball and ice cream. Instead, the mountain shook with each air strike. The jets were American-made and flown by Turkish pilots who bombed the Kurds from the PKK, a stateless people.

Once Shaun had arrived at Rojava, he tried to find a front-line *tabur*. He had heard rumors about the liberation of Shingal that was starting soon, and this was where he wanted to be. Shingal had become something of a mythical name, akin to the status attached to the heroic resistance of the Daesh-besieged Kobane. Its liberation was not about the small destroyed city in the desert but a powerful emblem. Shingal had become synonymous with the worst ISIS had done. Like Auschwitz, Mỹ Lai, or Wounded Knee, it would go into history books as a place where evil happened, where fanatics celebrated barbarism and collectively left the post-enlightenment consensus. The liberation of Shingal was about more than fighting for some rubble in the sand; it was a symbol to the world as well as to the enemy. Taking the city back was the beginning of the end for ISIS. Shaun understood this, and he wanted to be there.

Unlike John, the Marine who had been oblivious to the geopolitical nightmare around Shingal, Shaun was fascinated by this maze of checkpoints and different flags, including those of the KDP Peshmerga, PUK Peshmerga, the Turkish communists of the MLKP, the PKK, and the PKK-affiliated Yazidi militia of the YBS. Technically, he was back in Iraq via a detour through Syria, and although the PKK transit camp that was bombed by Turkey was only 100 miles away, here in Shingal, the F16s were fighting on the side of the PKK because they had American pilots. In Shingal, Shaun began to understand how power functioned.

Whilst the Hilux was plowing through mud and the usual rebel tunes were blasting, Shaun felt an increasing gap between his previous interventionist ideas and the reality on the ground. This place did not need some Western, blanket idea of liberal democracy but deserved a grassroots understanding. When the truck arrived at the front line, Shaun saw the Peshmerga forces on top of the mountain. Watching the endless columns of brand-new American MRAPs (armored personnel carriers) and Humvees that were staging on the muddy roads, he knew that the YPG/YPJ, and even the PKK, would only be spectators to the show.

In between the shiny new armored vehicles were hundreds of international journalists. Different to the more symbolic air strikes John had witnessed in Shingal 10 months earlier, now the Americans were hammering the relatively small ISIS garrison into submission. Acknowledging the symbolism, Obama wanted his jets there for the photo op. The part of the city Daesh held was not only destroyed, it was almost gone.

Before fleeing the city in August 2014, someone had painted "we want internationally [sic] troops" on one of the rooftops of the city. The Yazidis had hoped for the help of the international community in the form of the United Nations. Over a year later, the text was still there. Although CJTF-OIR's drones must have seen it every single day, the international community still did not care much for the Yazidis. Looking down at the graffiti from the hills, Shaun realized that the Yazidis would never see UN peacekeepers who would shield them from their next genocide. Now that he saw power working on the ground, he became disillusioned by the notorious absence of the supposedly humanitarian international organizations he had once believed in.

From the gravel of the city, and to everyone's surprise, Daesh still mortared Kurdish and Yazidi forces every morning. Using their tunnels, throughout the day, snipers would harass the Peshmerga and *hevals*. One day, a fixed-wing Daesh surveillance drone flew by. The homemade glider got stuck on a roof. With the mortaring having turned into a routine, this was the only event that broke up the boredom. Only before the big push to liberate Shingal did Daesh put up more resistance; although the gunfights increased in intensity, they remained harmless. It was the last attack by a wounded beast. The actual advance of the liberators on the city faced almost no resistance. Indeed, when the ground offensive began in November 2015, the attacking force was so overwhelming that the enemy stood no chance. The resistance in the city was minor. The only casualties Shaun saw were a result of the IEDs at the front lines. Once the *taburs* had pushed through this initial ring of mines, the advance was surprisingly easy.

Ultimately, the liberation became a logistical exercise to allow all involved forces to have a part in the victory parade. All over the city, fighters from various groups took photos that would soon flood social media. Later, Shaun watched the Peshmerga take down the ISIS flag from a grain silo and replace it with their own so that they could post a photo of it on Facebook. Shortly after, he watched how the same ISIS flag was hung back up on the same grain silo so that it could be taken down by Yazidi fighters, who replaced it with their own flag. That video too ended up on Facebook. Everyone wanted to be seen as the liberators, so the same ISIS flag was taken down and replaced by a different one several times for the waiting smartphones. From a soldiering perspective, this was a disappointment. From an academic one, it was a fascinating case study on power and propaganda in the social media age.

★

Meanwhile in Rojava, the al-Hol offensive was in full swing. In their very first small operation, the SDF advanced south of Hasake along the border with Iraq, closing the gap in the front lines between the Abdel

Aziz mountains in the west and the advancing Kurdish units south of Shingal in Iraq. In many respects, this operation was distinctly different from anything the YPG/YPJ had been involved with before, including the brief disaster south of Tel Abiat, where Arab lands had been occupied for some time. Although the area between the Cizire and Kobane *cantons* along the river was predominantly Arab, the belt along the Turkish border and the highway was still fairly heterogeneous. Over the centuries, Kurds, Arabs, and Christians had lived there in close proximity.

The al-Hol operation began pushing into the Arab heartland, the desert belonging to the Sunni Arab tribes that had ruled it forever. Throughout hundreds of years, many had tried to conquer these tribes but soon found that they were simply ungovernable. At best, foreign invaders would strike a deal and leave the desert warriors alone. Daesh's many attempts at commiting genocide on the tribes who rejected their rule ultimately led to the SDF's wide alliance, which would be the Islamist's doom. Alone, the YPG/YPJ would have never dreamed of advancing south of Hasake. Alone, the Kurdish militias had no business going there. It would have been a crass contradiction to their philosophy of democratic confederalism. The last time the SDF had compromised on their ideas there had been a spike in casualty rates. However, with the SDF, the YPG/YPJ were now in an alliance with tribes from the region and were able to liberate one village after another in a swift operation. And, although the al-Hol operation was fairly small and had been limited to open desert and a few smaller settlements, it was an important first test for the new SDF with a focus on the tribes from the desert south of Hasake.

The second test for the SDF would take place further west along the Euphrates. With some remnants of the Free Syrian Army and Arab forces from the Euphrates region, the SDF was about to advance south of Kobane along the Euphrates River. Having missed the al-Hol operation, Shaun wanted to be part of this next push. Since each *canton* had their own YPG and YPJ force, including separate command structures, he began the tedious process of being transferred to Kobane's YPG. However, with the official transfer leading nowhere, Shaun eventually took a shortcut and made it to the Jarablus front line, where he found a Kurdish *tabur* securing the banks of the eastern side of the Euphrates.

On the ground, this was the SDF's heyday. Many Kurdish fighters were still suspicious about their new Arab allies since there was a good chance that, at some point in the past, they had shot at each other. Shaun's *tabur* commander therefore warned him to keep his rifle close when the Arabs showed up. According to the Kurdish *tabur*, they could not be trusted. In consequence, there were constant rumors about standoffs between *hevals* and Arab units.

★

Parallel to Shaun and his crew, John was floating around the Euphrates front lines, where he noticed the same developments. The SDF was boiling from decades of hate, oppression, and prejudice between some of the Arab groups and the Kurds. One of the few people holding the coalition together was the famous Abu Layla. Born in Kobane to Kurdish and Arab parents, he had grown up in Manbij. Representing the remnants of the Free Syrian Army around Manbij, his Northern Sun Battalion had fought with the YPG/YPJ during the battle for Kobane, where Abu Layla had become a living legend. He now embodied the SDF. He was also one of the vetted Arab allies who received American military aid when the YPG/YPJ could not be sponsored for geopolitical reasons.

In the Euphrates, John ended up being dropped outside the Northern Sun Battalion living quarters, where he was greeted by a mannequin on a wobbly plastic chair with a shotgun slung across its chest. When John went inside, a fighter was fueling up a truck. However, when he saw John, he put the jerry can down, wiped his hands with his *keffiyeh* and welcomed him. Thus John met the famous Abu Layla, who would become a martyr shortly after, during the Manbij operation.

Although the Northern Sun Battalion was welcoming and hospitable—as is common in the region—it was not quite clear with whom some of the mainly Arab fighters had fought in the past. While sipping their *chai* together, given their anti-American sentiments, clearly some of these Arabs had problems interacting with the Marine and just stared at John irritated. John saw large blades he associated with beheading videos and although he was not scared, since he enjoyed the protection of Abu

Layla, he had no intention of staying with this rugged bunch. He had absolutely nothing against the battalion and wished them all the best for the upcoming battles, but suddenly, a YPG/YPJ *tabur* felt like home. He was nevertheless glad to have had this experience, since it gave him a new respect for the *taburs* he had been part of so far. John duly headed back to Kobane to seek out some friends.

★

Rolling with two other international volunteers, Shaun looked for a new *tabur* that would go on the upcoming operation. According to the rumors floating around, the target was the strategic Tishreen Dam and the affiliated town of Tishreen. He realized that the operation would start very soon when truckloads of very high-quality SDF flags suddenly arrived. It was obvious that they had not been manufactured in one of the small collectives around Derik or Qamishlo, where the usual YPG/YPJ uniforms and flags were made. Rojava was under an embargo, and the *hevals* would not waste their smuggling operations for shiny things like flags. They needed them to bring in medication, ammo, and the like. Given the complicated geopolitical situation around Rojava's borders, the only ones who could have pulled off that feat were the Americans, although this is just speculation on our part.

Prior to the operation, Shaun had seen evidence of America's secret arms deliveries to the SDF, including the Kurds. As a well-sourced investigative report by the Organized Crime and Corruption Reporting Project would later show, the Obama administration had begun a black op, buying up Soviet-style arms starting in September 2015. A month later, the first 50 tons of ammunition and RPG rounds were dropped with the YPG/YPJ. By summer 2017, hundreds of millions of dollars had been spent on the SDF. That translates into hundreds of millions of AK rounds that had weapon manufacturers in the Balkans working at full capacity. Furthermore, the United States Special Operations Command (SOCOM or USSOCOM) bought up stockpiles of weapons and ammunition in Bulgaria, Bosnia and Herzegovina, the Czech Republic, Kazakhstan, Poland, Romania, Serbia, and the Ukraine.[4]

In his five magazines, Shaun had rounds from five different countries, mainly the Balkans and Eastern Europe, but he noticed in particular Croatian ammunition showing up more frequently at the front lines. Although not listed in the report, brand-new Albanian AKs with underfolds and foldable bayonets also began flooding the front. However, as soon as Shaun picked one up, he knew that it was useless. The metal was cheap, and Shaun was able to scratch a notch in the handguard with his nail. He much preferred to keep his old Russian AK.

Driving south along the Euphrates, Shaun and two other *americani* were still trying to find a *tabur*. Hitchhiking to the front lines, they met an old *Asayîş* who invited them into his home for *chai*. On the wall, Shaun saw a photo of a younger version of their host and Öcalan shaking hands in the mountains.

With the old man's help, they finally hitched a ride with a logistics truck to one of the staging *taburs*. Right from the beginning, Shaun picked up an odd vibe from the unit. In particular, there was something shady about the commander. The other international volunteers agreed, and the group decided to organize their own guard shifts during the night.

Once the operation began and the *taburs* had advanced without meeting much resistance, the tensions between Kurdish and Arabic SDF elements continued. For instance, when Shaun's *tabur* secured a village, the YPJ celebrated by playing their songs on the stereo of their Hilux with the doors wide open and dancing. However, seeing happy women pissed off one of the new Arab units in the alliance, so they responded by playing songs about beheading infidels—a category that included the *hevalas*. That did not go down well with the YPG/YPJ *tabur*, and the tensions quickly turned into yet another standoff in an Arab village along the Euphrates. Given the numbers, the former Islamists and new Arab allies were forced to leave.

Drunk on their power, the kids in the Kurdish *tabur* celebrated this victory over the Arabs. Kurdish songs that had been forbidden in the past were blasted from distorted car speakers and when night fell, there was cheering around large fires where armed teens danced themselves into a trance. The unit had not seen any fighting yet, but to them, the Arabs had already withdrawn. A screaming kid with an AK slung around his shoulder smashed the concrete floor of a house with a sledgehammer to little effect and for no apparent reason but ancient hatred. To him and many others, "Daesh" and "Arab" were terms still used interchangeably.

When the frenzy stopped, the *tabur* sat scattered around the village. Waking from their trance, they quietly watched the remains of their fires glow red in the cold morning hours. Led by a commander who had a distinct Colonel Kurtz—the fictional antagonist in the film *Apocalypse Now*—vibe about him and a unit full of teenagers, the inexperienced and poorly trained *tabur* had tapped into some primal instincts that drive war: an ancient ethnic hatred and the urge to avenge the many people they knew who had been killed by "Arabs." For Shaun and the other international volunteers, it was time to leave before this got out of hand.

The group of *americani* around Shaun duly befriended the logistics truck drivers who could get them anywhere in this war. Having found reliable transportation, the friends began drifting around the front lines for the remainder of the operation. Whenever they merged with the command element of the offensive, who was usually set up on some rooftop, they saw French special forces.

At first, Shaun did not notice them. Out of all of the special forces that we ran into or worked with over the following month, the French were by far the most embedded ones. Different to the Americans, who never hid but relied instead on their superior firepower, the French special forces teams were indistinguishable from the rest of the SDF unless one stood right in front of the other. They operated in very small teams, wore the same cheap uniforms, had basic AKs, drove old-looking Toyota Hiluxes, drank the same horrible 3in1 instant coffee, and lived off the same scarce food. They even wore the same Mekap guerilla shoes that guaranteed foot rot in the desert. Only when Shaun saw the advanced communication devices and high-powered binos did he realize that they were special forces. The French were invisible in the chaos that every SDF operation eventually became.

Because of the January 2015 terror attacks in Paris that had killed 20, France had been looking for an opportunity to fight Daesh directly instead of waiting for America to move. As mentioned, in summer 2015, Baz and Jefferson had seen the French reconnaissance team at the Tel Abiat front line. Then, in September 2015, France rolled out an air campaign called *Opération Chammal*, named after the notorious sandstorms. On November 13 and 14, 2015, Daesh affiliates responded to the air campaign with another terror attack in Paris that killed 130. As a French operator mentioned to Shaun, now, in December 2015, closing in on the strategic Tishreen Dam, their deployment was France's response—the next stage of the escalation in the war between France and Daesh. It was around that time that Shaun decided to study international relations if he survived the war.

From their rooftop positions, coordinating with the YPG or YPJ commander in charge, the French special forces teams monitored the advance and called in air support. Although there had always been jets in the air, now that the U.S.-led coalition CJTF-OIR had their own eyes on the ground, they could assess the target, especially for collateral damage. Thus while the response time for the jets remained the same for the first flyover, the risk of civilian casualties was minimized, at least in the open countryside.

Eventually, the first SDF *taburs* arrived at the eastern end of the strategic Tishreen Dam leading across the seemingly endless river. Shaun and two friends followed the constantly moving command post and, when they caught up with them in a village overlooking the dam, they found an SDF general lecturing the civilians about their new freedom. Since they spoke no Kurdish, the Arab villagers just nodded, bored. After all, this was not their first lecture on freedom by an armed man since 2011. From a nearby rooftop, the French launched a small surveillance drone that quickly buzzed off on a reconnaissance mission. Shortly after the little drone left, air strikes around the dam started picking up and the town of Tishreen on the western side of the dam was bombed heavily.

Throughout the night, Daesh and the SDF fought each other with heavy machine guns, and tracers flew across the water whilst air strikes illuminated the night skies. In between, AC-130 gunships and A-10 "Warthogs" picked off smaller targets that didn't warrant a bomb worth tens of thousands of dollars. The next morning, Shaun and the gang walked across the dam. The enemy was gone. They could see the large IEDs on the dams, but Daesh had not blown them up.

When they reached the western side of the dam, the friends met confused *hevals*. Apparently, the enemy had given up the town as well. An old red fire truck came across the river to take the large Daesh flag off and replace it with one of those new high-quality SDF ones. As it turned out, the media team had missed the moment, so the Daesh flag had to go back up again. Once the director had given the "go," the *hevals* on the red truck once more took down the Daesh flag and replaced it with the SDF one. Shaun laughed. He had seen all of this before.

In the meantime, wider geopolitical tensions were brewing. The presence of any YPG/YPJ west of the Euphrates was the red line for Turkey as it would precede the connection between the Afrin and Kobane *cantons*. A land connection between all three Kurdish-dominated *cantons* along their southern border was Turkey's security nightmare. So, when SDF units attempted to advance beyond the town limits, Turkey responded with artillery and prevented any further advance west of the river. Consequently, the operation was declared over. The compromise that had been reached somewhere outside Syria foresaw Arab SDF units securing the bridgehead of Tishreen while Kurdish forces withdrew to the eastern side of the river.

Since there had not been much fighting, to Shaun, one of the noteworthy aspects of the operation had been the food. Throughout the operation, logistics trucks had brought fresh kebabs, falafel, or shawarma all day long from a famous kebab shop in Kobane town. During the battle for Kobane, the shop—run by a YPG veteran—had fed the besieged defenders. Employing other YPG veterans and always giving hefty discounts to SDF fighters, the shop now fed the Tishreen operation.

With fantastic food still coming in, Shaun and the gang continued hanging around the town of Tishreen. After all, they were not Kurdish and technically not part of the deal to withdraw. As Shaun still insists, in the following days, the group searched every single room, in every single building, in the entire town of Tishreen. They found networks of workshops for homemade grenades and IEDs and traces of chemical weapons, including used test strips that showed positive results. They found a strange pink ISIS flag for some weird Daesh project. There were DIY missile launchers and signs of further development and research everywhere. They found the bodies of executed civilians lying in the streets. All of them had been shot in the head and chest from the front.

The town was also littered with air-struck ISIS fighters. Shaun saw a dead Daesh child soldier who was not yet old enough to grow facial hair. Most of the dead were Arabs; the elite foreign fighters must have pulled out overnight, possibly as part of a deal that had been brokered behind the scenes. Tishreen had been a Daesh city ruled by Russian-speaking Islamists. Like Manbij for Westerners, Tishreen was the center for the infamous Chechen and Uzbeks who had come here to join the Caliphate.

In the school building, Shaun found coursebooks teaching Arabic to Russian speakers. These Islamists had clearly intended to stay long term. In the primary school, they also found little combat boots and tiny desert camo uniforms with matching tiny ISIS headbands. In the Daesh cartoons, faceless ISIS fighters were teaching hand-to-hand combat and the handling of firearms. On the walls were children's drawings of ISIS flags and weapons. In the yard, a small military-style obstacle course.

In the administrative buildings, Shaun found ISIS newspapers praising Jihadi John, Britain's most infamous ISIS member. Infographics on the walls showed that the enemy had been destroyed. Between statistics of tanks and armored personnel carriers, the wall poster showed an airliner. When Shaun looked closer, the plane depicted was Metrojet Flight 9268, which an ISIS branch had shot down over Egypt on October 31, 2015. To ISIS, the 224 dead civilians were legitimate military targets. Throughout the empty city blew leaflets American jets had dropped prior to the assault. They showed a black clock. It was five minutes to 12, and the two hands were squeezing a cartoon Daesh fighter. Time was up for the Islamists.

★

Just like at al-Hol, the Tishreen Dam operation was another test for the SDF. The alliance was still young and included actors who used to be affiliated with the al-Nusra front. The YPG, but especially the YPJ, continued to be wary of them. However, with two successful operations completed, the alliance grew closer as fighters understood its necessity.

None of the new allies had tried to kill each other, the enemy was gone, and the food was good. Trust was being built. The al-Hol and Tishreen operations were also the SDF's last move at the very end of the fighting season.[5] Now, the alliance had put their forces into strategic positions so when spring came, the first major Daesh city could be assaulted.

There is another possible reading of the Tishreen Dam operation. It was not only an internal test for the still young SDF but also America's, respectively Obama's, loyalty. In order to end Daesh, the SDF needed American air support, but first, they wanted to see how far America would go to support them. More precisely, would Obama stand with the SDF when Turkey grew agitated? In order to answer that question, the SDF pushed over the Euphrates and thus crossed the Turkish red line. To everyone's surprise, Obama stood by his word and held his protective wings in the form of F18s over the SDF units who secured a bridgehead west of the Tishreen Dam. Besides some minor artillery shelling, Turkey was thus forced to sit back and watch as the SDF got ready to cross the river in full force once next year's fighting season had begun.

For America's war against ISIS, the creation of the SDF was of strategic importance. It was more than a rebranding of the YPG/YPJ for practical purposes; it enabled attacks on the enemy's major strongholds. Once Obama stood with the SDF after they crossed the Euphrates, many *hevals* were certain they would go all the way to Raqqa. Together with Heval Obama, they would be the ones to defeat ISIS in Syria. *Hevals* spent the cold and muddy winter that followed, when operations are difficult for logistical reasons, debating what city the SDF would attack next year: Manbij or Raqqa.

Besides the intensified air campaign and diplomatic battles, this second phase of American involvement against ISIS in Syria was characterized by the deployment of special forces. Only weeks after the SDF had been created, about 50 U.S. Special Forces entered the theater. However, it was the French special forces who showed up at the front lines first.

★

Once the fighting season had come to an end after the Tishreen op in late December 2015, most people spent their time trying to stay warm around stinking paraffin heaters. In early January, Shaun found his way back to the academy for international volunteers in Rojava. Meanwhile, John, who did not care much for family holidays, had arrived there in late December. Hanging out in one of the barren rooms for all-international volunteers, a rather depressing place, John and Shaun thus met for the first time.

While the new recruits were going through their training, the two began talking, smoking cigarettes and drinking *chai* to kill time. Since John had been part of the legendary first batch of international volunteers, Shaun was curious to find out what it had been like back then. John soon realized that the war had changed significantly since he had last been there and tried to get some intel on the situation from a solid veteran. Eventually, Baz too arrived and, waiting for their marching orders, the three bonded as they sat under their blankets, huddled around a smelly heater, drinking *chai* and energy drinks all day long.

After the usual endless back and forth, John, Shaun, and Heval Zagros, one of the new recruits who had just finished his training, decided to find their way to Kobane. From there, they wanted to get to the Jarablus front line at the Euphrates, which was always somewhat active. Baz, on the other hand, wished to change his approach. Having decided to play it the YPG way, he waited until the commanders sent him to a *tabur* that was securing the front line in the middle of nowhere near the Abdel Aziz mountains.

The moment the unit Baz joined arrived at their new supposed base was to be the first and only time he doubted his decision to go there, and even his own sanity. The *tabur* had to occupy a village around a *tell* and serve as a quick reaction force in case the enemy attacked this part of the front line. During the offensives in the summer of 2015, the village had been bombed and all of the buildings had been damaged in some way or another. Now, cold wind pierced through every layer of the cheap uniforms. As per usual in the winter, there was mud everywhere. There was not enough food, no water, and even the few stray dogs just lay in a corner, trying to fall asleep and never wake up again. It was bad.

Yet, before darkness set in and without any of their own supplies or tools, the *tabur* had fixed up two houses and cleaned them while others scavenged for firewood, heaters, blankets, and mattresses from the surrounding deserted villages. A *heval* mended the ancient generator that ran a water pump and, by nightfall, the *tabur* was laughing in the warmth, playing cards, their spirits restored. Within two more days, the *tabur* had defenses, a kitchen, a football pitch, organized supplies, and had even found a bunch of puppies. An integral part of this process was Heval Bawer, the caring friend of Baz's from his time in Hasake. When Baz had to leave the village after a few weeks, he felt like he was giving up a home.

★

While Shaun, John, and Heval Zagros were floating around Rojava in January 2016 looking for clues on the next operation, they witnessed an interesting moment in the SDF-American alliance. It wasn't just the United States that understood the importance of the SDF, in particular when it came to dealing with the Arab tribes; Russia did as well and, although we have no insight into the negotiations, Russians were talking to the SDF in Qamishlo, trying to convince them into an alliance. At the Regime-controlled Qamishlo airport, Russian transports began flying in. Russian soldiers, in their characteristic blue-and-white striped shirts, were seen around the kebab shops in Qamishlo, and many Kurdish *hevals* began asking the international volunteers who the stronger ally would be: Russia or America. Indeed, many older *hevals* argued for Russia, referring to the American betrayal of the Kurdish people in 1991.[6] In hindsight, they were right. In January 2016, the SDF had a very strong basis for negotiations with the Regime and Russia.

Whatever was said, by February 2016, the SDF had made up their minds: they decided to stick with America as their ally. Although the details are unclear, the agreement between the SDF and America would have certainly included long-term promises to protect the SDF from Turkey and the Regime. Without such promises, the SDF would never have turned down Russia, who could have delivered on both points.

With the Russians thus disappearing from the scene again, the first rumors about the next operation began circulating within the alliance. There was talk of a place called al-Shaddadi, which no one had ever heard of before. Naturally, Shaun, John, and Heval Zagros found their way to Tel Tamir, one of the staging areas for the operation, where they were put in Tabur Şehîd Karaman.

★

It was February 13th or 14th when a Hilux pulled up at the village in which Baz's *tabur* was based. Being the only Westerner in the unit, the driver asked Baz, "*Tu Heval Askari Doctor?*—Are you the *heval* soldier doctor?" Baz nodded, and the driver yelled, "*Em bitchin şer heval, zu zu!*—We are going to war, Heval, hurry up!" Baz duly said his goodbyes to Heval Bawer and the others and left for the operation.

In a former dairy farm outside Tel Tamir, the driver dropped Baz with his new unit, Tabur Şehîd Arges. When he walked into the old cowshed, seasoned fighters welcomed him. As soon as they heard he was a medic, they laughed and told him that he would be busy very soon. At that point, everyone assumed the target of the operation was al-Shaddadi. Using the spotty cell network, some international volunteers managed to look up the place on Wikipedia. According to the encyclopedia, the city had about 15,000 inhabitants—a decent size for the region. Al-Shaddadi's true value, however, was not its size but its location. It connected Raqqa and Mosul, ISIS's two most important cities. With al-Shaddadi gone, ISIS would have to go far away via Deir Ezzor when traveling between their two capitals or else use dirt tracks. The rumored al-Shaddadi operation was to be the prelude to the battles for Manbij, Raqqa, and Mosul. Apparently, the Americans were pushing for the operation.

Along with Baz, several international volunteers were being put into the *taburs* that would lead the assault. The international volunteers had their first martyred, or *şehîds*; in the logic of the region, the international fighters had proved themselves and were allowed to play a more active role in the YPG/YPJ.

Amongst those fighters was Heval Rustem, a legend amongst the international volunteers who was also well liked and respected amongst the SDF ranks and their commanders. After almost a decade in the German Armed Forces, the Bundeswehr, Heval Rustem had spent another decade in the French Foreign Legion. He'd hunted war criminals in the

Balkans, evacuated French civilians from the burning Beirut, and fought Congolese child soldiers for France's economic interests. Heval Rustem was a warrior through and through, and well beyond the point at which he could function in a peaceful society. Very much like Şehîd Mazlum, he needed war because war brought out the best in him.

Drifting around in between wars, the 50-plus-year-old came across a book called *Revolution in Rojava*, written by a group of German leftists and Kurdistan activists.[7] Usually, he would not have read a book like that, but it had war in the title, so he opened it. He read it seven times and began a self-reflection on the battles he had fought and who had profited from the people he had killed.

At the end of this reflection period, Heval Rustem packed his bag and followed the ratline of the German Islamists to Turkey, flying to a popular tourist destination and then winging it to the Syrian border. However, whereas the Islamists could cross into Syria very comfortably under the eyes of supportive Turkish border guards, Heval Rustem had to crawl through a minefield to get into Kobane. Once he had made it to Rojava, he'd asked the YPJ if he could join their revolution. The YPJ loved Heval Rustem for that, and he had been granted a kind of grandfather status that allowed him to spend more time with the fighting women.

Since Tel Abiat in June 2015 had barely been a fight, al-Shaddadi would be the first enemy city the SDF would assault. The time to test alliances was over. This operation would not push into an empty stretch of desert but would attack a strategically vital city. A city the enemy had fortified during the winter. This operation would be the real deal.

In the evening, the logistics truck brought more fried chicken and plum sauce than the unit could eat. During dinner, it got very quiet. Even the seasoned vets had never seen that much pre-operation chicken, and everyone interpreted it as the SDF's version of a last supper. Looking into the fire, stuffed with chicken, sipping *chai*, smoking his extra-strong Ardens and occasionally breaking off the filter, Heval Rustem told Baz that he was here for forgiveness. Following orders, he had done bad things in the name of France's economic interests. For the first time, Heval Rustem had found meaning and peace. Rojava was his home. Here, he wanted to die. The following day, the operation began.

CHAPTER 10

Operation *Wrath of Khabur*: February–March 2016

The staging area for the three *taburs* that would spearhead the operation was on top of the *tell* with a water treatment plant just outside Tel Tamir. In the chaos, we all met, and Shaun, Baz, and some of the Kurdish snipers who were still alive looked down at the Christian village they had defended together just a few months before. Now the village and surrounding lands visible on the horizon were free, and soon, the enemy would have been pushed even further south. The *civîn*, a large pre-operation briefing, began in one of the plant's former engine rooms. In the sticky heat, about 200 *hevals* listened to their highest commanders.

The operation would indeed liberate the strategic city al-Shaddadi. This operation's name was *Wrath of Khabur*, and it was a retaliatory action to punish the abduction of the 200 Christians Daesh had taken from the Khabur region outside Tel Tamir. Moving along the Khabur River, the Kurdish, Arab, Christian, Yazidi, and American coalition would fight the enemy until the last hostages had been released. As the YPG's highest general explained to the assembled fighters, "There will be no peace until all of our Christian brothers and sisters are free." The Kurdish fighters who would lead the assault answered with "*Biji Rojava, biji azadi*—long live Rojava, long live our freedom."

Although Kurdish *taburs* would lead the assault, the city would later be handed over to a local SDF militia made up of mainly Arab fighters. Kurdish forces were only to fight and die in Arab lands, not occupy them. Again, the Kurdish fighters cheered because this was about their version of democracy. Once the city had been liberated, a military council of local men and women would secure it so YPG/YPJ forces could move on.

The operation was a two-pronged assault with a second battle group attacking from al-Hol. The battle group leaving Tel Tamir would attack via the Abdel Aziz mountains. The operation would begin as soon as the *civîn* was over. With adrenaline pumping, the *taburs* ran to their Toyotas, mounted up, and a convoy with trucks rolled down the *tell* to the deserted Christian villages, where more units were staging.

With about a hundred Toyota Hiluxes all packed with fighters, the battle group drove into Tel Tamir. At the first large roundabout in the city, more *taburs*, including the Tabur Silah Grand (the heavy weapon units), were waiting. An ever-growing convoy that included the Cizire *canton*'s two old Russian tanks and two BMPs, and thousands of fighters of both genders representing all of the region's religions and ethnicities rolled through a city that had been deserted just months before. While their defense force was riding into battle, the people who had returned came out onto the streets to celebrate them, waving the victory sign.

Right then and there, these SDF fighters knew they were in the right. It was their moral responsibility to liberate al-Shaddadi and to kill the enemy before they could commit more crimes. The world agreed that ISIS had to be destroyed, and they would be the ones to do it. Yet it was not a testosterone-laden affair with men in tight shirts promising each other over and over again to fuck up the enemy. With a third of the fighting force being female, the moment was full of smiles and happiness. Somehow, this operation was not about taking the lives of the enemy but preserving the lives of these people. Riding on the back of a pickup was a glorious feeling that left Baz thinking this was probably what religion must be like.

Leaving Tel Tamir, the convoy processed through the villages Shaun and Baz had defended eight months previously. The convoy even drove by the old shitter that had hosted a very fat snake. On the northern slopes of the Abdel Aziz mountain range, the Tel Tamir battle group stopped again, and *taburs* lined up for the actual assault. There was excitement, adrenaline, tanks, coalition bombers, and hundreds of Hiluxes with thousands of fighters crawling up a muddy mountain. It was cold, and no one knew where the enemy was waiting. Everyone still felt nice and fuzzy from the ride through Tel Tamir.

Suddenly, Shaun and John ran toward Baz, the Marine mumbling something about German intel he, Shaun, and Heval Zagros had found in a Daesh house in an abandoned village a few days earlier. When Baz unfolded the piece of paper John handed him, he discovered it was a very bright and colorful photo of a naked baby wearing sunglasses, chilling on an air mattress in a swimming pool. This picture was so utterly out of place and unexpected that Baz burst into loud laughter that made a hundred heads turn. The baby seemed to epitomize the phrase "zero fucks given" and was a comical contrast to the environment and circumstances the photograph was found in.

The moment over, the friends then had to split up as their *taburs* were on the move again. When the sun set, the SDF units were on the peak of the mountain. By the time it was pitch black, the first *taburs* had descended into Daesh heartland.

Floating along with Heval Rustem, Baz ended up in the second Hilux behind the first front-loader and three *hevals* from Tabur Sabotage, the SDF's IED guys on foot. Having developed their own way of spotting Daesh IEDs, every once in a while, the convoy would be redirected away from the dirt road to evade enemy mines. When the sun came up, Baz's Tabur Şehîd Arges had reached the first settlement on the southern slopes of the mountain. The YPJ secured one compound while Heval Rustem, Baz, and a couple of other fighters were securing another. Whilst doing this, Baz heard warning shots fired nearby. After a few seconds, every rifle in the vicinity opened up at once. This meant only one thing: an SVBIED was on the loose, looking for targets.

An RPG missed the suicide bomber in his up-armored van, and the "Dushka" truck was too slow to react. Heval Rustem and Baz could hear how the desperate suppressing fire shifted further toward the second compound, the *tabur*'s YPJ *takem* having been secured. For a brief moment, they saw the SVBIED before it disappeared again behind a small hill. Next, a flash blinded them and, while they shielded their eyes by pure reflex, the shock wave of the explosion hit them in their guts. Tense silence followed while everyone listened around the radio for news. "*Civil brinda*—Injured civilians." The bomber had found targets.

When the SVBIED came their way, the YPJ retreated behind a solid structure away from the tarmac. This was the only way to survive this sort of chase: get into the fields where the heavy SVBIED cannot follow and seek the cover of a house or ditch. The suicide bomber saw the retreating YPJ through the slits of the steel plates, drove straight into the house, and detonated himself. When the entire structure collapsed, it turned out that the women of the family who lived in the compound had hidden in there.

As Baz ran up to the site, *hevalas* were digging for survivors with their bare hands. A *heval* from Tabur Sabotage carried a small child covered in grey dust. When the medic looked at the *heval*, he shook his head. In a nearby ditch lay some injured people. Baz signaled for the other casualties from the collapsed building to be brought over. Beside the pile of dead lay the wounded: a grandmother with a severe head trauma, her daughter, and two grandchildren as well as a mentally disabled young man. However, there was little that could be done for them in the field. Their injuries, caused by both the blast and the falling rocks from their house collapsing, were internal. They needed surgery.

This was not about putting on bandages but transportation. Baz made that very clear to the driver of one of the *tabur's* trucks. Looking at the civilian women who lay on the ground moaning, the driver agreed to transport them toward a unit further in the rear. This was the best deal Baz would get. For the kind of warfare the SDF was fighting in the open countryside, the Hilux was vital for a *takem*. Without the Toyota, they were stranded in a Daesh desert. That was to be avoided.

Everything that followed was beyond what German EMT training could prepare you for. In order to get the unresponsive grandmother into a recovery position, Baz had to roll her onto her dead granddaughter while he stabilized another child who was still alive. During the maneuver, the blanket that covered the body had moved, and now the dead girl was staring at Baz. That morning, when Tabur Şehîd Arges descended into the enemy's wasteland, they felt the hopelessness and evil that was waiting on the horizon. There was no laughter, just pain. There was no beauty, just despair. There was no life, just death. Darkness and death. It was almost palpable.

Once Baz had found another driver willing to head toward the ambulances up on the mountain, the race against time continued. Halfway up the mountain, while the Toyota was evading the two tanks on their flatbeds that were now coming down, the young mother of the two girls slid into unresponsiveness. Baz knew that she needed fluid. However, these were his first casualties ever; he'd only had three weeks of training and had never put in an IV before. All he knew about the procedure was what he'd learned from a YouTube tutorial. Now he was in the back of a pickup on a dirt track up a mountain, alone with a dying family. He had to decide if he wanted to stop and try the procedure he knew nothing about or hope the promised ambulance would finally materialize.

He decided to continue the mad race and, when the Hilux came around a corner, the flashing lights of the Heyva Sor ambulance finally appeared. In the end, all of the injured civilians survived. Once Baz had made it back to the front line, Heval Rustem patted him on the back and muttered a "well done."

About three hours after the attack, French soldiers showed up with Javelin ATGMs to protect the advance from future SVBIED attacks. Even though they arrived a little late, these French Fusiliers were some of the first Western combat forces at the front lines.

★

With a foothold in the enemy's territory, Tabur Şehîd Karaman, including John, Heval Zagros, and Shaun, came down the Abdel Aziz mountains and began clearing operations in the villages north of al-Shaddadi. Similar to the operation during summer 2015, SDF *takems* would take a village and, while it was still being secured by the main battle group that moved up, another *takem* would advance on the next village. About three or four *taburs* participated in those clearing operations, meaning that about five *takems* continuously advanced with the support of the "Dushka" trucks and BMPs of the heavy weapons *tabur*. In a force with very limited means of communication, these operations always appeared extremely chaotic, but on a meta level, they worked. With their close air support, the *takems* found themselves in a headlong advance, liberating small villages from Daesh by the dozens. In the countryside, the enemy had nothing to stop the SDF and CJTF-OIR.

During the advance, Tabur Şehîd Karaman was mainly clearing villages the enemy had already given up. Occasionally, there were small skirmishes over some distance, or else the *taburs* were harassed by snipers before CJTF-OIR dropped a bomb on their position. John and Shaun's *tabur's* "highlight" was being chased by a suspected SVBIED. Most of the time, the *hevals* were just trying to stay warm.

Due to the fact that his team leader was a woman, during this operation, John began noticing all the female units. This was in contrast to the static trench warfare he'd experienced during his first trip, when John had not come across the YPJ much. In the villages, they had their separate *nocta*, living quarters, and their own fighting positions along the berms. However, during operations, this clear structure was being broken up for practical reasons and, suddenly, John was fighting next to the women of the YPJ.

At first, he was skeptical. Based on his experience in the Corps, the equality project of women in the Marines had in reality been a failure. From day one, women had been treated differently than men. Where John would get a rifle butt as a wakeup call, the women got actual wakeup calls. He had nothing against women in the Marines in general; to him, they just had to suffer the same as the men because that's what the U.S. Marine Corps was about: to make its members suffer. Following the idea of "train hard and fight easy," the American military keeps its Marines in a constant state of misery so that when they are unleashed, they thrive. This all means that infantry Marines look down on cooks, mechanics, military police, and anyone else who isn't hiking heavy weapons, running daily PT death runs, or spending as many nights as them in the wet and miserable field. Applying different levels of misery according to gender therefore creates resentments. Yet, during his time back in the United States, he'd promised himself to be open, so he was.

One of the first things he learned was that the YPJ is not part of the YPG but is in fact its own independent force with its own command structures, weapons caches, training facilities, bases, and academic discipline called *jineology*, the Kurdish science of women. The PKK's female wing is called YJA STAR. YJA stands for Yekîtîya Jinên Azad (which translates as something like "units for the freedom of women"), and STAR is a reference to the Babylonian goddess Ištar. Although the goddess of sexuality and war may seem a paradox at first, she actually represents the female fighting units precisely. In their struggle against the repression they've experienced at the hands of the Turkish state, the women who join the guerilla movement join for life. With this step, the *hevalas* sacrifice their privilege to bear life for a greater good: the freedom of their sisters. They join the YJA STAR so other woman can give birth in a better world, free from oppression, death, and destruction.

Ištar is also a reference to Öcalan's fascination with Neolithic society. Öcalan argued that the beginning of female oppression and patriarchy correlated with the emergence of the first state-like structures and the new concept of capital that manifested itself during that age. When women are enslaved by the state and capital, the liberation of women by other women is seen as an inherently anti-capitalist and feminist action. As *jineology* and the movement argue, the liberation of people begins with the liberation of women. To the YPJ, feminism[1] means to not rely on men in any way. In war, feminism means that women fight for their freedom themselves instead of needing armed men to protect them.

The *hevalas'* gender equality was utterly uncompromising on the battlefield and in everyday lives, as well as in theory. The women in the movement were not *given* their freedoms; they had *fought* for them in endless battles going back to the 1980s. When the Regime withdrew from Rojava in 2012, the movement immediately restructured the police in an ongoing attempt to make at least a third of the force female. The women of the movement introduced *Asayîş Jin*, women's police, to protect their sisters from abuse. In the recent past, Daesh had kidnapped or killed their sisters, and now the Islamists were feeling the wrath of the YPJ breathing down their necks. This was equality and feminism John understood almost instinctively. Hell, many of the women in his *tabur* were saltier than he was. They were warriors, and he respected that.

They could also do things that men couldn't. For instance, there was a time when John's squad had just taken a village. Having experienced years of Daesh in the vicinity, the civilians were now scared of men with guns and were consequently all huddled up. John tried to tell them that everything was OK, but all they saw was another foreign fighter with a rifle, so they were terrified. He understood there and then that armed men can't liberate traumatized people. While he was still trying to explain that he and the other men were good guys, the YPJ arrived—15 confident armed women driving up in their own Toyota Hilux, their hair flying in the wind. Boom, that's how you win hearts and minds. Within moments, the civilians understood what Rojava was about: women and their freedom—because if they felt free, everyone else would, too. Although John could not understand the details of their conversation, he could see that the people immediately trusted the YPJ, and indeed went on to provide fresh intel on the enemy. So, just in terms of interactions with civilians, the YPJ in all its radically uncompromising form was an invaluable asset. This force was not about marching X miles with Y pounds in a backpack during training, but liberating people every day. And the YPJ was really good at it.

Thinking about the role of the female militia, John noticed something else: the absence of any sexualized violence, including all so-called "locker room talk" amongst the YPG. Up to this point, he had spent months in one of the most notorious war zones, where systematic sexual abuse had become part of warfare, and yet he never witnessed a single case of any form of sexual harassment against the YPJ or civilians. Besides the occasional consensual love affair between young people who would probably die very soon, it was as if sexuality did not exist. Thanks to the YPJ, the SDF as a force kept the moral high ground and, as we know, fighting from any high ground is always preferred.

John understood that without the YPJ, the YPG would be just another gang of men with guns and good intentions. It is thus the YPJ that sets apart and defines the YPG, not the other way around. Having implemented democratic confederalism, the revolution worked in practical terms because of the YPJ. *Jin-jiyan-azadi*, "women-live-freedom," in that order. Only free women can bring a free life. John therefore fully appreciated the YPJ and was increasingly proud to fight alongside these women.

★

During the swift advance along the fertile lands of the Khabur River, Tabur Şehîd Arges had to trail behind the front line. Morale amongst the *hevals* in the unit was getting low. The *tabur* was itching for the battle their commander had promised them. Only Heval Şoreş, Baz's *takem* commander, was completely relaxed. With his trademark smile and green eyes, he would say, "*Swei swei. Em bitchin ser*—Patience. We are still going to war."

On February 18th or 19th, SDF forces were staging outside Umm Ahzar, a large village just north of al-Shaddadi. The village had to be taken and secured before the city could be assaulted. The enemy knew that and was planning to put up a fight. At dawn the following morning, the SDF attacked Umm Ahzar from different directions. There was little resistance until the SDF encountered fortified positions where the village morphed into the city. For the rest of the afternoon, the SDF attacked the neighborhood with the support of American air strikes.

During this stage of the assault, Baz and Heval Rustem's *takem* was tasked with securing the western flank of the assault. With the two SDF tanks that were deployed to act as mobile artillery and fire over their heads at the burning city, Heval Rustem and his M16 fitted with a decent Chinese knock-off ACOG sight were battling a Daesh sniper who was harassing the advance. Suddenly, the YPJ's *takem* commander pressed Baz into their ranks. In a place where most local fighters were legally still too young to drive and had no training, and most international fighters could not handle a proper, nonautomatic car, the only medic around had to drive a Hilux behind the front line while on the radio, he could hear how his friends had been injured.

By the time the Toyota was tucked away nice and safe, it was evening, and Baz was being hosted by the YPJ. Still steaming, the big angry German sat in the corner of the roof they occupied and ate the food his sisters provided.

Later that night, fighters from Tabur Şehîd Arges and other units took the most northerly two blocks of al-Shaddadi right next to the banks of the Khabur River. When the YPJ and Baz were finally shuttled to that front line by the BMP, the advance was stalled by a Daesh sniper and his security team, who were operating within the maze of mud huts, low walls, chicken coops, water tanks, and two-story buildings with fighting positions all over the walls.

Having made it to the city and organized himself some hot *chai*, Baz lay down with the others and waited for the A-10 "Warthog" to finish its first and second overflies. While Baz was still sipping his hot beverage, the A-10 came down and opened fire on a building just 30 yards in front of their position. After the strike and with his tea finished, Baz found Heval Rustem, who had made it to the front line sometime during the night. When Baz sprinted over to him, Heval Rustem's smile stretched over his whole face as he beamed, "Today is my second birthday. I could feel the sniper's round go through my hair just a couple of hours ago." Apparently, Heval Rustem's duel with the Daesh sniper had continued throughout the morning.

Heval Rustem had encountered this Daesh tactic before during operations around Kobane. One or two snipers would target advancing forces from pre-prepared firing positions that were connected by a network of paths broken through walls and backyards. On their flanks, the snipers were protected by a small security team of regular fighters and IEDs planted for just this purpose. Given the labyrinthine nature of the poorer neighborhoods in Syrian cities, the sniper could only fight at distances between 100 and 500 yards, rarely more.

Daesh used the base of an M16, attached a heavier barrel, a good bipod, and put a 15,000-dollar scope on top. With such rifles, neither the sniper nor the security team with their AKs needed to be good marksmen or well-trained soldiers. In fact, so far, this particular sniper had missed several *hevals* at less than 300 yards, yet a team of between five and 10 enemy fighters were able to stall the entire advance. In coming operations, the enemy would perfect this way of fighting and use it for their very own messed-up psychological warfare.

After the A-10 strike, Tabur Şehîd Arges's commander was looking to put together a small team to advance first into the main city. Given his reputation within the militia, Heval Rustem was going in and, since Baz was the only medic, he would go too. The team would be led by their charismatic *takem* commander, Heval Şoreş. Following his example, the team of five sprinted across the street into the chaotic, narrow network of alleys. While the core city was built along strict plans, these outskirts had developed unregulated. With no clear streets visible, the team advanced carefully.

The neighborhood was completely deserted. There was no sign of life, and every time a cat jumped up with a sudden movement, several rifles were immediately trained on the animal. Every once in a while, Heval Şoreş climbed onto a roof to get a fix on the team's location. Climbing over walls and walking through houses and back alleys, the team eventually found its way to a house at the most northerly corner of a large open square that was the size of four large blocks. The team took a defensive position on the roof and, with the small sledgehammer he carried for such purposes, Heval Rustem began smashing murder holes (openings from which to shoot without losing cover) into the concrete walls.

The entire brown and dusty square was empty. There was no movement. In the middle of the square stood a burned-out car. All over the place were freshly dug-up patches in the earth, suggesting mines. At the southern end of the square was a large school overlooking the northern part of the city. It was the most important building the SDF had to take in order to control the neighborhood and secure a strong foothold in al-Shaddadi. This also meant the enemy would be positioned in the school.

Once Heval Şoreş had radioed in the team's position, three or four snipers moved up and took over. Supported by a YPJ RPG gunner and two more *hevalas*, the team continued their advance. However, instead of creeping toward the school, Heval Şoreş led them away from the square. Every so often, before the team continued their advance, he would check the tablet the Americans had provided showing high-resolution images of the area, or climb up on a house. Suddenly, the team stood in front of a Daesh building. In the entrance lay the bottom half of an enemy fighter. The top half and the surrounding walls had been annihilated by another A-10 strike. Inside the building were traces of Daesh administration, shaved-off beards, and ISIS uniforms. The enemy was trying to blend in with the civilians.

After searching the building, the team continued until they were almost at the same level as the school, just one block northeast of it. Here, they secured a rooftop, and Heval Şoreş fired a couple of rounds in the air. Baz and Heval Rustem exchanged a worried glance. Their commander was trying to give away their position. As expected, an old man appeared in the streets and looked at them. Heval Şoreş waved at him excitedly, then the startled man disappeared again. Once he had made sure the team had been spotted, Heval Şoreş led them into a back alley running parallel to the street on which Heval Rustem and Baz could see the old civilian running. Slowly and silently, the team advanced toward the school. Suddenly, there was a commotion on the street where the old man was running parallel to their axis of advance. Men were now running past the small SDF team in the opposite direction on the main road.

Coming around another corner, the team met two SDF *Asayîş* and a civilian wearing a balaclava. Ahead of any SDF unit, the three were collecting intelligence. Whenever their own masked informant pointed at a building, the two *Asayîş* entered the house with their pistols drawn.

Heval Şoreş and the team sprinted the rest of the way to the school and climbed the high perimeter wall at the northeastern side. Firearms at the ready, safeties off, the team searched the building quickly before securing the large rooftops overlooking the north of al-Shaddadi. As soon as Baz reached one of the murder holes in the northern wall, he came under small arms fire from the street down below. He also saw the old man who had spotted them in their previous position.

With his maneuver, Heval Şoreş had given the impression that the SDF was outflanking the school. Informed by the old man, the Daesh fighters had fallen for the ruse and left the only high ground. By the time they had realized their mistake, Heval Şoreş's team was waiting for them on top of the school. In hindsight, it was an ingenious move, a textbook example of urban guerilla warfare and small team's tactics. With his blatant confidence, Heval Şoreş had simply outmaneuvered the enemy. He turned one of Daesh's most effective weapons systems, a network of civilian informants, against them. He had the guts to lead his team past the enemy in this game of hide, seek, and kill. It had been the SDF team's mission to find the enemy and initiate the battle. Thanks to Heval Şoreş's tactical genius, his team was now in the best possible position to do that.

At first, the gunfight went well. Firing from a well-fortified position occupying the high ground is as safe a position as there can be in a reasonably wild shoot-out. For about an hour, all went according to plan. The enemy undertook several attempts to retake the school, but the team could fight them back. From the roof of the school, they could hear other SDF teams fighting their way through the quarters next to the large square. If all went well, they should pass the school soon and outflank the enemy.

About 15 minutes later, Heval Şoreş came to the section of the roof from which Baz and two YPJ *hevalas* were fighting. According to their commander, the enemy had breached the perimeter, and the notorious sniper team was in the building in the squad's dead angle to the left. Unless they left the cover of the murder holes, the YPG/YPJ team could not fire at the Daesh sniper's position. At the same time, other SDF units who were meant to fight their way up to the schools and past it were under heavy fire. Around the mosque just west of the square, the enemy had set an ambush, and the advance of the SDF *takems* had come to a halt.

Another 15 minutes later, Heval Rustem, who had been elsewhere this entire time, appeared in the school's courtyard. He knew enemies were behind the perimeter wall and wanted to ambush them. However, approaching the wall from the right, Heval Rustem exposed himself to the sniper team within the perimeter to the left. As soon as they saw him in the courtyard, the two *hevalas* and Baz had their rifles up, waiting for the inevitable. "Heval Rustem, no no," hissed one of the *hevalas*. In that moment, a round hit the wall next to their friend. They saw how he turned around to them, waving as if to say that it was he, Heval Rustem. He must have thought it was his *hevals* who had shot at him by accident. Most likely, the language barrier was the reason why he had no idea that his nemesis was waiting for him just 77 yards away. The Daesh sniper was clearly a horrible shot, but he knew the place well and was prepared for this. With an escape route in place, all he had to do was wait for the SDF to advance, and while he was turning toward his friends, the sniper adjusted his aim and killed Heval Rustem.

Immediately, the enemy became more aggressive and, with their dead friend lying unreachable right in front of them, the SDF team continued to fight back. "Heval Baz, mouth open!" yelled the 16-year-old(ish) *hevala* YPJ. To protect her eardrums from the blast, she put a pencil between her teeth and fired two RPGs at the Daeshis, who were closing in on Şehîd Rustem's body.

However, some two hours into the shoot-out, the first *hevals* were now running low on ammo. In the streets parallel, the enemy pushed up with gun trucks, firing mounted double-barrel "Dushkas." Given the terrain, the SDF could not yet bring in their own "Dushka" trucks or any of the heavy armor. On the ground, the SDF teams were thus now severely outgunned. Consequently, the SDF *takems* on the flanks were hunkering down.

The small SDF team in the school was now surrounded on three sides. The fourth side was the open square, where the sniper could pick them off one by one. Although taking casualties, the enemy continued their aggressive attempts to retake the school. After about three hours of gunfighting, the school was about to be overrun. The enemy had breached the perimeter wall at several points, occupied two of the three school buildings, and the defenders were finally running out of ammo. The sun was starting to set, and it was clear they could not hang on to the position much longer. Once it was dark, the enemy would come for them. If they lost the school, the SDF would be pushed out of the city again, and the momentum the operation had developed so far would be lost.

Suddenly, a jet appeared and took out one of the enemy's gun trucks about 110 yards southeast of the school. Heval Şoreş ordered Baz and the two *hevalas* to go to the ground floor and take cover. He had given the Americans the coordinates and told them the enemy was all around. Soon, Heval Obama would bomb within the school's perimeter. It was likely that the team would not survive the air strike.

When they lay down on the cool floor waiting for the bombs to fall, a content tear was running down his cheek, Baz made peace with death. It was OK because it had meaning. He would die fighting the darkness so others could live and love again. "What a poetic death," he thought while the American jets were coming in for their third deadly bomb run.

Baz had lived a happy life and would die in a cause he was somehow meant to fight in. Now he would burn together with his sisters, and they looked at each other and smiled. Blasts from several explosions shook the building. "*Serkeftin hevalas*—Goodbye, *hevalas*." While on the roof their machine gun still fired, holding back the fascists, a wall of fire rolled toward the windows.

For a few seconds, there was a complete silence. Baz and the two women opened their eyes. To their surprise, they were not dead. This short moment of silence was followed by sudden strong winds that were rattling on the chains of the barricaded school doors. The bombs had burned all the oxygen in the vicinity, and the air was now equalizing the pressure. The three got up slowly, dazed. Outside, the gunfight had stopped abruptly, and SDF fighters who had been waiting for the air strikes were using the enemy's confusion to push up to the school's northern doors. After the two *hevalas* and Baz had removed the makeshift barricades of chains and school tables, snipers and machine gunners came in and relieved the team of seven. It had gotten dark outside and, after reloading his magazines, Baz fell into a restless sleep on a tiny couch in the school's hallway.

★

The remainder of John, Shaun, and Heval Zagros's advance on the city was best described as chaos. Although all three were in the same *tabur*, John was in a different *takem* than Shaun and Heval Zagros. There was a lot of driving around on the back of Hiluxes whilst being harassed by snipers. Occasionally, Shaun and Heval Zagros saw French special forces on the roof with the command element. They saw a Hilux with blacked-out windows and a .50cal on the back engage a target about a mile away. "Probably Americans," they thought. At the outskirts of the city, Shaun and Heval Zagros's *takem* rested at the command element's temporary base. When the American operators noticed the two Westerners, one of them fetched cold orange juices. "You guys want a drink?" Shaun and Heval Zagros said "No" and walked away. Being intimidated and starstruck, in their panic, they both came up with the dumbest answer possible.

Once the first school building had been secured in the immediate aftermath of the air strikes, it became the hub for the advance to the next school or other strategic buildings, including the hospital. When Shaun and his team arrived in the school to get their next orders, he found Baz in full battle rattle folded up on a tiny couch. Baz told him about Şehîd Rustem's death. Shaun could not believe it at first. If a warrior like Rustem could die, how could they stand a chance?

Once the two friends had swapped the little intel they had, Shaun's team pushed up to another school and secured it. When the night was the coldest, the first call for prayer rang from the mosques in the city and, in order to prevent himself and his team developing hypothermia, the German leftist and teacher began burning books and little wooden tables inside the school building. When one of the *hevals* highlighted the historical bizarreness of the situation, they all laughed. In a desperate situation, humor is often the only way through.

The morning after the neighborhood around the school was liberated, a shy, hunched-over father showed up with his son. The 12-year-old child carried a tray bearing hot *chai*, some yoghurt, and some stale bread. They did not have much but they knew the SDF fighters in the school had less, so they shared their precious little. Despite the trauma that had made father and son the submissive people they were, their eyes showed genuine gratitude. They understood they had just been liberated. To the team, the father and son were not the enemy, they were the people the SDF was fighting for, so they enjoyed the simple meal with two Arab representatives from the city.

Having been defeated, Daesh subsequently released the remaining 43 Christian hostages in return for safe passage out of the city. Of all the forces that would fight Daesh effectively throughout the war, the SDF had some of the poorest equipment and highest casualty numbers. Fighting as few enemies as possible was therefore a strategic necessity in February 2015.

★

In the following days leading up to February 20th, the official end of the operation, all of us spent time searching neighborhoods of the city or surrounding villages. With about 30 other international SDF volunteers, we were amongst the first Westerners to see the Caliphate from the inside. This was the first city in Daesh heartland that had been taken from the Islamists, and it allowed unprecedented access to Daesh's inner workings. Up to this point, to all of us, Daesh had been an organization of black-masked men who performed a constant trickle of exceptionally brutal execution videos and terror attacks.

Indeed, places where such horrors had been filmed and used for propaganda videos were everywhere. We saw cages and other instruments of public humiliation and punishment. There were whips and lashes, cable binders, and handcuffs. There were places that served the systematic abuse of enslaved women. For example, in a private home he searched, John found a room that was secured by a large padlock from the outside and had its windows bricked up. Inside was a bare mattress on which lay some women's clothes. On the floor were food bowls, whips, and blindfolds stiff with dried blood. Similar "rape rooms" could be found all over the city, as if it had been normal practice.

There were mines, IEDs, and piles of suicide belts. There were fighting positions connected by sophisticated networks of tunnels. There were warehouses full of United States government-issued M16s and AKs from all around the world. There were bomb factories containing chemicals from Germany, Turkey, and other NATO countries. There were stockpiles of diverse military gear from Turkey. There were even more shaved-off beards, but we had expected all of this.

What we did not expect was the "banality of evil," as the political philosopher Hannah Arendt[2] once called it, that was still lingering throughout the city. Every small neighborhood had a Daesh administration office filled with a ridiculous amount of papers regulating the most trivial aspects of life. To Daesh, one of the defining aspects of their self-declared statehood was a bureaucracy that governed everyone's lives.

To the people who had lived in the Caliphate, Daesh was not a series of extraordinary events the Islamists carefully choreographed, but in fact the opposite. Daesh governed everyday lives with a set of draconian rules and hypocrisy. Yet most of the Daeshis were no monsters; when we saw them, they were scared young men who had their hands tied behind their backs. What they had done was follow orders in a system that did not tolerate any form of refusal or objection. They were not devils but nobodies. They were average, just as Eichmann had been.[3] In a system in which every aspect of life was formalized, individuals became irrelevant. Reduced to an administrative process, people had become interchangeable. Eichmann, as well as ISIS prisoners, said they just followed orders and their oath without thinking too much. From their perspective, they had done nothing wrong. They had just fulfilled their duty and implemented existing law. Indeed, what Shaun witnessed reminded him a lot of the Gestapo Museum in Berlin.

The Daesh fools who defended the city when it was already lost were only small, exchangeable parts in the bureaucratic beast that was the Caliphate. While Daesh had their evil poster boys they used to communicate with the West, to the people internally, it was a bureaucracy that included everyone and eventually made most somewhat complicit. The evil was not about devilish individuals but an administrative machinery that had created a totalitarian system. Following Hannah Arendt's argument,[4] this does not put individual guilt into perspective but rather enables an understanding of fascism and the absoluteness of moral breakdown. To the people of al-Shaddadi, evil had become a mundane affair. Gaining insight into the Caliphate, Sinjar, and the genocides, it all suddenly made sense to us. This place was evil and wrong, yet it was also somehow normal.

However, it wasn't just its bureaucracy that was responsible for the almost palpable sense of fear in Al-Shaddadi. On all the advertisements, boxes in grocery stores, books, and even some bank notes, every face had been covered with black marker pen since to Daesh, the graven image of a face was blasphemy. In a strange attempt to keep them usable, in children's books, instead of drawing over all the heads, Daesh had just scratched out the eyes of the cartoon characters. Imagine your child reading a comic book in which Mickey's eyes have been scratched out. Very creepy indeed. When we opened the wardrobes while searching deserted homes, there were just black abayas (long black dresses that hide a woman entirely, similar to the Afghan burka), all of which looked exactly the same. School books by the Caliphate talked about 72 virgins for nine-year-olds. Yet, for its most fanatic members, the Caliphate was perfect. There was the diary of a 16-year-old girl from the UK. After joining Daesh, she had been smuggled to the Caliphate in Syria. Over dozens of handwritten pages, she talked of happiness and joy.[5] She was perfectly fine with the brutal executions and madly in love with a fighter she was too young to have married.

Many of the civilians who experienced this banality of evil had become submissive, with hunched backs just like the father and his son who'd shared their food and tea. They either looked at their shoes or over their shoulders, and although it was images of cheering women taking off their black robes that made international news, to us, this continuous fear was a much more common response to their liberation. Over the years, the entire social fabric of their society had changed. Daesh had enforced a system in which the unimaginable became normal. Children drove armored trucks on suicide missions. At the end of the school term, the adolescents decapitated an innocent. If a Daesh fighter lusted for a woman, he found an imam who would somehow sanction her rape. It was insanity and desperation, and it was everywhere. Physically being there gave many a cold rush down our spines. In terms of its inner logic and functioning, this city was all about destruction.

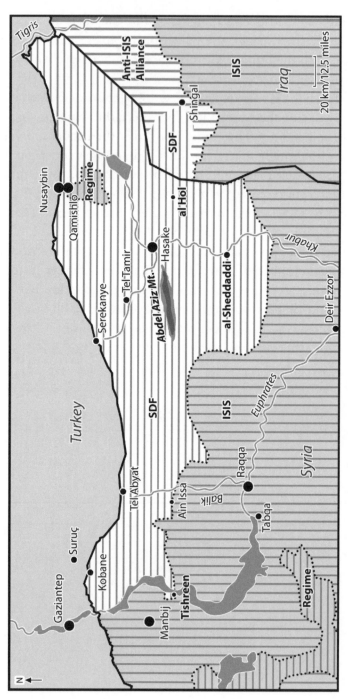

Map 5: Front lines in April 2016 around the Kobane and Cizire *cantons*.

Early July 2014. Peshmerga outside Mosul securing the new border with the Caliphate. (Courtesy Till Paasche)

Early July 2014. Kurdish flag flying over an abandoned Iraqi Army Humvee after Peshmerga had rushed in to fill the security vacuum. (Courtesy Till Paasche)

October 2014. In Camp Newroz, Rojava, Yazidis retells their genocide—that was still on going—after their escape from Mt. Shingal through a corridor opened by YPG/YPJ. (Courtesy Till Paasche).

December 2015. YPG/YPJ position at the front in Arja. A front-loader piled up mud two stories high around a school building, creating a large bunker. (Courtesy John Foxx)

December 2014. Daesh position on the only high ground for miles, opposite Arja. (Courtesy John Foxx)

January 2015. John on guard in Shingal. (Courtesy John Foxx)

January 2016. Daesh lighting fires to obscure their positions from U.S. drones and aircraft in Shingal City. (Courtesy John Foxx)

January 2016. Daesh IEDs found during a raid. (Courtesy John Foxx)

March 2015. Air-struck Daesh position opposite the Christian village Shaun and Baz defended with a Kurdish unit next to Tel Tamir. (Courtesy Shaun Murray)

Church near Tel Tamir destroyed by Daesh on Easter Sunday 2015. (Courtesy Shaun Murray)

May 2015. Daesh lighting dry field on fire to obscure their positions from coalition jets. (Courtesy Hanna Bohman)

May 2015. YPG/YPJ units waiting for orders during the Tel Abiat operation using basic held radios. (Courtesy Hanna Bohman)

May 2015. Baz on guard during the advance, with the Abdel Aziz mountains in the background. (Courtesy Shaun Murray)

June 2015. Baz in a BMP racing towards the next Daesh village south of Suluc during the Tel Abiat operation. (Courtesy Till Paasche)

June 2015. Kurdish armoured personnel carriers (BMPs) staging during the advance on Tel Abiat. (Courtesy Hanna Bohman)

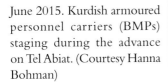

June 2015. Coalition airstrike hitting Daesh position ahead of advancing YPG/YPJ units. (Courtesy Hanna Bohman)

July 2015. Burning front line between Hezbollah and Daesh in southern Hasake. (Courtesy Till Paasche)

July 2015. Seeing war through children's eyes. Paintings in a school building in Hasake. (Courtesy Till Paasche)

December 2015. Recently taken Daesh position in Tishreen. (Courtesy Shaun Murray)

December 2015. Shot-up Daesh position in Tishreen. (Courtesy Shaun Murray)

December 2015. Staging area for an assault around Tishreen. Two assault units, one logistic Bongo van and two "Dushka" trucks from the heavy weapons unit. Supported by the "Dushka" trucks, the assault units would take and secure one village unit while the unit leapfrogged forward to the next village. Often, two or three assault groups would operate alongside one another in the countryside. (Courtesy Shaun Murray)

Leadership of the Cizire *canton* representing two genders, two religions and the right not to be religious, plus three ethnicities, taken by Baz during a research trip in October 2014. (Courtesy Till Paasche)

February 2016. Air-struck Daesh Humvee during the al-Shaddadi operation. (Courtesy Shaun Murray)

Leaflet dropped by American jets to prepare the population for the coming offensive. (Courtesy Till Paasche)

April 2016. Baz playing at being the dummy after his IV class for a YPJ assault unit. (Courtesy River Rainbow O'Mahoney Hagg)

April 2016. Baz teaching combat first aid to a YPG/YPJ assault unit. Heval Ciwan, who plays the victim, fell şehîd four months later during the battle for Manbij. (Courtesy River Rainbow O'Mahoney Hagg)

May 2016. Baz and his spirit animal at a staging area before the Euphrates crossing. (Courtesy River Rainbow O'Mahoney Hagg)

May 2016. Medic team breakfast (cigarettes and Iraqi instant café au lait in the notorious plastic cup) at the Euphrates watching all of the Cizire *canton*'s tanks. One flying the new SDF, the other the new Manbij Military Council flag. An hour or two later, U.S. Navy Seals ferried the ambulance across the river. (Courtesy Till Paasche)

May 2016. John and *Şehîd* Armanc at the same staging area on Al Jazeera news. (Courtesy John Foxx)

June 2016. Medic team and heavy weapons unit advancing on Manbij. (Courtesy Till Paasche)

June 2016. The inside of the ambulance after a run to the field hospital. On the race through the desert, nothing stayed tied down or in place and at times resupplies including tourniquets and chest seals were scarce. The medic team did not have the best medics, but within days "adapt, improvise, overcome" became their mantra. (Courtesy Till Paasche)

March 2014. Şehîd cemetery in Qamishlo, Syria. During the war there were always rows of fresh graves. (Courtesy Till Paasche)

October 2014. Mother and sister mourning their son/brother somewhere in Rojava. (Courtesy Till Paasche)

CHAPTER 11

Between Operations:
March–April 2016

Shortly after the al-Shaddadi operation had finished, all foreign fighters in Tabur Şehîd Karaman were sent back to the academy. In these kinds of situations, usually no explanation was provided. Heval Zagros, John, and Shaun grabbed their bags and had to leave their *tabur*. They were furious. It was not the first time this had happened to them. As soon as they found a *tabur* and established rapport, some dumb order would come down the chain and force the *americani* back to the rear.

While John and Heval Zagros eventually made their peace with the fact they would be fucked around again, Shaun had had enough. His six months, the minimum length for a tour with the YPG, were almost up, and he wanted to get out. There would be no more operations any time soon, and he wasn't going to spend several weeks in that horrible academy. He therefore headed to the Tev Dem *nocta*. Usually, the Tev Dem only hosts international volunteers who work in the civilian society outside the YPG/YPJ, but given the poor physical state Shaun was in, it agreed to an exception.

In brief, the Tev Dem is the group of diplomats who communicate democratic confederalism to the people of Rojava. It is one of the organizations that advance the movement intellectually. Enjoying the honor of receiving the Tev Dem's hospitality, while there, Shaun translated some documents and wrote a report to SDF's high command. Within the militia, every fighter has the right to compose a report that will go up the command chain until the issue can be addressed adequately. The subject of Shaun's report was his argument for a CASEVAC unit, a team in a lightly armored fighting vehicle that would stabilize and evacuate the wounded from the fighting arena. Listing his observations, especially those gleaned from the al-Shaddadi operation, he identified a large gap between the fighting *taburs* and the staging civilian ambulances. As a consequence, casualties were getting stuck at the front lines and could not reach the ambulances, which were often more than 30 minutes away. This is not ideal, since when dealing with combat casualties, the first hour is the most important one. In his report, Shaun therefore suggested closing this gap. In all, Shaun stayed with the Tev Dem for 10 days, until in mid-March 2016, he left Rojava to be smuggled back to Erbil.

Meanwhile, Zagros and John were stranded at a transit base just west of Qamishlo, only a couple of stone throws from the Turkish border. Once upon a time, this place must have been some kind of resort. Now it looked like the set of a post-apocalyptic Tarantino movie; the only reminder of its former glory was an utterly fucked-up old peacock.

Trying to stay productive, John used the time to reflect on the conversations he had had with Şehîd Kosta. Given his own experiences during the al-Shaddadi operation, the words of his slain brother began resonating with him. John thus told Heval Zagros of Kosta's ideas for a combat medic team roaming the front lines for casualties. From the beginning, Kosta, too, had noticed the absence of medics as well as state-of-the-art combat medicine. Understanding the potential for such a team, Heval Zagros was on board for the project. At times, the relatively small battle in al-Shaddadi had been a shitshow. The next operation would take on either Raqqa or Manbij. Those were major cities hours away from the next friendly hospital. Not having combat medics at the front lines could potentially turn these assaults into a disaster. Like Shaun, the pair therefore wrote a report to SDF high command suggesting that there should be a medical team that would stabilize combat casualties at the point of their injury on the front lines and evacuate them to the civilian ambulances.

While all of this had been going on, Baz's Tabur Şehîd Arges had been sent to the notorious Balikh River valley south of Tel Abiat, where once again Daesh had launched a counterattack. By the time the operation was over, it was March. The last time Baz had showered had been in January. Using personal contacts, Baz negotiated to stay at the Tev Dem *nocta* in order to avoid having to go to the academy for international volunteers, and arrived just a day or two after Shaun had left.

The Tev Dem liked intellectuals, so Baz shamelessly used his PhD in order to get hot food and an even hotter shower. Then, Baz too wrote a report to SDF high command suggesting that there should be a medical team that would close the gap between front-line and civilian ambulances. After translating all three reports, a good friend of ours put them into one folder and personally drove them to YPG's high command.

After a week, Baz eventually had to leave the cushy Tev Dem *nocta* and move into the fucked-up resort with John, Heval Zagros, and the old peacock. Then, the waiting began. After a few days, the three were ordered to the academy, where they hung about to see the commanders. After more waiting, the commanders said this was the responsibility of the Health Committee, so the three went back to the resort until they could be seen by them. When the Health Committee responded by saying that they had no idea why they'd come to them, it became evident that actually implementing the idea of a medic team would take a while.

Elsewhere in March 2016, just a couple of hundred yards away on the Turkish side of the border, the Turkish military was shelling a Turkish city with artillery. The reason? The city, Nusaybin, was predominantly Kurdish and, for the Turkish nationalists, that was a problem. As was usually the case when facing an ethnic issue, Turkey resorted to genocide. According to reports by *hevals* who had come through the base, there was also regular fighting at the front south of al-Shaddadi.

To John, it felt like the battle was still going on without him while he just sat around all day long, waiting for meetings that never took place. After about a week, the Marine lost his patience. "If you get this thing started and need me, I will be there. In the meantime, I need to go fight this war." He followed Baz's suggestion and joined Heval Bawer's *tabur*, which was still somewhere south of Tel Tamir.

★

Possibly fueled by Rojava's recent autonomy declaration, the inner Kurdish border tensions escalated. In particular, the Iraqi-Kurdish

Kurdistan Democratic Party, led by the Barzani family, was trying to close all existing smuggling routes. When Shaun arrived at the academy after his six months with the YPG were officially over, a group of other international volunteers was already waiting to cross back into Iraq and fly out of Erbil. With the smuggling routes closed and tensions between the KDP and the *hevals* growing, the foreign fighters had to stay put.

As the wait dragged on with no solution in sight, some international volunteers lost their shit and came up with their own smuggling plans. The issue was not the actual international border between Syria and Iraq since the *hevals* still held a corridor to Shingal Mountain. The problem was the KDP checkpoints on the route to Erbil. Some could be avoided, but eventually, the international volunteers would be forced to go through the main checkpoint outside Dohuk, the first major city on the way to Erbil, and its international airport. No *Asayîs* would ignore a group of white guys who obviously came from Syria.

Desperate enough, a YPG commander gave Shaun and a couple of other guys a lift across the border to Shingal city in Iraq, where the small group of foreign fighters wanted to link up with a journalist. In exchange for an exclusive story, the journalist's fixer would smuggle them through the checkpoints through Dohuk and into Erbil. However, when it became clear the journalist was a no-show, they simply tried their luck and took a taxi. Technically, Shaun was already in Iraq; but he was tired and exhausted, and there was no way he would go back to Syria to stay in the academy indefinitely.

They made it through a couple of smaller KDP checkpoints between Shingal and Dohuk. "Tourist, tourist, Kurdistan *bash*—good, hahaha." As expected, at the *Asayîs*'s main checkpoint outside Dohuk, their luck ended. After an *Asayîs* officer muttered "PKK" to his men, Shaun and the others got pulled out of the taxi. For the KDP *Asayîs*, the PKK was synonymous with all *hevals*. When the KDP *Asayîs* interrogated him in a little cabin, Shaun played it cool, aka dumb. They looked at his phone, hoping for juicy intel, but all they found instead were the notorious shit/dick pics a mutual friend of ours had sent around.

From the cabin, the international volunteers were taken to a hotel in Dohuk, where they spent the night with *Asayîs* guarding the entrance.

When they came down to the lobby the following morning, they met another group of guys who had tried a different route. Everyone, including the *Asayîs*, had a good laugh because there was little else they could do. While the guards were telling Shaun they would take them to Erbil so they could leave, a prison van pulled up outside. The six guys were driven instead to a prison in Erbil and put into a cage holding about 50 inmates. After three days, the guys were moved to the political wing of the prison. They were considered PKK, and political prisoners were imprisoned separately from the general population.

The cage for the political prisoners also held about 50 men, including various Islamists and Daesh suspects. When the group of international YPG volunteers walked into the cage, they were therefore tense and ready to be jumped by a crowd of crazy suicidal Daeshis armed with long beheading shanks. Instinctively, they looked around for possible weapons, but then they saw the group of men with very big mustaches smiling at them. "*Heval internacional?*" the men asked, and Shaun relaxed. Just like in Shingal, the PKK would have his back.

At this point, Shaun was not too concerned about the situation. He was Irish, and being a political prisoner was somewhat of a tradition in his family. Although he was completely broke in the Western sense of the term, Shaun was still in a better position than the local prison population, who had next to absolutely nothing. With the only lighter in the cell hanging from a string at the other end of the cage, international volunteers and the PKK guys made sure that someone was always smoking a cigarette. This way, they could light the next cigarette on the burned-down one, and no one had to get up and walk through the crowd to the lighter.

When Shaun and the others arrived, another international volunteer had already been there quite some time. Soon after, this guy's 21 days were up, and he was allowed to make his only phone call. Since the lad had no one to call, he was about to turn down the offer, until Shaun intervened. The dude therefore talked to Shaun's mom because, until this point, no one on the outside knew they were jailed in Erbil.

The entire time, the interrogations continued. Soon, Shaun felt dizzy from the incompetence of his interrogators. "What weapons does YPG have?" "What are the Americans giving them?" Eventually, the *Asayîş* googled his mom's number and found her in the Irish online phone book. "Is this lady part of the PKK in Ireland?" That made Shaun actually laugh. Yet he was grateful at the same time. He knew very well that his European passport protected him from the kind of interrogations the locals faced on a regular basis. When they came back from their interrogations, many would break down crying.

The alarm having been raised by Shaun's mother, a British diplomat showed up after a few days, questioned the Brits in the group and, since the Irish had no diplomats in Erbil, Shaun as well. To him, the whole process felt more like another interrogation instead of a helping hand. The diplomat looked him in the eyes and told him he had to stay in jail since there was nothing he could do. They both knew this was a lie because just weeks before, some Italian diplomats had walked straight out of jail with one of their citizens simply by insisting on their liberation.

However, after a couple more days, the foreign volunteers were released. Together with the Brits, Shaun was driven to the British consulate based in a fancy hotel outside Erbil. Pissed off, Shaun took a taxi to a hotel in Erbil that was known to be friendly to foreign volunteers. He had been there a couple of days trying to decompress when a group of shady international Peshmerga volunteers started showing up. When these dudes began selling sawn-off shotguns in the hotel room he shared with some other guys while the *Asayîş* were still watching from a car outside, Shaun decided it was time to leave.

Having been paid for an exclusive interview, he began floating around Europe, wondering what to do next. Reflecting on his time in jail, Shaun felt the prison had been probably better than those in Ankara, Baghdad, or Damascus. At the same time, it was way worse than any Irish prison. In a way, the prisons were an accurate description of the autonomous Kurdistan Region's state of democracy.

★

By then, it was early April 2016. Baz and Heval Zagros were still waiting outside Qamishlo. Standing on top of the resort's roof, watching the ongoing genocide in Turkey as well as the peacock, smoking Ardens, and sipping *chai*, Heval Zagros suddenly said, "Is that an ambulance?" It was. Together, they walked over to the next compound, a junkyard where a refugee family and their three chickens were squatting. Turned out, it was a junkyard for ambulances. How bizarre; all this time they had been trying to set up a medic unit, and over a dozen old ambulances were rotting away right next to them.

Fortunately for them, Heval Zagros was a boat mechanic who had spent his childhood at illegal races in old beaters somewhere in the bush. After Baz had watched his friend do his mechanic stuff for a while, he asked, "Which one, Heval Zagros?" With a filterless Lucky Strike sticking out of his beard, he mumbled, "The Ranger."

The ambulance he picked was a single-cab Ford Ranger with a box on the back. The truck was painted in coyote brown and already had several bullet holes. In the back, dried blood covered the sides and floor. The old beast had clearly seen its share of action and had been parked here to die slowly. Heval Zagros would change that. After more waiting, someone showed up with the ignition key. Once Heval Zagros managed to get it started, the *heval* who had the key got into the Ranger and drove away. In order to be allowed to keep the Ranger, they had to write a new report to the Health Committee.

The idea of a medic team was turning into a nightmare. Eventually, the commander of the base got annoyed with the two men. This was a transit camp, and Baz and Heval Zagros had been leeching around for weeks. When he finally had enough, he sent them to the new Tactical Medical Unit, or TMU.

The two knew of the TMU and had absolutely no intention of joining. The name alone was idiotic. The unit should have been called Tabur Şehîd Kosta, after the first international volunteer who had had the idea for such a team. Giving the unit an English name showed a lack of respect. The unit was part of a TV documentary, but neither Baz nor Heval Zagros wanted to be filmed, for their own legal and personal reasons. However, the base commander was determined to get shot of the pair, so he explained that this was their only option if they wanted to work as medics. Still believing in their idea, Heval Zagros and Baz decided to check out the TMU before giving up altogether.

★

Baz found the following weeks leading up to the next operation to be his worst time in Rojava. To be diplomatic, let's just say that the so-called Tactical Medical Unit was simply not his thing. For good reasons, the commanders in Tel Tamir where the team was posted on a large base had soon had enough of the constant drama the Tactical Medical Unit was causing around the city and were ready to declare the whole medic team project dead.

Despite this, the entire time, Baz and Heval Zagros continued to bond and began doing their own projects. So, refusing to partake in the TMU drama much longer, Baz started drafting a teaching manual for possible combat lifesaving classes while Heval Zagros worked on various designs for tourniquets and stretchers that could be produced locally with the scarce materials available in the embargoed Rojava. While the TMU telenovela continued, those two projects developed their own dynamic. In time, other guys began to help and feed into them.

The highlight of this period was the guys' meeting with the Health Committee, who really liked the idea of an ambulance directly at the front lines. Their main issue, however, was the many crazy people amongst the international volunteers who had been in Rojava over the last two years. This meant that they wanted to meet Baz in person, to check him out. Since they too had heard of the endless drama surrounding TMU, the Committee made it clear to Baz in a private chat after the meeting that they were giving an ambulance to him and Heval Zagros, not TMU. From now on, the two friends had their own wheels with which to implement their idea.

With the help of a friend, Baz recruited a man called Heval Rezan as an extra medic. Heval Rezan was a practicing Mormon from Utah, and a U.S. Army veteran who had deployed to Iraq for 15 months. Out of all the international volunteers, he'd always stood out for his honesty. Instead of the boasting about the usual heroic antics, he always insisted he saw no action whatsoever and had spent most of his time watching movies and drinking milkshakes. He wasn't a party pooper though, and, although he looked like a 16-year-old kid, he could pull a trigger when triggers needed to be pulled.

In terms of his personality, Heval Rezan is rather sharp and has a weird, slightly dark sense of humor. He was also used to the politically very incorrect, often homoerotic Western soldiers' humor from his time in the U.S. Army and could tolerate it because he understood the reasoning behind it. While he had his religion, the rest of the medic team used messed-up humor as a coping mechanism to deal with the shitshow all around them. In the team, Heval Rezan was the voice of reason and fact.

Next, Baz remembered that Heval Tekoşer, the American documentarian shadowing the medical unit, had mentioned having attended EMT school during his time in the U.S. Navy. Given the distinct lack of medics in the medic unit, Baz pressed Heval Tekoşer into their ranks. Heval Tekoşer was clearly mad, but also caring and compassionate, and gave Rojava absolutely everything he had.

Leading by example, Heval Zagros and Baz gave the project momentum and, by the time the commander for all international volunteers drove down to Tel Tamir to shut down the TMU, Baz and Heval Zagros were able to show him tourniquet prototypes and a combat lifesaver training manual that was based on the American Tactical Combat Casualty Care (TCCC) guidelines[1] but modified to fit the needs of the SDF in Syria. That presentation was convincing enough to keep the project alive, with the geography teacher in charge. To Baz and Heval Zagros, TMU was over. This was new medic team project, consisting of Heval Zagros, Heval Rezan, Heval Tekoşer and Baz. To Baz the team was simply "the medic team" or Tabur Askari Doctor—"soldier doctors," a name given to them by many *hevals*, even though it grossly inflated their medical skills and knowledge.

At this point, all professionally trained combat medics had left the medic team for their own reasons. Nevertheless, the atmosphere in Tabur Askari Doctor was finally positive. The team was able to conduct training relevant for the mission ahead and compatible with the way the SDF fought. Having tested various prototypes who's creation had required the involvement of the bazaars in Tel Tamir and Hasake, the medic team began producing hundreds of improvised tourniquets made of seat belts and welded metal rods. Armed with SDF's first combat lifesaver training manual, which included a section on improvising all lifesaving items in the Individual First Aid Kits, the medic team now began approaching different *taburs* to see if they were interested in training. They were not.

By May 2016, most SDF units had seen their fair share of insane international volunteers and were skeptical of the *americani*. Eventually, though, a small group of international volunteers from Tabur Silah Grand, the heavy weapons *tabur* that was based next to the medic team's *nocta*, came over to receive some combat lifesaver training. After four hours, they went back to their own *nocta* and showed their *hevals* the medical kit they had received.

The sitiation was helped by the fact that some of these *hevals* had seen Baz evacuating the blown-up family at the beginning of the al-Shaddadi operation. Slowly, the story of Baz, the Western *tabur* commander who had saved civilians, began circulating amongst the large heavy weapons *tabur*. Since this was conducting training with the various mobile *taburs* based around Tel Tamir, the story began circulating there as well. In this region, you do not get respect for what you claim to be. You get respect for what you have proven yourself able to do. According to the inner logic of the Kurdish fighters within the SDF, the story of his involvement with the injured civilians gave Baz valuable credibility. Soon, Tabur Silah Grand asked for more training, and the Kurdish *hevals* enjoyed it. (To improve the experience, the medic team cleaned their *nocta* and made it a habit to offer cold Pepsi and cookies alongside the usual *chai* to any of the visitors.) Partially due to the fact that Daesh had just blown up the city's hospital with two truck bombs, slowly, *hevals* began consulting the medics for mundane things, such as diarrhea, foot rot, and scorpion bites. Others just stopped by for a cold Pepsi and a chat. Finally, the fighters began trusting their medics.

During the day, the medic team drove around in the ambulance, visited the nearby *taburs*, and provided very basic primary health care. At that point, Baz was one of only two Western unit commanders. Showing up in the militia's first and only ambulance left an impression with the *hevals*. During one of those trips, Baz ran into Heval Şoreş, his team commander from the battle in al-Shaddadi. Heval Şoreş understood the possible impact the medic team could have on the battlefield and put on his most charming smile when he told his *tabur* the exaggerated story of Baz saving the family. Eventually, *taburs* were lining up for training and, in the 14 days leading up to the next operation, the medic team trained and equipped more than 150 *hevals* from eight different *taburs* in combat lifesaving. During the next couple of months, those classes and the provided materials did indeed save lives.

Around mid-May, reliable rumors were beginning to make the rounds. The fighting season for any major operation would end around November when the rain turned the desert into sticky mud. With spring on the way, the operation had to begin soon. During this buildup for the next major operation, more U.S. Special Forces arrived in Rojava, bringing their official total number up to 300.[2]

After al-Shaddadi, American operators slowly left their secret bases and started showing themselves. Kurdish SDF units received rudimentary training on the tablets loaded with the American "air strike app" and on the GPS devices. Thanks to American pressure, flatbeds full of 7.62 caliber rounds began arriving via the autonomous Kurdistan Region in Iraq. When the order came down for all Tel Tamir *taburs* to be ready to move out within minutes' notice, U.S. Special Forces began training units in amphibious landings on a small lake. Although it was clear to everyone in the medic team that they were not nearly ready for what was to come, spirits in the unit were high. What other choice did they have?

In the cities, the civil defense units were mobilized to run the checkpoints in order to free up the *Asayîş*, who would support the military operation. During the night, convoys of empty trucks with their lights on were driven around different parts of Rojava to confuse the enemy.

Finally, the order to mud up the trucks came in. All units, including the medic team, began smearing wet beige mud over their white trucks to camouflage them in the beige desert. The operation was imminent when the front-line commander suddenly dropped Heval B., also an EMT, at the medic team's doorstep. The team did not really know him, but there was nothing they could do about it. They had already almost been shut down, so any more bickering on their part would only cause trouble.

All *taburs* from the base were ordered out to a staging area south of the city. When the medic team showed up, they were received warmly by the Kurdish grunts. The medics had trained half of them, and the other half had heard stories about the team. These were the fighters on the ground who knew that many of them would soon be dead. Having medics roll with them in an already shot-up ambulance somehow had a positive effect on morale.

CHAPTER 12

Crossing the Euphrates: May 2016

After the exhilarating four-hour ride in the convoy leaving Tel Tamir, the Cizire *canton's* *taburs*, including Baz and Heval Zagros with the medic team and John with a regular *tabur*, took shelter behind a large grain silo at a junction around Ain Issa. The road south led straight to Raqqa, the road west to Manbij. Soon, the excitement of the convoy faded and was replaced by pre-operation boredom in yet another staging area. After a few days in the shadow of the silos, the *civîn* was called in. Given the Kurds' paranoia when it came to operational safety, this meant that the actual operation must be about to start very soon.

In the pre-operation strategy meeting, the SDF units who would spearhead the assault were briefed on the operation's aims and objectives. The mission was to cross the Euphrates and take al-Bab and Manbij. For the enemy, both cities were of vital importance as they were ISIS's lifeline to their strategic ally, Turkey. With al-Bab and Manbij gone, Daesh would be cut off from the Turkish border and have a serious logistical issue. The operation would pave the way for an assault on Raqqa in the following summer.

While these were the arguments the SDF used to persuade their American partner to support the operation, there was a second motivation: a successful operation would connect all three Kurdish *cantons*—Afrin, Kobane, and Cizire. Controlling the entire north of Syria, including the border to Turkey, would put the SDF in a very powerful position for any future peace talks. For Turkey, this scenario was a strategic nightmare and just as it had been with the Tishreen operation, it represented a red line. From their perspective, the PKK would occupy the entire border with Syria except for a section in Idlib. Without the support of America, the SDF would not have even dared to think about an operation like this given Turkey's constant threats. Seizing this opportunity, the SDF wanted to try connecting the *cantons*, hoping the American F16s would keep the Turkish ones away.

The primary target of the operation was Manbij. Of the original 100,000 inhabitants, between 30,000 and 50,000 were still in the city. The coalition estimated between 3,000 and 5,000 well-prepared Daesh fighters were waiting. In comparison, al-Shaddadi, a city of 15,000 with few civilians left, had been, according to rumors, defended by about 200–500 enemy fighters.

The SDF would assault the city from two directions. While the Kobane *taburs* would cross the river via the Tishreen Dam they had liberated in December 2015, the Cizire *taburs* would cross at the bridge of the M4 highway. The enemy had blown up parts of the bridge, so the mobile *taburs* would be shipped over by American special forces. On the other side, they had to secure and hold strategic hilltops until the main battle group could follow. When John realized his *tabur* was tasked with conducting an amphibious assault and taking and holding a hilltop, he got very excited. This was a Marine's wildest fantasy.

Next, the *civîn* turned to a highly political subject. Up to this point, Kurdish *hevals* had continued to refer to the militia as YPG/YPJ, not SDF. Kurdish *hevals* were still wary of sections of the Arab fighters, in particular, the former Islamists. In addition, YPG/YPJ was their identity. Giving that up was not something that would happen overnight. It had to grow. This is why the test runs in al-Hol, Tishreen, and al-Shaddadi were important: these operations built up trust between all involved partners, including the Americans.

Drawing on this trust, their commanders were now asking the YPG/YPJ fighters who would lead the assault to take off every single YPG/YPJ logo, patch, or flag. They were no longer YPG/YPJ; they were SDF as soon as they crossed the river. It is easy to explain this step as yet another American attempt to appease Turkey. It meant that, officially, it was not the Kurds who were going to cross the Euphrates, it was the SDF. This explanation, however, fails to take into account the wider issue.

As the SDF commanders continued their explanation, similar to al-Shaddadi, two military councils had been formed: the al-Bab and Manbij military councils. Both consisted of people representing each city, people who had fled Daesh because they believed in democracy. Now, these councils wanted to liberate their city and had asked the SDF for assistance. According to the plans, as soon as Manbij and al-Bab were free and both military councils were in a position to hold them on their own, the YPG/YPJ elements of the SDF would withdraw east of the Euphrates and leave the control of the western Euphrates's banks to their local Arab allies.

The concession was free passage between the Kurdish Afrin and Kobane *cantons*, following the model that was now in place between the Kobane and Cizire *cantons*. As proof that the YPG/YPJ had no intention of occupying and conquering Manbij and al-Bab, behind the front line, local Arabs trained by the Kurdish *Asayîş* would establish a tight network of checkpoints that would keep the SDF's back clear. Consequently, the mainly Arab civilians in the liberated towns and villages would not interact much with Kurdish fighters but rather with their former neighbors and fellow Arabs. Insisting that it was the SDF who crossed the river was not just about fooling Turkey; it was about democratic confederalism and keeping the moral high ground.

Soon after the *civîn*, the first *taburs* were deployed to another staging area. Sometime during the night, a *heval* in a Hilux showed up and told the medic team to follow. On the road to the river, they overtook unmarked flatbeds carrying pontoon elements for a temporary bridge. The trucks were being driven by American soldiers wearing night vision goggles. The medic team arrived at a staging area in a village on the eastern banks of the Euphrates near the M4 bridge. The first volleys of mortars were exchanged with the enemy over the massive river. Adrenaline began pumping.

A little further down the river, John was about to lose it. He was ready to go on this mission but expected to get blocked at the very last second again. Not this time. When the sun was about to set, Tabur

Şehîd Karaman and other *taburs* began moving out. While the sky was turning pink, John and Lenny, his new battle buddy, a Christian kid from Georgia, were riding on the back of a Hilux through a deserted village close to the river. Suddenly, another Hilux gunned it up the road, raced past the *taburs*, and took the lead. When the Hilux passed John, he saw the Mk 19 grenade launcher on the back. Since the SDF did not have those, he deduced that they must be U.S. Special Forces.

By the time the convoy made it to another deserted village near the river, it was dark. The assaulting force unloaded and hiked through the high grass until they were close to the riverbanks. Since there was no info on their departure, John lay down and zoned out for a while. He was woken up by the sound of English being spoken, and although he could not see what was going on, he noticed the green glow of the night vision goggles. The U.S. Special Forces were clearly trying to communicate some kind of issue with the Kurdish *hevals*. However, their interpreter only spoke Arabic and these Kurds did not. "I need everyone in four fucking lines, that's all!" barked the American, who was increasingly worried about the operation's tight schedule.

With his Kurmanci, or Northern Kurdish, being good enough at this point, John took over as interpreter and organized the *hevals* into four single-file columns before they hiked to their designated staging areas at the riverbank. On the way, they walked past a house that was occupied by an American reconnaissance team. They had not seen any enemy movements at their designated landing zone (LZ). This was the first intel John and Lenny had received.

When they reached the river, several black Zodiac inflatables were already waiting. The boat operators wore black contractor-style clothes and had no visible weapons. Once his Zodiac had departed, John and the boat operator started talking. When John mentioned he was a Marine, the boat operator paused for a second before responding that he was a Marine, too. Apparently, they were MARSOC guys, which made sense; the United States Marine Forces Special Operations Command are the Marines' own special forces and are highly trained in amphibious assaults.

Here, the Euphrates was between 1¼ and 1¾ miles wide. The moon was covered by clouds, and a thick fog hung over the water. Around the halfway point, the fog lightened up, and John could see the hills on the other side. After some time, the fog grew thicker again. Suddenly, the boat operators killed the engines. In complete silence, the rafts floated on the water out in the open. John could hear the four engines of an AC-130 above them. As soon as the plane was orbiting over the river, its guns sprang into action, marking the LZ with red flares. Go time. The Zodiacs sped up.

With the fog hanging thickly, John could still not clearly see the LZ. From the back, the boat operator yelled, "When I say go, you guys go. Marine, you need to push back my boat, otherwise, I am beached and stuck." There were a couple of hundred yards between each Zodiac when the boats slowed down. "Go, go, go!" the boat operator yelled, but the *hevals* just stared at him. They could not see any land, just fog and water. John noticed a rock on the shore and whisper-screamed "*Bitche, bitche! Zu, zu!*—Let's go, let's go! Fast, fast!" All at once, the *hevals* tried to get off the boat. Since they were all bunched up and he had no idea where the enemy was, John jumped off the side of the Zodiac into the Euphrates.

Immediately, he knew he had fucked up. The water was much deeper than he had anticipated. In the river up to his nipples, John tried not to go under whilst at the same time keeping his AK nice and dry. The MARSOC guy yelled, "Push the boat back, push the fucking boat back!" Once John had made it out of the river, he pushed the Zodiac off the beach and took cover behind a rock next to Lenny. Together, they watched Heval Ali, John's *takem* commander, check their surroundings. On Heval Ali's orders, the *takem* searched the nearby road for IEDs before taking up defensive positions. Sitting in the cold night next to a wall, a soaking wet John observed the *heval* from Tabur Sabotage, which had been attached to their unit, continue the search for mines. Eventually, a *heval* from the SDF's own special forces led the *takem* up a small path while first light illuminated the skies.

★

The same night, the medic team was deployed to the M4 bridge. When the sun came up behind them, they were lined up behind several *taburs* and an old Russian armored personnel carrier. There was a fantastic chaos on the endless bridge. Just before the section Daesh had blown up, a SEAL team was using a pontoon segment originally intended to build a bridge as a raft. However, since the Euphrates was too broad at this point, individual segments or rafts were instead used as a barge to shuttle the SDF forces. Powered by a Zodiac on each side, six Hiluxes (two full *taburs*) were shuttled over at once.

On the bridge, more MARSOC guys were trying to clear the traffic jam caused by the old Soviet tanks. Drinking nasty 3in1 instant cappuccinos out of foldable plastic cups that never got cleaned, Baz and Heval Zagros took in the scene. This was like the beginning of *The Longest Day*, in which the Scottish major drove along the tank columns, chitchatting with everyone. This was exactly where they wanted to be: at the beginning of a big battle.

When it was time for the medic team to cross, one of the SEALs jumped on top of the ambulance for better visibility and directed the raft across the wide river. At the other side, the banks of the river were rather steep, and a SEAL asked Heval Zagros if he needed any help getting off the raft. Seriously offended, Heval Zagros made a horribly condescending clicking sound the Arab fighters did all the time that signaled "no" and raced up the hill, leaving the SEALs in a cloud of dust.

★

When John and Lenny's *takem* secured their designated hilltop, they encountered no resistance. While other units nearby had come into contact with the enemy, John was watching the landscape. As soon as the sun was up, the temperature turned from freezing to sweaty hot, so the team waited for new orders and tried to stay hydrated. Even though there wasn't much fighting, in the morning, this Marine and Lenny participated in an amphibious landing and secured a strategic hill until the main battle group had crossed. This was everything John had ever wanted to do.

When night fell, they started moving again. Snipers with thermal optics led the way. After several hours of hiking, they reached another hilltop and secured it again. The sun would come up soon, and John needed to get some sleep.

When he woke up, it was already hot, and he was dripping with sweat. There was very little shade and even less water. The *takem* had no idea what the course of action was going to be, and eventually, the YPJ element at the side of the hill got fired on by a "Dushka" truck that ISIS had snuck through a gap in the premature front line. Luckily, nobody was seriously wounded. Trying to find a spot that was clear of goat poop, the *takem* settled for the night.

The following day, they made it to a rendezvous point with the BMP. The *tabur* was meant to assault the large village where the hills turned into flat desert. However, as soon as they got near the rendezvous point, they were mortared. Since the Cizire *taburs* only had two BMPs, the plan was scratched, and they hiked toward the village along a dry riverbed. Eventually, a Hilux picked them up. Completely overloaded, the truck almost flipped when climbing up the dry banks.

Driving forward, they soon heard a different unit being fired upon by the enemy mortars. The Hilux raced to a compound where *hevals* were firing at a suspected Daesh SVBIED. The threat having passed, John and the other *hevals* with him from Tabur Şehîd Karaman were finally sitting down for some food when a civilian holding a baby appeared. Desperately, the man waved at the *hevals*, coming closer. Several *hevals* yelled at him to stop, but he kept waving and walked ever closer. Then one of the *hevals* shot him. When they got closer to the old man's body, they saw that the "baby" was in fact an IED.

For the following few days, John and Lenny's *takem* secured some rich folks' deserted house overlooking a large field that marked the front line. As usual, it was miserable and hot. The only food options were old, fermented-smelling rice or chocolate bars. John opted for the chocolate. This decision was not about taste but choosing between nasty diarrhea or 10 days of constipation and stomach cramps. John always felt that constipation was the lesser of the two evils.

From this point onward, Daesh began harassing the SDF advance through the countryside until Manbij. Along the M4 highway, the enemy would constantly take pop-shots in the general direction of the SDF.

Amongst the buildings at the other end of the field, John and the *hevals* could see the enemy running around through buildings and alleyways, but they were too far away for their AKs.

With time, the constant harassment began rattling John's cage. The concussion waves of hundreds of mortars and thousands of close rounds were taking their toll. The mortar rounds had become omnipresent, yet they were completely unpredictable. Although the enemy was ineffective in stopping the advance, they wrecked the SDF's nerves and, once in a while, even hit a target. With American jets and drones around, the enemy could not use mortar batteries in their classic sense because the mortar position would be immediately air struck. Thus, they used them for taking seemingly interminable pop-shots in the general direction of the SDF forces. After firing a few mortar rounds, Daesh moved back into shelter to fire another couple of rounds a bit later from elsewhere. Eventually, John would feel every shockwave from every mortar in his guts, where they shook the solid block of half-digested chocolate.

★

After the river crossing, the medic team hit a dead end again. Despite there being casualties at the front line, the unit was kept in the rear. Morale was low. They were under the command of one of the front-line commanders who had strongly voted in favor of the team's abandonment the base in Tel Tamir. Everyone hoped they would have forgotten about the drama, but it seemed not since now, the only medic unit was sidelined. Having slowly grown into his war persona, after delivering a rather loud and slightly threatening speech, Baz asked the team to trust him. They did, and the medic team kept waiting for their opportunity.

The SDF was still advancing through the countryside, where the enemy did not put up much resistance anymore. Here, there was no hiding from the jets, and the enemy wasn't going to waste the lives of their experienced fighters for nothing. All that was left for Daesh between the river and Manbij were villagers with AKs, mortars, IEDs, and SVBIEDs who popped up occasionally just behind the front lines, where they would chase the medic team around.

So far, the front-loader continued to be an effective weapons system against SVBIEDs. Wherever the advance halted, the front-loaders would put earth berms across the highway that were too big for any driving suicide bomber to negotiate. Now the *taburs* had moved into a more densely populated terrain, though, SVBIEDs have more places in which to hide—in garages, under tarps, and in houses—while they waited for an SDF *takem* to roll in. When an SDF unit was close by, the bomber would drive out of his hiding place and straight into the *hevals*, where he detonated himself. In a landscape of interconnected villages that slowly morph into a city, this tactic left very little time for the SDF fighters to set up proper defenses or coalition jets to bomb the SVBIED. As a consequence, each Hilux of the Cizire Taburs began carrying a spike-chain that they could throw across the street to impede the progress of SVBIEDs.

Sometime in early June, Baz ran into one of the French *hevals* he had taught during one of the combat lifesaving classes with Silah Grand, the heavy weapons *tabur*. Since this included all "Dushka" trucks, BMPs, and the two tanks of the battle group, the *tabur*'s surprisingly young commander was always accompanied by Hevala Roza, the front-line commander in charge of the assault, and the French special forces, who coordinated the air campaign. As the French *heval* spoke good Kurdish and was well liked, he stayed around the command element to help translate and assist with overcoming any cultural barriers.

Seizing the opportunity, the French *heval*, who was highly supportive of the medic team, introduced Baz to Hevala Roza and told her of the problem of being stuck in the rear, where they could not help the wounded. Seeing the logic in having their own medics ahead of, not behind, civilian ambulances, she told Baz to bring up his team and stay with her command post. For a couple of days, the medic team tried to keep up with Hevala Roza's command element, which was constantly changing positions. Baz always made sure Hevala Roza's aids knew where their medics were. All the medic team needed was an opportunity to prove themselves; yet advancing through the countryside remained relatively easy, with few casualties.

During the following days of the advance, though, some other SDF units got into small skirmishes and, occasionally, a house was blown up by a jet. Then, on June 11th, Hevala Roza and her entourage occupied a tall white villa. From its roof, parts of Manbij could be seen. From up there, Manbij just looked like a big, burning city. SDF units had surrounded it and were preparing for the assault. In the past, the SDF had left the enemy a corridor through which to retreat. This time, the SDF and the Americans intended to kill or capture all of the enemy's elite foreign fighters rather than allowing them to escape to fight another day.

★

After a few days, John and Lenny's *takem* was relieved by just two Arab *Asayîş*, who had to defend the position alone. With their Hiluxes, Tabur Şehîd Karaman moved up to a completely different front line. At a staging area, they waited for an air strike the front-line commander there had already called in. There were three houses about ⅔ mile away and, after the usual flyovers, one of them was blown up. The *takem* moved up to the position and secured it. Inside the destroyed building lay some dead Daesh fighters. In the other two buildings were families, all of them unharmed. All the *takem* suffered from was some ringing in their ears.

Heval Ali, John's *takem* commander, sent the families toward the rear to find one of the many empty houses. The front line would only be there for a couple of days. They could return without a problem once the units had moved forward. The *tabur* knew they were at the very front line but had no clue where the enemy was. Soon, locals began walking their cows around, and kids were out playing. Thanks to the incident with the guy with the "baby," the *tabur* was already on edge when Daesh ambushed them from a nearby tree line. In the subsequent skirmish, one of the cows was shot and went bottom-up in the middle of the field as dozens of villagers ran for safety. After then, no one walked their farm animals around anymore.

The gunfight was still going on when John, who was posted covering the rear sector, which included a couple of houses and compounds, noticed three men on motorbikes coming toward them. Contemplating the lack of clear-cut rules of engagement, John called for Hevala Rojin, his team leader. However, Hevala Rojin was still engaged with the firefight taking place in the front sector and was unavailable to give orders. The decision was on John. On one hand, he could be a hero if he were to take out three possible ISIS suicide bombers; on the other hand, he could be a murderer of three civilians who had heard gunfire and were speeding over to check on their family in the area. John sent a volley of very close warning shots over the heads of the bikers, who took cover behind a nearby farmhouse about 150 yards away.

When the men reappeared on foot in front of the house, John fired right above their heads, blowing chunks out of wall. He wanted to send a strong message, not kill them, since there was still a slim chance those poor bastards were just in the wrong place at the wrong time. All the while, the firefight was still raging in the front sector. John suddenly heard the beautiful sound of what Marines call "The Hand of God"—an A-10 Thunderbolt jet unloading its Gatling gun into the tree line, quickly quieting the battlefield. Once the Daesh fighters out at the front sector were either dead or had retreated, the three guys John had watched sneaking around at the rear sector left as well.

With other *taburs* leapfrogging forward, John and Tabur Şehîd Karaman secured this flank of the advance for a few days. Eventually, they were repositioned to yet a different part of the battlefield. Rolling through an area that had been liberated days before on the back of a Hilux gave the Marine a strange warm and fuzzy feeling on the inside. People were cheering the fighters. Children showed the victory sign, and the YPJ handed out some candy. Little shops were openly selling cigarettes that were banned under Daesh while old men were puffing their Alhamras or locally grown tobacco in the open. From the Hiluxes, Kurdish music was blasting. People were smiling again.

The *tabur* arrived at the rendezvous point just behind the front. Several units were gathered around a large farm building. A group of Arab women with their children had gathered amongst the Kurdish YPJ *takems*. The women had dropped their full black Daesh niqab for hijabs, scarfs of colorful material loosely draped around the head just covering the hair in the way it had been normal before ISIS came on the scene. John watched the women and children interact. They all felt cool and safe while American jets were dropping bombs just across the field.

The Arab women trusted their Kurdish sisters who had just liberated them from their common enemy. This is how the YPJ could generate real-time intel on the enemy. A platoon of U.S. Marines in full battle rattle could never have pulled that off.

After some chocolate bar burritos made with stale bread, Tabur Şehîd Karaman mounted up again, drove toward the city, and passed the "White House" from where Hevala Roza and a small team of French special forces were watching the advance, calling in constant air strikes.

CHAPTER 13

The Meat Grinder: June 2016

For the medic team, hour zero was June 11th. After all the drama, waiting, arguing, and being fucked around, on this day, the medic team began saving lives. Overnight, the enemy had retaken a strategic village northwest of Manbij. In early morning, the enemy continued their aggressive counterattack, and SDF *taburs* were taking casualties.[1] When the medic team arrived at the rendezvous point at the outskirts of the village, the fighting was close. Within seconds, a Hilux arrived from the front lines, and two wounded YPJ fighters were unloaded.

One had fallen *şehîd* during the drive; the other was badly wounded from an RPG blast. She had shrapnel in both arms and her head. Her right hand was partially burned off with the fingers reduced to charcoaled sticks. While the team began stabilizing her, a second truck arrived and unloaded a *heval* who was lying on his back and in the process of drowning in his own blood. While Baz was pulling him out of the vehicle, the *heval* was gasping for air but couldn't stop swallowing the blood that kept pouring into his throat from a gunshot wound through the neck. On the way out through his mouth, the round had chipped a couple of teeth. The team scooped the blood out of his mouth and applied an occlusive dressing to the neck. Baz noticed the tattoo under the dust on the *heval*'s arms. This dude was one of the American volunteers.

Somewhere in between all of this, a third casualty arrived with a large caliber gunshot to his leg. The fighting had picked up, and the incoming rounds were getting more precise by the minute. Zagros had the team's back the entire time, keeping Baz updated on the changing tactical situation. Amidst all the chaos, outside a small house, an old lady continued cooking lunch over a fire.

With the enemy advancing, the team's situation changed from tactical field care to care under fire.[2] Behind the team was an open field and, with all casualties somewhat stabilized, Baz ordered an immediate evacuation. While Zagros maneuvered the minivan, Baz raced the Ranger over the fields while bullets were hitting all around. As the ambulance was ferrying the casualties to the hospital, Baz arrived back at the "White House," where Hevala Roza was waiting for him. "Will Heval *Americani* be OK?" she asked. A dead international volunteer this early into the fight would not be good for morale. With more confidence than he actually had, Baz answered, "Of course, Hevala Roza."

While the medic team cleaned the ambulance and loaded new syringes with their various drugs, Hevala Roza watched them from the roof of the "White House." When Baz met her gaze, she gave him a friendly nod. The medic team had proven themselves. They had gained the *hevala*'s trust, and together, they would find a way to deploy the medics most effectively.

The following weeks would not only be a learning process for the medic team but also for the YPJ commander, who was not used to there being a medic team at the front lines. Previously, the *hevals* had used PKK's guerilla tactics, which did not have a strong emphasis on medics. If a guerilla fighter was injured during a fight with the Turkish Army and could not retreat into the mountains, he or she would die or be captured. Medics played no part in this kind of warfare. Slowly, the SDF was finding its own style of fighting, and from now, that would include combat medics.

★

On the night of June 16th, Tabur Şehîd Karaman first entered Manbij. The Hiluxes rolled up to a staging area from where the *hevals* continued their patrol on foot. They were led by someone wearing basic night vision googles, but even without them, John and Lenny could see that they were hiking through a network of olive groves and small villages.

Occasionally, Heval Ali would relay the *tabur*'s position to the CJTF-OIR. John's *takem* cleared a large farmhouse in between the bushes. After some more walking, Tabur Şehîd Karaman made it to their target: a building where about two other *taburs* were already staging. The whole building reeked of decomposing bodies, and the *hevals* were happy to continue their advance. They continued through more olive groves until they'd reached and secured the next compound.

Staring into the darkness during his guard shift, John heard the calls to morning prayer from nearby mosques. John looked forward to this call as it meant that soon the sun would come up, and units from the rear would move up and relieve them. He would eat and have some *chai*. It meant their job was almost done. However, this time, just before the sun came up, they got the order to continue their advance.

The *takem* now entered an urban area, where they cleared another compound. The people must have left in a hurry. During first light, they moved to the next building, crossing a street. At this point, the SDF only operated at night. Thanks to CJTF-OIR, they had more night vision capabilities, and the AC-130 gunships with their all-seeing eyes could give close, easy, and effective air support. Now, clearly visible to everyone in the vicinity, the *takem* had just secured the single-story building when a firefight broke out just down the street. John had never heard such a high volume of small arms fire. It sounded like being in the rifle pits during Marine Corps rifle qualification with exponentially higher volume. Heval Ali and the squad's RPG gunner lost their cool. Heval Ali failed to take charge as the squad leader, and the RPG gunner yelled and took badly aimed shots toward the enemy. John tried to balance the situation by staying extra cool. Looking out of a window, he saw an almost cartoon-like hailstorm of lead hitting all around their building and its surroundings. Moving in the morning light, the enemy had zeroed in on them. They were sitting ducks for some fuck with an RPG, a grenade, a mortar round, or a machine gun. The squad was caught in a frontal ambush with unsecured territory to its left flank, which John recognized as a possible means for ISIS to maneuver on them and execute an L-shaped ambush, pinning them all down until death. John knew the clock was ticking and kept a close eye on the tree line and houses to the left flank.

The team's command structure was down with everyone screaming and panicking. In order to get out of the structure, the *takem* finally prepared for a 55-yard sprint across the kill zone back to the house the squad had cleared previously. The first group made it unharmed. The second group made it safely as well, but every time *hevals* were in the open, Daesh lit them up from their ambush positions. It sounded like a steamroller driving over bubble wrap. When the third pair had almost made it, they took a casualty. The enemy had finally zeroed in on the only doorway leading into the saving compound. John, Lenny, Heval Ali, and Hevala Rojin were cut off and had no idea where the rest of their *tabur* was.

While the enemy still engaged the building they were in, John spotted a little shack at a five o'clock position to the front. He sprinted over first. As with each previous sprinter, the volley of fire increased tenfold as hundreds of rounds were fired in John's direction with every step. Surprised yet elated, John made it to the small shack and ducked around the corner to take cover. Lenny and Hevala Rojin followed. Heval Ali, their *takem* commander, never arrived. Without knowing what had happened, Hevala Rojin broke down completely. Lacking much cover, John took control of the three-person fireteam and maneuvered Lenny and the *hevala* across the rest of the kill zone into yet another compound. Unable to hold off a large attack, John worried about being outflanked and overrun.

They searched the compound—John went left and Lenny went right. John walked into a room that looked like a small guard shack in which he noticed a bed. On top of it was a gas mask and plastic bags filled with a brownish substance with what looked like cotton balls. He didn't get time to inspect the plastic bags before he began feeling dizzy and lightheaded—and he realized what the gas mask was for. John had entered a room used to store some form of chemicals. The compound itself was therefore utterly useless, and they had to leave it before they became stuck in a situation they could not get out of. Yet the *hevala* was still in a state of panic and, despite having a radio, was unable to get a grip on the rapidly deteriorating situation. Small arms fire was tearing away at the compound's outer walls. John was encouraging the *hevala* to radio the rest of the squad and find their position so they could unite the teams, but she was frozen in fear.

John's plan was to move down a nearby alley to get as close to the rest of the *tabur* as possible. However, as John and Lenny got ready to sprint, the *hevala* refused to join them. Worried about snipers waiting in the alley, she wanted to run back across the entire kill zone in a direct route to the house in which she believed the rest of the squad was located. Outranked, Lenny and John conceded, but as soon as the three broke cover, they took heavy fire that split John and Lenny, who was at the front of the group. As feared, ISIS had effectively outflanked them and executed an L-shaped ambush, pinning the group down for 270 degrees of movement. John grabbed the *hevala* and pulled her back to safety, but Lenny kept running. Stuck with the panicking *hevala*, John was trying to figure out their next step when he heard Lenny on the other side of a nearby wall.

"Lenny, what the fuck!" John yelled.

"John, is that you? Wait a second." Then John heard gunfire from where Lenny was hiding. Although not penetrating the wall John was behind, bits of concrete were coming off. John yelled, "Lenny?! Lenny?!" No answer. He assumed Lenny had been shot whilst climbing over the wall, but then Lenny suddenly ran through the compound entrance.

"I tried to shoot a hole into the wall, but it did not work." Just happy to see Lenny was still alive, John reminded himself this was not the moment to lose his shit, so the two discussed their options. Suddenly, two more *hevals* from their *tabur* who were also lost showed up. Unfortunately, they were in a similar state to Hevala Rojin and also unable to function effectively.

Having run out of options, the *hevala* finally agreed to the plan involving the alley. Being lit up again, the small team was forced back to the previous compound. Luckily, a second squad that had been sent to locate John's fireteam stumbled across the compound and linked up with them. Then, instead of calling in support, the group embarked on another run through the kill zone in an effort to outmaneuver ISIS.

The morning operations having gone completely sideways and several casualties having being incurred, the orders were to regroup before pushing forward. Having used up their luck, another *heval* was hit during the run through the kill zone but made it to safety. Now the ragtag group was stuck behind yet another dusty, beige compound. With the assault clearly having gone awry and the enemy advancing, they were waiting for yet another ambush. They therefore had to pull back, and embarked on a sprint into the cover of an olive grove while some asshole fired his PKM, a belt-fed machine gun, at them from the hip.

After several hours, an A-10 came to end the situation. Having held out in the olive grove while the rest of the force continued attacking with air support, the *tabur* now moved back to regroup. Around their compound were fruit trees bearing little green cherries that tasted like pears. John ate a shit-ton of those. He liked them because they had a high water content and because he could stuff them into his drop pouch to eat at a later time.

★

After another particularly bloody day, the medic team stayed with an inexperienced *tabur* that had just arrived to the fight. When the medics began hosing down the ambulance, streams of blood washed out, and the young fighters who were watching the scene fell silent. They had to go into the city next, and the campaign was not going well. Years later Baz noticed the similarities between this scene and the children's drawing he had found in Hasake in July 2015.

What followed from there on was a feverish nightmare of sweat, blood, and tears. The medic team was racing death for the souls of their brothers and sisters. Together with the SDF, the team walked through several circles of Dante's *Inferno*. There was no more hope, just mutilation, children's bodies torn apart by mines, and young girls hunted by ISIS snipers. The only constant was the pain and suffering. The desperation was so absolute, so all-consuming, that it would change the survivors forever. And while the devil—the regional Daesh commander—was waiting in Manbij's center, he was surrounded by Dante's Sowers of Discord, the hypocrites, and the barrators who were ripped apart by American bombs. Different from *Inferno*, however, the innocent were suffering the same fate as the guilty when they crossed the minefields that lay around Manbij in concentric rings.

★

SDF, male, caught in RPG blast, 20 to 30 shrapnel wounds, large chunk of shrapnel in right thigh. Possible pierced lung. SDF, male, caught in mine or RPG blast and shot by ISIS sniper. Right arm, right leg, left leg, all shredded, bones shattered. Gunshot wound to left shoulder. It took five tourniquets to control the bleeding. SDF, male, shot by ISIS, gunshot wound entered high on the thigh, did not exit, severe bleeding. SDF, male, shot by ISIS, gunshot wound between abdomen and chest cavity, no exit wound. Applied decompression needle in chest. SDF, female, shot by ISIS sniper, gunshot wound to the head: entered forehead, exited back of head. SDF, female, shot by ISIS sniper, gunshot wound entered back over left clavicle, exited back near spine. SDF, female, shot by ISIS sniper. Gunshot wound entered top of arm near shoulder. No exit wound. Civilian, female, shot by ISIS three days prior, two gunshot wounds to right leg, one went through, one stuck, gunshot wound to the arm. SDF, male, shot by ISIS, gunshot wound to abdomen exited near spine. No feeling below the waist. SDF, male, shot by ISIS, gunshot in extremity, entry and exit. SDF, male, stepped on landmine. Severed right foot. SDF, male, caught in mine blast, small shrapnel wounds on all extremities and on chest and abdomen.

SDF, male, caught in blast, shrapnel to the eye, possible internal bleeding, vomiting blood. SDF, male, shot by ISIS, gunshot wound through left thigh, arterial bleeding, tourniquets applied. SDF, male, shot by ISIS, gunshot wound entered high inside of left thigh, exited high on outside of thigh, arterial bleeding, tourniquets applied. Civilian, female, shot by ISIS, gunshot wound entered side of left chest cavity, exited right side of abdomen, two chest decompression needles, performed cricothyroidotomy. Child, gunshot wound to chest, three chest decompression needles. *Asayîş*, male, shot by ISIS, gunshot wound to thigh. SDF, male, shot by ISIS, entry wound on back of head, cricothyroidotomy. Child, hit by shrapnel, shrapnel entered side of chest and exited back, two chest decompression needles. SDF, male, mine, broken left leg, shrapnel all over body. SDF, male, gunshot through chest, decompression needle and chest tube. SDF, male, mine, body peppered with shrapnel, chest wound, large part of right hand missing. SDF, male, multiple gunshots, through and in left hand, gunshot in leg, gunshot in stomach. SDF, male, multiple gunshots, shot in right leg twice, shot in right biceps. SDF, male, gunshot to upper left thigh, arterial bleeding, two tourniquets. SDF, male, bullet in abdomen, bullet traveled upward through abdomen, coughing up blood, decompression needle. SDF, male, large caliber gunshot in left leg, broken bones, and severe bleeding. SDF, male, mine, shrapnel to face and body. *Asayîş*, male, mine, left leg amputated, calf on right leg missing, tourniquets on both legs. *Asayîş*, male, same mine, right leg half amputated, injuries to chest and head, decompression needles to both lungs, tourniquets. SDF, female, shot through eye, exit at side of skull. Child, shot through back, exit in lower abdomen, evisceration. SDF, female, shot through left arm, arterial bleeding and broken bones, tourniquets. SDF, male, shot through left chest. Exit on side. SDF, male, shot through left chest, exit on side. SDF, male, mine, shrapnel in eye. SDF, male, shot through chest. SDF, female, multiple gunshots, shot through both lungs, shot through left foot. SDF, male, RPG, left foot open, tourniquets. SDF, male, shot in side, exit in abdomen, evisceration, intestines stabilized. SDF, male, shot in abdomen. SDF, female, mine, shrapnel to chest and arms. Civilian male, multiple gunshots, shot through left hand, shot through upper chest, no exit wound. SDF, male, shot through leg, arterial bleeding, tourniquets. SDF, male, mine, injury to head, back, legs. SDF, male, shot in inner thigh. SDF, male, mine, shrapnel to entire front apsrt from the chest. SDF, male, mine, injury to eyes. SDF, male, mine, shrapnel to leg. Parts of thigh missing. SDF, male, shot in left thigh. SDF, male, shot in back. War is hell, and those who think otherwise have not seen it from up close.

★

On June 20th, Tabur Şehîd Karaman was sent into the city for another night operation. From their staging area, they could see the dreaded Daesh berm that ran around Manbij. Without any intel, the three *takems* sprinted to the berm and took cover. John and Lenny's team commander, Hevala Rojin, had never mentally recovered from the ambush a few nights before and was scared, just like the rest of the *tabur*. Above them, an AC-130 was hammering targets in the neighborhood they would breach soon.

Once the gunship had destroyed all known enemy positions, Tabur Şehîd Karaman received the order to cross over the berm. The *tabur* sprinted to a nearby compound, *nocta yek*-one, the next known rendezvous point. With Heval Ali injured, their new *takem* commander transmitted their position to CJTF-OIR. Using *nocta yek* as their hub, three *takems* advanced in different directions.

Carefully, John and Lenny's *takem* moved past a row of houses, and while John's head was just below a window of one of the homes, he heard a woman cough. The neighborhood was supposed to have been abandoned except for Daesh fighters. Was the cough from a civilian? Was it an ISIS bride trying to wake her husband to alert him to the invading fighters? Whatever it was, it had to be investigated. He signaled his new *takem* commander, and they searched for the front door of the building so they could look for the person who'd coughed. At the front of the building there were three doorways: two doors that were wide open and a third door that was closed. The two open doors led to areas of the house that were completely empty. John mentioned to his *takem* commander that the cough he had heard had undoubtedly come from the area of the house behind the third, closed door, but the commander wanted to continue pushing forward. John had a very bad feeling about this.

Ignoring the possible threat, the *takem* advanced through another olive grove until they got to a square. Right in front of the square was a half-finished three-story building with dozens of dark windows staring down at them. In the quiet of the night, John heard the ever-familiar sound of feet shuffling on a concrete floor inside of a window on the second floor, again, right above his head. John slowly moved into a defensive position behind a wall while covering the window with his rifle. Lenny followed suit.

"Did you see that?" whispered Lenny.

"What?"

"The red light."

Civilians do not use red light, the military does. John felt the noose of an incoming ambush tightening around them. He tried to warn his *takem* commander, but he ignored him. The *takem* continued their patrol into the city with John and Lenny being tail-end Charlies. As soon as the patrol broke the cover of the olive growth, an AK opened up on their point man from the third story of the building. John, who patrolled with his rifle with the safety off because the Russian design of the safety mechanism was the opposite to that of a NATO weapon and inconvenient for a rifleman, was the only person in the squad who was ready to return fire. He immediately opened up on the Daesh position. Once the smoke and fog of war had cleared, John realized he was alone in front of a building infested with ISIS fighters. He had been abandoned by his squad. John backpedaled to a side alley and began yelling his battle buddy's name. "Lenny! Lenny!" Having walked straight into the ambush, the *takem* had dispersed, and he was on his own. Many *hevals* had panicked and run. In fact, their PKM gunner had thrown away her machine gun and radio in her desperate attempt to escape the ambush.

"Lenny, Lenny, are you hit?"

"I am OK, John. I am coming over."

From the houses around them, Daeshis were screaming and opening up on Lenny. Unharmed, he made it into the alley, and the two pulled back into the life-saving thick olive grove to regroup. The two debated back and forth about the proper course of action. Lenny wanted to launch a rescue mission to locate the other seven squad members. John wanted to pull back to *nocta yek* and set up a defensive position in which to wait for reinforcements.

Every squad member knew where *nocta yek* was, and that was the place the first reinforcements would be sent to. It was also the last position CJTF-OIR knew of and would undoubtedly recon with a drone so they could identify the new front line once the dust had settled. With the sun coming up, John pointed out to Lenny that if the pair were to take a rooftop like Lenny wanted to, they'd be pinned down in the morning light by every sniper in the city—there would be no getting off. Suddenly, an RPG was launched from somewhere on the ground into the third story of the Daesh building. Now that the building was marked, a unit made up of several former Marines lit up the Daesh position, giving John and Lenny a fighting chance of getting out of the olive grove alive.

While the ISIS fighters in the building were distracted with heavy combat, John and Lenny ran to the closest house they felt was far enough out of immediate danger. John booted the door and cleared the house while Lenny searched for a staircase to the roof. The sun was half up, painting the sky in yellow and blue. While John got a fix on *nocta yek*, he heard voices from the next building. He could hear that they were panicky and listened in to figure out if they were Kurdish or Arabic. He decided he had to peek through the window to find out for sure. He found his *takem* commander and their RPG gunner.

Before exposing himself in the window and risking accidentally being killed by two panicky *hevals*, John yelled out the window in Kurdish to let the anxious pair know there were two Americans in the house and not to shoot. John and Lenny then joined the two Kurds, and John communicated his plan of falling back to *nocta yek* and holding the line while waiting for reinforcements. That way, the SDF wouldn't completely lose their breach over the berm and get pushed back out of city limits. So, after firing a rocket at a Daesh position, John, Lenny, and the two *hevals* pulled back to *nocta yek*. After about 40 minutes of the group of four holding the two-story building, John saw reinforcements coming over the berm under constant sniper fire. It was broad daylight, and crossing the berm had become a gamble. Practically cut off, *nocta yek* slowly turned into one of the few remaining SDF positions inside the berm.

With time, several of the *hevals* who had been separated arrived. The *takem* made up of international volunteers, mainly former U.S. Marines, arrived as well, got some intel, and advanced again. SDF fighters, meanwhile, began breaking murder holes into the walls of *nocta yek*. Giving away their position, Daesh snipers with large caliber rifles began walking their rounds through the walls of the room, trying to kill anyone hiding behind them. John, Lenny, and a couple of other *hevals* made it out just in time. However, one of the squad leaders required someone to be posted in the room watching down the road, so John volunteered

Sitting on a wobbly plastic chair, John watched the road through a murder hole, waiting for a SVBIED to come around the corner. Suddenly, he saw dust shoot out from the concrete wall in front of him, and heard the loud *SNAP* of a sniper round punching through the wall. Something hit John in the face and sent him tumbling with his chair onto his back while rounds kept punching through the wall. John rolled over onto his stomach then felt his head with his left palm to check for blood. There was only a little, so he crawled out of the room and pulled his original Marine Corps-issued goggles off his face. He felt blood and debris but luckily he had not been hit directly. The impacting round had turned the cheap concrete into shrapnel that had buried itself within his skin. He was cleaning himself when more *takems*, including YAT, SDF's Anti-Terror Units, came storming over the berm.

Trying to push Daesh back, the remains of John and Lenny's *takem* was ordered to secure a farmhouse at the edge of an olive grove. Rather than be elevated in the farmhouse, John and Lenny chose to occupy the barn in the olive grove. Shortly after, the advancing units, especially YAT, got into a major gun battle that lasted for several hours. During that fight, the Anti-Terror Units took heavy losses, many of which the medic team medics treated and evacuated. Since the enemy made no attempt to attack the flank, John and Lenny held their fire so as to not give away their position. What followed was hours of seemingly endless guard shifts.

Sometime in the afternoon a couple of days later, John and Lenny heard a heavy engine driving around behind them. For a moment, John hoped Tabur Silah Grand had made it across the berm with one of their BMPs. However, when he heard gunfire picking up, he knew he was wrong. When the SVBIED detonated in one of the nearby houses, he again flew out of one of those wobbly plastic chairs that seemed to be omnipresent in this war. While the gunfight continued, dust lingered in the air. All they could see was dust; John could not even see Lenny in the same barn as him. Around them, everyone was firing, and the positions around them were lit up with heavy fire, though the barn remained untouched. They fought for more than two hours with Daesh trying to push them back over the berm. Finally, when the sun was about to set, an A-10 "Warthog" stopped by to save the day.

The following night and the better part of the next day were calm until they heard yet another engine. With everyone's nerves unraveled, the *takem* had their rifles at the ready when a truck came up the road toward them. According to their last information, this was still enemy territory, and the SDF had not yet breached the berm with any vehicles or armor. Hence, they fired warning shots. The truck did not stop or slow down. Instead, it kept racing toward their position. The *takem* opened up.

Immediately, the truck turned and hid behind a wall. John could hear the yelling *hevala*, who came running toward them. John's heart dropped. He had fired warning shots, but the truck had kept coming toward them, indicating it must be an enemy vehicle. Now he worried that they'd just killed a truckload full of refugees who were trying to flee ISIS. In his worst nightmare, he'd pictured a scenario a little like this. John and Lenny watched the ensuing chaos hoping, and in Lenny's case, praying, for the best. As it turned out, it was a civilian family who had been sent their way by another SDF unit without informing them. To everyone's relief, no one was seriously hurt or wounded. A little boy had received a scratch from shrapnel and would be OK, but John had had enough. He did not feel respected as a soldier. His advice had been ignored over and over again and essential, bare-minimum of information was not even being passed along. This could have ended an innocent life. John requested a transfer out of his fighting unit. Half of his *takem* was missing or dead; his *tabur* was combat ineffective. It was only a matter of time before John's *tabur* was pulled off the front line due to its losses anyway.

To John's relief, they were pulled back on the other side of the berm in mid July. In their new *nocta* just behind the front lines, John slept for the first time in weeks and, when he woke up, he felt recharged. In hindsight, analyzing the mistakes the unit had made, Tabur Şehîd Karaman had served as a dramatic reminder of the situation the SDF was in. Facing a severe shortage of trained and experienced *tabur* commanders, being alive and over 23 was sufficient qualification during a war with very heavy casualties. With no experience and absolutely no leadership, the *hevals* stumbled from ambush to ambush. With first contact, the entire command structure went down, and fear spread like a disease. In their panic, inexperienced and poorly trained young *hevals* ditched their weapons and ran away. With panicking friendly forces running around everywhere, CJTF-OIR could not provide air support without risking friendly forces being accidentally killed. In response to these situations, the few remaining experienced *hevals* took the lead and often died first.

★

On June 23rd, the medics received another call about injured civilians. That morning, there was only Baz, three medics, and the rattled ambulance when the first *Asayîş* trucks pulled up, and panicking *hevals* began unloading one casualty after another. About 60 civilians had tried to escape the besieged city through an exploding minefield.

More trucks pulled up, unloading more people and bodies. There were about 20 casualties, several bodies, and dozens of panicking civilians and *hevals* who were not sure what to do. People were screaming in agony; others were moaning over the corpses of their loved ones. Several children had parts of their small bodies ripped open. One of the young girls' back was open with a large piece of skin and flesh missing. The blast had simply blown it away, and now Baz could see her left lung trying to get oxygen. Every time he attempted to triage, casualties were moved or new ones arrived. The chaos was so ultimate and absolute that, for a split second, he just wanted to run into one of the houses and hide in a dark corner, eyes closed, holding his ears shut whilst screaming.

Pulling himself together, Baz told the *Asayîş* and *hevals* to fetch mattresses from inside the deserted houses. He yelled instructions to his medics. "First children, then parents, then elderly. Only lifesaving interventions. No CPR. Save the ones that are savable. Let the others die." Heval Tekoşer, the documentarian/medic, pulled up with the ambulance. Tearing everything out of the vehicle, the *hevals* covered the floor with mattresses from the houses before the medics began loading nine or 10 critically injured little ones. Ripping the babies and children away from their parents was by no means ideal, but with the next surgeon well over two hours away, it was either that or death. With Heval Rezan in the back, Tekoşer and the ambulance took off.

The team was down to two medics, Baz and Heval B., and no vehicle. What they did have was 10 casualties and a ton of chaos. Heval B. and Baz worked their way through the adult casualties. Although Baz started seeing the scene through a cloud of teary eyes, his head worked just fine. He was worrying about transportation when out of nowhere, a Bongo van with a flatbed pulled up. Some civilians must have heard what had happened and had come to help their neighbors.

The *Asayîş* covered the flatbed with mattresses, and the two medics began loading all casualties, including another baby who had shown up from somewhere. Heval B. stayed behind to represent the team near the fighting, while Baz and the Bongo van took off.

With Baz hanging on to the side of the van, he could communicate with the driver about where to go whilst also trying to stabilize casualties in the back as best as possible. About a minute into the ride, the unknown civilian driver pointed at the fuel control. It was blinking red. Baz had thought the day could not get worse, but it somehow managed to. Instead of leaving the front toward Kobane and the next hospital, the Bongo van was now speeding parallel to it. Silah Grand's fuel truck had been in a village nearby, but when the van arrived, the fuel truck was gone. The geography teacher and the Bongo van from hell were stranded in a remote village with no means of communication. Baz's body was producing such insane amounts of adrenaline that his legs began shaking uncontrollably.

Suddenly, a small band of tribal fighters showed up. According to rumors, they had been fighting with the Islamists before. So far, they had gotten along great with the medics, despite some irritating decapitation jokes. However, seeing their people on the flatbed, the tribal fighters grabbed a hose they had handy for such purposes and began sucking the diesel out of their own truck. From behind his seat, the driver of the Bongo van pulled out a funnel. Bit by bit, the tribal fighters managed to get the diesel into the funnel.

When the driver gave his thumbs up, the Bongo van took off again. With a two-hour drive over dirt tracks ahead, Baz needed help. He remembered that John and Tabur Şehîd Karaman was based nearby. They went to pick him up. Having thus recruited John into the medic team, the van began its journey toward the Euphrates. While Baz still hung on to the side directing the driver, John tried to comprehend the situation. The girl to his right had had her fingers blown off, and they were hanging by the skin. There was a boy with a head wound, a young mother with a kid with Down's syndrome, vomiting on himself, and a gentleman was laying down with his feet sticking up into the air; his toes were either gone or hanging on by their skin. Somewhere in between was a baby.

John stabilized an unconscious boy on his leg. A few minutes later, he felt a warm sensation. John looked down and saw his left thigh was covered in blood. John reached under the kid and felt a puncture wound on his leg that had been resting on John's thigh. John's Marine Corps training kicked in and he packed the wound with gauze from his Individual First Aid Kit, as he had been trained to. The girl with no fingers asked for "*mai*—water," and John gave her some. When the van sped over a bump, John tried to shield her from the dust because she had no hands with which to do it herself.

At the checkpoints, Baz yelled, "YPG! YPG *Askari Doctor!*" The *Asayîş* knew Baz by that point and cleared the road, firing rounds in the air. The Bongo van made it onto the M4 and flew down toward the bridge that had been somewhat, very temporarily, fixed. Finally, the van made it to the SDF field hospital on the eastern banks of the Euphrates. With one of their medics taking over, the Bongo van continued to the hospital in Kobane. The field hospital, basically a medical station with minor surgical capacities, could not handle such casualties. The ambulance containing the injured children had also arrived. Seeing the complete desperation at the hospital where civilians were moaning over their loved ones showed John the dark side of war; the receiving end of weapons had nothing glorious about it.

Something had clicked with John during that ride on the Bongo van. He had kicked in enough doors by now. After seeing so much insane death, saving lives made him feel like he was being repurposed again. This made more sense to him now. The Marine had come to this war in 2014 eager to kill the enemy, and he would leave it as a passionate lifesaver. Somewhere in between, he had met Kosta, his brother-in-arms, and now it all made sense.

★

For weeks, the SDF had been trying to establish a foothold in the city, but wherever they breached Manbij's perimeter, the defenses were overwhelming. Within hours, *taburs* that went on the attack were torn apart and driven back out again. During that time, the involved units routinely had casualty rates of more than 60 percent. Most *taburs* were no longer operational after their initial deployment.

Given the distinct lack of experienced fighters, the SDF had assaulted a fortified position with numbers equal to those of the defenders. From a tactical perspective, this is not ideal. Usually, fortified positions are attacked with superior numbers. Even with the help of American air strikes, the SDF had lost the momentum it had built since summer 2015.

After the initial assault failed, the commanders had to stop the operation and reassess the situation, bring in new fighters, and so forth. With all of their test runs and al-Shaddadi having gone so smoothly, it seems that the coalition had underestimated the enemy. However, fighting ISIS left no room for mistakes. Surprised by Daesh's resistance, the death toll of SDF fighters continued to rise. One morning, Baz and John's friend, Heval Bawer, fell *şehîd*. Baz could not believe it and had to open the body bag to see it for himself.

Later, Heval Armanc was severely injured. He'd blown up an SVBIED that had attacked his unit with an RPG and been injured by the subsequent explosion. He later fell *şehîd* in the early stages of the Raqqa campaign. Just like Heval Bawer, he was a truly good human being who had sacrificed his life for humanity and so that the rest of the world could live in peace.

The tactics the Islamic State used were essentially the ones the SDF had seen before. The main difference was that the Islamists had perfected them in the meantime. Even though the odd villager with an AK might suggest otherwise, the Islamic State was an extremely deadly opponent. Given their organizational structure, Daesh adapted very quickly to changes on the battlefield. Even with little in the way of electronic means and no real freedom to move between cities anymore, they were able to analyze and understand changing situations, such as the American air strikes, learn from their own mistakes, and come up with countermeasures.

In Manbij, Daesh made SVBIEDs a better and more effective weapon than any American smart bomb would ever be. Those Daesh trucks had steel plates welded to their front, meaning that AKs and PKMs couldn't stop them. Hidden all over the city, their drivers sat and waited. Once a target, such as a SDF *tabur* or fleeing civilians, was nearby, the SVBIED would leave its hiding place and chase them down. During the period between leaving their hiding place and their detonations, SVBIEDs were only exposed for seconds. This was too short a time for any air force to respond.

Explosive factories and workshops were spread over the entire city, so even when American jets took out one, two, or three there were still several others mass producing explosives. In the SVBIED around the actual explosives, the enemy would stack barrels with diesel and ball bearings or screws—all materials that were readily available. With 50,000 civilians still trapped in the city, the enemy also had an almost infinite number of suicide bombers at their disposal. When Daesh ran out of brainwashed teens and fanatics who volunteered for the mission, the Islamists took some regular dad's kids hostage, forcing daddy to go on a suicide mission to save his children. Indeed, many SVBIEDs had big locks bolted onto the outside and were detonated remotely, to stop the drivers fleeing. At one point, the Americans began jamming the frequencies for remote triggers, and suddenly, many SVBIEDs stopped exploding.

Eventually, SVBIEDs became a psychological weapon. Just like the constant danger posed by unseen American drones, the threat of SVBIEDs hidden amongst them caused the SDF at times to stop all civilian traffic, resulting in severe danger for the people caught in the battle, who were thus unable to escape.

The regional Daesh commanders must have also revisited their sniper tactics from al-Shaddadi and other battles and made them more deadly. In Manbij, Daesh commanders sent a band of disposable fighters on a full-frontal, suicidal attack against an SDF unit. While the *hevals* were killing this cannon fodder, snipers would wait on the SDF team's three or nine o'clock positions. As soon as an SDF fighter exposed him or herself fighting off the frontal attack, they were shot by the waiting sniper. Depending on the mission, Daesh snipers would use pimped-up M16s for distances under 100 yards or .50cals for shots over 1½ miles. The snipers and their security teams would move through a network of tunnels, pathways, and fighting positions with water and some food. This way, the sniper and his security detail could move fast and light between their different positions. This was how the enemy shot the American *heval* in the neck; this was how they almost got Heval Rezan a few weeks before when the medic team was ambushed; this was how they killed and injured dozens, if not hundreds, of others.

As with all their weapons systems, Daesh began using their snipers as a psychological weapon. The first time the medic team documented this was mid-June 2016 when the SDF tried to breach Manbij's eastern extension from the north. For days, Daesh snipers were only targeting the YPJ. Male fighters would move around unmolested, but as soon as a woman showed herself, she was sniped. For the medic team, this meant attending to a constant stream of YPJs with rounds to the head, neck, and shoulders. Using just a few 5.56 rounds, the Caliphate was still preaching death to women's rights.

The second time the medic team came across this nightmare was once Baz had already left the unit. Then, Daesh snipers would exclusively shoot children who tried to flee the city. Later, in 2017, during the battle of Mosul, Baz saw Daesh hunt girls who were fleeing the city. Just girls in their early teens. Being singled out by an unseen enemy does something to the target group's heads. It creates an almost maiming fear.

When it came to IEDs, Daesh was always good. What changed in Manbij was not necessarily the mines' quality but their quantity. In one single house, Tabur Sabotage found more than 20 IEDs hidden under rugs, behind curtains, under the stones in front of all doors and windows, in boxes with Snickers bars, or under a bottle of Pepsi sitting in an otherwise empty room. Daesh bomb makers were masters at their art, and everyone who did not take them seriously enough was either dead or missing the odd limb. The psychological warfare of mines is well documented. It is a constant fear of pretty much everything.

Combined with these weapons systems were possibly thousands of well-trained and experienced Daesh fighters turning Manbij into a meat grinder. Consequently, the medic team and civilian Heyva Sor ambulances could simply not cope anymore. Although the team had turned their supply minivan into a makeshift ambulance, it was not enough. Being constantly beaten through the fine desert sand was also taking its toll. By July, absolutely all nonessential parts of both ambulances were broken. As one vehicle sat in the shop in Kobane while something critical was being fixed, the other was already starting to die again. Every trip with a casualty to the field hospital on the Euphrates took well over three hours and a lot of energy.

The unit was running out of essential supplies, such as tourniquets, chest seals, pressure bandages, and so forth. While improvising them works for regular *taburs* in emergency cases, a medic team working in a high-stress environment with regular mass casualties needed a minimum standard of supplies in order to be able to operate. Securing plastic bags with duct tape as a makeshift chest seal had its limits when reaching the hospital could take anywhere from 90 minutes to several hours depending on various circumstances (new people at checkpoints, traffic jams at the improvised bridge over the Euphrates, changing front lines, and unpredictable weather conditions).

Eventually, then, the medic team had to call a crisis meeting with Hevala Roza. Since the team had just treated two of her favorite aids after a mortar attack, Hevala Roza saw them immediately. As Baz instantly spotted, the *hevala's* black hair had begun to turn grey from the stress and all the dying during the last few weeks. Forced to send more and more inexperienced *hevals* into the carnage, the *hevala* had learned to like the medics.

What happened next was truly bizarre. Having apparently really gained her trust, Hevala Roza gave Baz the freedom to do whatever he needed in order to get his job done. Now, the medic team could order *tabur* drivers to transport all non-critically injured *hevals* to the hospital themselves. For the fast guerilla-style warfare the YPG/YPJ fought, the Hiluxes of the *taburs* were of vital importance. Without their truck, a whole *takem* is unable to move longer distances. For a regular *tabur* commander like Baz to commandeer the trucks of another *tabur* was unheard of. *Tabur* commanders who protested were dealt with by Hevala Roza.

What sounds banal freed up enormous resources. Baz could send exhausted medics to a private hotel in Kobane for a couple of nights when they needed to sleep and eat away from injured people for a little while. Under Hevala Roza's wing, the medic team was the only *tabur* exempt from the order not to drive around the front line at night in case casualties needed immediate transport. In addition, one of the Heyva Sor ambulance drivers, with his new ambulance, was now attached to the medic team. All of this was an incredible support for a team that was working on its absolute limits.

Within days after that meeting, bags with much-needed medical supplies started to appear, dropped off without comment by some *heval* who left right away. The medics had an idea where those came from. Once the SDF had reached the outskirts of Manbij, the French special forces had begun making way for the American operators, who had started to roam around at the fringes of the battlefield. Until this point, the French special forces had been the ones who had had the most impact on the front lines. However, once the offensive had reached the city limits, the U.S. administration in the White House changed their approach and pushed U.S. Special Forces teams up to the front lines as well, to take a more active role. As soon as America decided to take a more hands-on approach on the ground, the sheer numbers of American operators and hardware simply pushed the limited French teams to the side.

John was burned-out though and had reached the end of his six-month agreement with the SDF. He had survived several suicide missions with his previous *tabur* during which his commander had ignored the very basic rules of warfare as well as John's advice. The situation had driven him almost crazy and drained his batteries. He had to tap out.

CHAPTER 14

Rolling with the Operators: July–December 2016

For some time now, the medic team had increasingly spotted the U.S. Special Forces teams, who, unlike the well-embedded French special forces, did not really try to hide despite being a prime target for ISIS mortars. Only a few days earlier in late June 2016, the medic team was next to the operators somewhere near Hevala Roza's command post. Baz and Heval Zagros were minding their own business, smoking cigarettes on the hood of the ambulance, drinking 3in1s from their plastic mugs, when the commander of the special forces team came over to talk to the pair.

Pointing at the ambulance, he said, "You guys might want to park that thing behind the wall over there. In 10 minutes, we will receive precise mortar fire." Baz repositioned his team and exactly 10 minutes later precise mortar fire indeed was targeting the compound. One of the special forces guys returned fire with a .50cal. When Heval Zagros asked, "Well, having fun yet?" the youngish American soldier smiled but tried to hide it in order to maintain his ultra-cool operator image.

When the third volley hit, an American jet appeared and dropped a very large bomb on the mortar position. "We just took out their top mortar guy," the special forces dudes updated Heval Zagros and Baz. Without letting the medics know, the operators had used them and the ambulance as juicy bait to make Daesh send one of their mortar commanders to take them out. Using their technology, America's military triangulated the Daesh commander, who was harassing American soldiers, and dealt with him accordingly. After that, mortars remained a constant threat, but they lost a bit of their scare power.

Starting in July 2016, the American and British special forces who were supporting the Cizire battle group began pushing even further up to the front line and Hevala Roza's position, just as the French had done beforehand. Hevala Roza's command post was now at the so-called chicken factory, a poultry farm at a critical junction just north of Manbij. However, being that closely involved in an operation that was beginning to derail created an unexpected conundrum for the special forces team. The ongoing stream of casualties was too much for their own medics to deal with, so the entire team had to help out on a regular basis, distracting them from their actual mission: to call in air strikes and provide fire support with their own mortars. The solution for this problem was driving around in a shot-up ambulance and a beaten-up Hyundai minivan.

The next time the medic team had a mass-casualty scenario, the operators stopped by and watched. Heval Zagros overheard them on the radio; apparently, the Americans were checking the medics' backgrounds. What they discovered was a guy with an open arrest warrant for spitting at a cop, a convicted felon who'd lost a tooth in LA county jail, a hairy bushwhacker who had lied to them about his name and citizenship, and a Mormon who looked like he was 16, all led by a leftist geography teacher who was highly critical of the "War on Terror." Nevertheless, the special forces team got the OK to work closely with the medic team. That's how bad the situation around Manbij had become.

After a week of working with the medic team just behind the front lines, the operators were out of medical supplies. Based on past experience, they had packed supplies for a month's time. Within just this one week, the special forces medics had seen every single injury from their textbooks. Open skulls, destroyed airways, chest wounds of all varieties, open fractures, open abdomens, amputation, and so forth. After another mass-casualty case late at night when everyone was having an Arden or two, the adrenaline slowly giving way to exhaustion, one of the special forces medics told Baz, "Right now, there is not a single trauma team on this planet seeing more shit than you guys." Later, Daesh mortars came in again, and while the U.S. Special Forces were pulling back for political reasons, the geography teacher and his gang of misfits advanced. Apparently when entering a Daesh city, nothing made sense anymore.

Within days, the medic team and the operators developed a routine. Their two medics would take the lead stabilizing casualties, and Baz would organize appropriate transportation and check what medics would go with the transport while the rest of the medic team assisted the operators. This was a good arrangement that helped save many lives, including those of uncounted civilians. However, any time the medic teammembers asked the special forces guys who they actually were, they did not really answer. If Baz were to speculate, he'd say they were a mix of the various special forces, including U.S. Navy SEALS, the U.S. Army 5th Special Forces Group, the Horse Soldiers from the heyday of the War on Terror featured in *12 Strong*, and Air Force Combat Controllers.

At that point, the American military must have realized the potential of this alliance with the SDF. From a relatively safe position, the special forces teams were able to force multiply[1] most effectively. It would have been foolish not to have an unexperienced generation of operators not rotate through this front line.

In the case of the British teams, the answer to who they were is much easier to answer since there is just one Regiment trained for this sort of warfare. Asking the guys with the strong British accents in the field, however, produced only one answer: "We are Americans." After having spent some time with the medic team, even they couldn't keep a straight face when saying that.

Food had again become a serious issue, and whenever the special forces team had to pull back, the medic team scavenged through their trash. Seeing five grown men crouching in a pile of garbage squeezing nasty jalapeño cheese into their mouths was definitely not a pretty sight, but it was war. For the team, but especially Baz, the EMT who had come up with protocols for the unit, it was a relief to know that special forces guys were happy with the way his team stabilized the wounded. Their main feedback was that the medic team was being too reserved with the drugs, so Baz increased the standard ketamine dose by 400 percent. The operators also updated the team on the latest research on administering fluid, but that was it.

The only skills the medic team were missing in order to become more effective medics was inserting cricothyroidotomies, an alternative airway through the throat, and chest tubes in case a chest wound involved blood filling up the lung space. American and British special forces taught the team both techniques and, within days, they had the opportunity to assist in the procedures. However, in reality, none of the casualties who needed either of the two interventions survived the ride to the hospital. Although the medics would fight for their lives, injuries involving blood in the lung cavity or a destroyed face were too severe to allow them to survive the tedious transportation to the limited surgical facilities in Kobane.

On July 15th, on a run to the Euphrates, Baz bumped into the French special forces again. Instead of their previously very light footprint, these French operators now came in full force in a long convoy of about 10–15 armored vehicles, wearing their own camouflage and so forth. There was nothing embedded about those teams anymore. Just like the American teams, this convoy projected power. As Baz would find out later, the day before, the Islamic State had executed a terror attack in which a 19-ton truck had driven into a crowd in Nice, France, and killed more than 80 people.[2] The driver was killed by the French police. In the escalating feud between France and the Islamic State, this convoy was the next step. To Baz, this convoy looked like the French president was determined to finish off the Caliphate once and for all.

Around mid-July, rumors were confirmed that the operation would no longer include al-Bab. This meant the Afrin and Kobane *cantons* would not be connected, which was a blow, especially to the YPG/YPJ element of the coalition. Turkey had made it clear it would not tolerate the connection of the *cantons*. Even the Americans could not hold them back any longer. At the same time, it was evident that taking Manbij was all the SDF could possibly chew right now. A second operation like this was not within the capabilities of the militia. Later, Turkey's debacle in taking al-Bab confirmed that, similar to Manbij, Daesh had no intention of giving the city up easily.

The SDF finally made progress in Manbij when they managed to cut off the eastern extension of the city at the hospital and began clearing the neighborhoods. As soon as they were free, the civilians fled the besieged city. All over the desert, first hundreds, then thousands of civilians were stranded in groups. Some would squat in deserted homes; others slept in the open. Some had cattle; most of them had nothing. Parents would feed their children grass soup, in the absence of a single international aid organization. Trying to stay neutral in a very messy war, the international community stayed out completely. Every time the SDF pushed a hole in Daesh's defenses, columns of hundreds of civilians fled the city until the enemy plugged the gaps again. With no journalists present, unknown to the world, yet another small humanitarian crisis took place.

★

In late July, Baz was done. Having constant stomach cramps and vomiting up everything he ate, his body told him it was time to leave. Plagued with nightmares foretelling his death in the city, he became snappy and a liability for the medic team. Altogether, he had spent a year in the war. He had helped set up the medic team so many of them had envisioned and had gotten the unit to a point where they were working closely with the U.S. Special Forces. The special forces guys had just opened a casualty collection point, or CCP, behind the front line and out of mortar range. Consequently, the medic team's commute was cut in half. A former U.S. Army Ranger, and experienced medic, arrived and would take over the team.

Heval Tekoşer had tapped out a little earlier, and Heval Rezan had been injured in a mine blast a couple of weeks prior and was in an American facility in Baghdad for treatment. Although parts of the casualty list were lost or got blown up, the team estimates that they treated well over 200 victims of war, including many civilians, children, and the odd Daesh fighter. By the end of the campaign on August 27, 2016, Heval Zagros, Heval B., and the new guys would double that list.

In light of the mounting casualty rates, the SDF had to retract their previous promise to "kill or capture them all." Daesh and the SDF negotiated a deal: the remaining ISIS fighters would leave the city with their personal weapons. The SDF was trying to keep the deal a secret and did not tell all of their own units about it. Consequently, the medic team ran straight into the convoy of hundreds of the most fanatic fighters.

Luckily for the medic team, ISIS kept their end of the bargain and retreated without more fighting.

★

As soon as the SDF liberated Manbij, the Manbij Military Council (MMC), took control of the city and its surrounding countryside in the so-called Manbij pocket west of the Euphrates. Once the people of Manbij and al-Bab were organized and the MMC strong enough to resist the attacks by the Turkish-backed militias, the Kurdish element of the SDF withdrew in November 2016 from the western side of the river. Just as they had promised at the beginning of the operation, the SDF would liberate, not occupy, Manbij or indeed any other Arab lands.

Simultaneously, at the end of the battle for Manbij, Turkey launched Operation *Euphrates Shield*. Still concerned the Kurds could try to take al-Bab and connect the *cantons*, the Turkish military invaded Syria and positioned itself in the way of a possible corridor between Manbij and the Afrin *canton*. With the American elections just two months away and Obama's two terms coming to an end, Turkey felt emboldened. On its way to becoming a lame duck, America momentarily lost its power, and Turkey went ahead with their operation, presumably against American advice. The Turkish military and its affiliated Islamist gangs occupied the area between Jarablus, Afrin, and al-Bab, creating a buffer zone that prevented the Kurdish *cantons* from being connected. Thus, Turkey stopped Kurdish forces from occupying most of the Syrian–Turkish border.

With the Turkish invaders becoming ever more aggressive, constantly probing Manbij's defenses, the MMC had to concede territory south of Manbij to the Syrian Regime's Syrian Arab Army (SAA), which was moving in to stop any further Turkish advance. Turkey wanted to check the Kurds' power, not start a war with Syria, thus Turkish forces had to hold their incursion. In the north, American soldiers began patrolling with the MMC. In order to prevent Turkish attacks on the MMC, America had to be there physically. Ignoring American advice was one thing. Firing at American soldiers was a line Turkey would not cross. In order to prevent the SDF from being attacked by Turkey or its gangs, all America had to do was drive around and enjoy the countryside. It was neither a particularly costly nor complicated task, nor was it a war.

Not completely lame yet, in September 2016, Obama extended the Train and Advise to a Train and Equip mission, enabling the United States to arm the SDF directly.[3] Also, the State Department changed their rhetoric. During the operations in al-Shaddadi and Manbij, the YPG/YPJ's role within the SDF had been played down. From September 2016, however, the State Department began differentiating between the YPG/YPJ and the SDF entirely. America dealt with the SDF, not the YPG/YPJ, because as of now, the two were different.[4] This rhetoric was yet another attempt to justify the close cooperation between America and the SDF in front of Turkey, the latter being, after all, still a NATO ally. At the very last minute in December 2016, Obama sent additional special forces to Rojava, bringing their total numbers up to 500.[5]

Once the beginning of the rainy season had made every large-scale military operation impossible, the people of Rojava began closely monitoring the American elections that would take place on November 8, 2016. In the past, the Kurds had been betrayed by most of the partners they had aligned with. Together with the Palestinians, they were the losers when the region was split up by the colonial powers (France, the UK, and the Ottoman Empire). They were the underdog. Their allies simply did not profit from being loyal to the Kurds in the long term. Thus, the stateless people had learned to understand realpolitik. Whatever promises had been made by one United States president could become meaningless overnight when power in the Oval Office changed hands. For many United States American's, elections are about heated debates over Thanksgiving dinner; for the people in Rojava and many other places, the decision those voters make determines if there is going to be another genocide within the next four years.

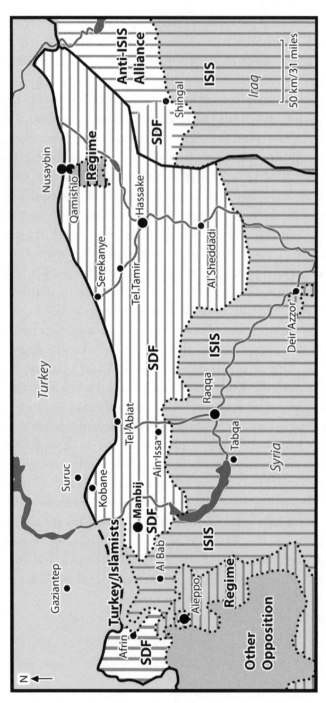

Map 6: Front lines in September 2016 around the Afrin, Kobane, and Cizire *cantons.*

PART III

DEFEATING THE CALIPHATE: AN AMERICAN SUCCESS STORY: JANUARY 2017–SEPTEMBER 2019

PART III

OPERATING THE CAPITAL:
AN AMERICAN SUCCESS STORY,
JANUARY 201?–SEPTEMBER 2019

CHAPTER 15

Rojava Becomes Formal: January–February 2017

By early 2017, the SDF had proven themselves. With al-Shaddadi, Manbij, and all the space in between liberated, the SDF had become one of the most effective fighting forces in the war against ISIS. Handing the liberated cities over to local military councils, the SDF signaled to the Arab tribes that this alliance would keep its word. In 2017, the SDF offered the tribes around Raqqa and Deir Ezzor a far better deal than they would have ever gotten with the Regime or Daesh. The SDF had proven that their version of democracy was about the protection and autonomy of the minority, not the rule of the majority, as was the case with everyone else in the region.

To fully appreciate the power and appeal of the SDF and their complicated, often oversimplified relationship to the PKK, it is worth going back to the 1970s. Back then, the continuous genocide of the Turkish state against the Kurds within its territory had broken the resistance, and generations of Kurds were assimilated by Turkey, forbidden to speak their own language, eat their own food, or dance their own dances. Any Kurdishness was punished with uncompromising brutality or public humiliation. It was a time when Turkish children learned that Kurds had an animal tail because they were half beasts, and while it was bad to kill humans, it was OK to kill beasts.

Parallel to the atrocities in eastern Anatolia, the Turkish state was pushing for a massive water dam project across the Euphrates and Tigris. The so-called Güneydoğu Anadolu Projesi (Southeastern Anatolia Project, or GAP) was supposed to boost the Turkish economy and the nation's general development. The project would create jobs, power parts of Turkey, enable agriculture, and so forth. At the same time, the GAP had a distinct geopolitical component. It would not only advance Turkey but also weaken Syria and Iraq, both regional opponents. The GAP was a vehicle for Turkey to re-establish itself as a serious power broker in the region. The Euphrates and Tigris were literally Syria and Iraq's lifelines. At the banks of those rivers, the people grew their food and powered their countries. Being upstream, the GAP suddenly put Turkey in a position to control the water flow of both rivers, possibly stopping them completely, causing an almost immediate famine in Syria and Iraq.[1]

Since the GAP had become a serious threat to Syria, Hafez al-Assad, the pseudo-socialist ruler at the time, began looking for ways to sabotage the massive building project that was spreading across hundreds of miles in often-isolated terrain. His answer, as was usual during that time, came in the form of young communist intellectuals who wanted to revolt and liberate their people from capitalism and oppression. More specifically, he found Abdullah Öcalan and a small band of other Kurdish leftists.

With the support of the Assad Regime, the PKK was formed. In camps in Syria and other friendly places, such as Lebanon, the Regime trained the first *hevals* in guerrilla warfare and supplied them with weapons and explosives. Using Syria and Iraq as safe spaces, the PKK began their war against the Turkish state in the early 1980s. While many attacks targeted the Turkish military and affiliated groups, it was little surprise that the PKK also bombed the GAP and began slowing down its construction.

Although many *hevals* understand an open debate about the movement's origins as an insult to their claim for autonomy, it is not intended as one. Historically, most guerilla movements had to make a deal with a lesser evil in order to get their insurgency going. Starting as someone else's proxy in an ancient power game is, unfortunately, how geopolitics for a stateless people or any guerilla movement works. In order to fight the Turkish state, the PKK had to give up much of their autonomy and independence in order to get the needed support from Syria's Assad clan. The reason for highlighting the deal between Hafer al-Assad and the PKK is the small print that came with it.

Since Syria had a large Kurdish population that Hafer al-Assad was himself oppressing, the PKK was not allowed to fight a general Kurdish struggle, only a very specific one. In other words, the PKK had to fight exclusively for a Kurdish state seceding from Turkey, not more. If the PKK ever broke this promise, Öcalan, who lived in Damascus partly as a guest, partly as a hostage, would be arrested and handed over to Turkish intelligence.

In the 1970s, leftist nationalist liberation struggles were in vogue, and the PKK agreed to the deal. For the rest of the 1980s and 1990s, the PKK and Turkey engaged each other in an exceptionally brutal war. While Turkey practiced genocide and a counterinsurgency warfare they might as well have copied from the Wehrmacht, the PKK forcefully recruited youth, collected revolutionary taxes (i.e. protection money), used suicide bombers, and occasionally killed not only their enemies but their families as well. After tens of thousands of deaths, by the mid-1990s, the conflict reached a stalemate. On the one hand, the PKK was still being forced to fight for a Kurdish state in Turkey. On the other was a NATO member, Turkey, who would most certainly never secede any territory. The killing continued without a possible solution. The PKK was waging an unwinnable war that was traumatizing generations.

As argued elsewhere,[2] the solution to the conundrum came in the form of the abduction of Öcalan by Turkish intelligence. As part of the Adana Agreement between Turkey and Syria, Öcalan was evicted from Syria. Subsequently, Öcalan began an odyssey through parts of Europe and Africa, but no one wanted to shelter the leader of a stateless people. Then, in February 1999, Turkey got to him in Kenya, Africa.

Although many *hevals* still demand his release, we believe his imprisonment was a blessing in disguise. Until his arrest, the movement had a geographical center: Abdullah Öcalan and his physical whereabouts. However, the PKK was a guerilla movement. Having no geographic location, no center that is open for attack, is the guerillas' preferred way to fight. Syria's ruler being able to blackmail the PKK with the possibility of Öcalan's arrest had paralyzed the movement. The PKK's war had turned into a struggle to find shelter for their leader. Practically and intellectually, a free Öcalan had become the open flank for the PKK. His arrest and subsequent imprisonment on Imrali Island thus practically despatialized Öcalan. His whereabouts became irrelevant. Kept in isolation, Öcalan physically left this world. The PKK had no geographic center anymore. The movement shed themselves of their obligations to Syria.

By facilitating Öcalan's arrest, Hafer al-Assad and his son Bashar had broken their previous deal with the PKK, including the small print that was part of the arrangement. By the late 1990s, the PKK had tens of thousands of fighters who occupied impregnable mountain fortresses in Turkey, Iraq, and Iran. With their own supply routes in place, the PKK did not need a regional power to support them anymore. With Öcalan's arrest, the PKK could thus emancipate themselves from Hafer al-Assad.

Not bound to Syria's goodwill, the movement could finally think beyond their obsolete national liberation struggle. No longer needing to worry about his arrest, the walls of Imrali prison freed Öcalan's mind as well. By being physically irrelevant, Öcalan was at liberty to think of the ideas that would eventually lead to democratic confederalism. By arresting Öcalan, Turkey ultimately paved the way for the Rojava that is now spreading along their southern border.

Being intellectually unleashed, Öcalan began reflecting on the political situation of the Kurds. During this process, he identified the modern nation-state itself as the root cause for the Kurds' oppression. In a geopolitical world structured around state lines, stateless people can only lose. Within the existing order, the Kurds, just like the Palestinians, could only be someone's puppet in a much bigger power game that did not foresee an independent Kurdistan. But if the state was the problem, why would the PKK fight for their own? Öcalan and the movement began to understand this contradiction. Consequently, they turned toward the rich literatures on grassroots, or direct democracy, communalism, Swiss and other federalisms, and anarchism. In particular, the works of Murray Bookchin began resonating with Öcalan.[3]

As he acknowledged himself, Öcalan did not reinvent the wheel in his writings but rather drew on more than a hundred years of critical reflective thinking. What makes Öcalan's writings so exceptional was his analysis of Western and Russian ideas for their relevance to Kurdistan and the Middle East. Instead of simply copying the concepts, Öcalan understood how they connected to the ancient history of his people. Identifying different commonalities, he expanded on them and began formulating his own theory.

From Imrali Island, Öcalan's new ideas of a radical federalism found their way into the movement. In 2014, Baz discussed this moment of Kurdish history with several of the movement's intellectuals. They all described it as one of the most painful moments of their biography. For two decades, so many had died for the dream of their own state. Kurds had been displaced, raped, humiliated, and tortured for this idea, and suddenly, they were supposed to give it up. At first, to many, these new ideas felt like a betrayal of their cause. Indeed, some thought out loud that Turkey had broken Öcalan, and this was a plot to weaken the Kurdish resistance. It took years of debate before the people began seeing the true value of democratic confederalism. It was not about betraying the idea of a state; it was about evolving beyond it.

In 1969, Rudi Dutschke, a charismatic German student leader, defined revolution as a collective intellectual process that reflected on the status quo.[4] The revolution was not about fighting but thinking. The violence that often followed was simply the result of the reflection. In this sense, the often-ignored period of the collective debate about democratic confederalism was the true Kurdish revolution. It was this intellectual undertaking that would, years later, legitimize the armed struggle in Rojava and rally the resistance around.

The event that started the Kurdish resistance against an oppression led by Arabs was a football game in 2004 in Qamishlo, Syria. The mainly Arab supporters of a team from Deir Ezzor provoked the Kurdish fans by mocking their systematic oppression under the Assad Regime. During the subsequent riots, Kurdish activists toppled a statue of Hafez al-Assad. In a dictatorship, this was a symbolic attack on the ruler himself. Showing little humor, the dictator sent his security forces, who killed several protesters.

In response to this latest escalation of violence in their ongoing oppression, Kurdish youth and members of the movement formed their own self-defense group based on the ideas of democratic confederalism, in particular the self-defense of a free people. The Arab Spring happened and, in 2011, the war in Syria began. Governed by their underground party, YPG/YPJ's predecessor was slowly transformed from youth with bats, shotguns, and knives into an armed militia with the mandate to defend the Kurdish people in case of an attack by the Regime or one of the many other militias that were sprouting all over Syria. By late 2012, Bashar al-Assad had come under so much military and political pressure that he had to pull together his remaining forces to secure his "rump state,"[5] which consisted of the densely populated areas further west in the country, including the capital Damascus. Trying to survive the war, the Regime gave up all nonessential territory.

Having actually understood democratic confederalism, Assad knew he could give up the Kurdish-dominated areas because the Kurds were no threat to Syria's territorial integrity. The Kurds wanted to be left alone, and that's exactly what he did. Assad pulled out of the Kurdish-dominated areas in Cizire, Kobane, and Afrin. The Syrian Regime kept control of a small corridor connecting a Turkish border post, parts of Qamishlo airport in the north, and Hasake in the south.

In term of the wider war in Syria, the Kurds tried to stay neutral until late 2013. Quickly, the Islamists had grown into some of the strongest factions in the war in Syria, and they hated the Kurdish atheist movement. To them, the YPG were infidels, unbelievers. The sheer existence of the YPJ drove them insane. Consequently, the al-Nusra front, an al-Qaida affiliate, attacked Kobane and Cizire. For the following two-and-a-half years, the YPG/YPJ were fighting for their survival. Different Islamist groups, but foremost Daesh, threw their entire arsenal against the Kurds and their few local allies but could not break them.

When the Regime withdrew in late 2012, they left more than a security vacuum, which the newly created YPG (the YPJ was created in early 2013) had to fill. Almost overnight, the previously illegal movement was in charge of governing hundreds of thousands of people and several cities. At that point, the idea of democratic confederalism had only been practiced in some villages in the Qandil Mountains in Iraq, where the PKK held territory. It had never been tested on a heterogeneous society like northeastern Syria. The idea was still a theoretical utopia, so the *hevals* began translating the theory into practical governance guidelines. In January 2014, the three Kurdish-dominated areas of Afrin, Kobane, and Cizire declared their autonomy and Rojava as a political entity was born.

In March 2015, the same month he joined the YPG, Baz published an article in *Middle East Policy*[6] arguing that the PKK and the YPG/YPJ are not the same entity. There had not been much academic debate on the subject and Baz's plan was to turn himself into one of the few experts around. In case the German government came after him for being PKK—not an unreasonable concern—Baz could be his own expert explaining his innocence to a state prosecutor who had no idea about the conflict. After all, his argument had been convincing enough to pass the review process of *Middle East Policy*, a journal by the Middle East Policy Council, a think tank that forms part of Washington's power landscape.

Baz argued that while the PKK had in the past been self-declared Marxist-Leninists who wanted to secede territory from Turkey, this was not the case anymore. When the movement made democratic confederalism their guiding idea, they shed the obsolete notion of a dogmatic communist regime that had not worked in the past. In a war dominated by the Syrian Regime and Islamists, the Kurds were actually the good guys. The paper furthermore argued that democratic confederalism was simply about a direct democracy in autonomous spaces. Democratic confederalism is a political theory advertising decentralized power and for minorities to live their own identity. What it is *not* about is secession, terrorism, and Marxist-Leninism. Time and the sprouting of Arab *cantons* have confirmed the argument. The idea of democratic confederalism had become Rojava's social fabric and in the process, the intellectual ownership of the theory had changed.

For almost 10 years, the movement experimented with the practical issues that arose when translating theory (democratic confederalism) into practical policies. The Tev Dem, Rojava's diplomatic and intellectual organization, spent years traveling villages to explain democratic confederalism to Kurds, Arabs, Christians, and many others. Making the theory work was a difficult trial-and-error project that experienced many setbacks. Yet the people, many of whom never read the original Öcalan (Öcalan himself wasn't able to write it down, and instead had to tell his ideas to his lawyers, who subsequently wrote the five volumes from memory), continued to implement the utopia of direct democracy and federalism despite the Islamists' vicious attacks and economic embargo. Since the Regime had withdrawn its force in 2012, Rojava continuously worked on its constitution as well as the practical implementation of the idea, including free health care, women's shelters, the establishment of *Asayîş Jin*, and so forth. While everyone was fighting for their stagnating status quo or some medieval Islamist nightmare, Rojava was creating from the ashes something original, something positive.

★

After returning from the al-Shaddadi operation in March 2016, Shaun spent the rest of his six-month tour in Qamishlo to see how Rojava's civil society worked instead of wasting time in the academy. Justifying his stay in the Tev Dem *nocta*, Shaun wrote a report about a medical unit and helped out with English translations. In return, he got 24/7 electricity, hot showers, Wi-Fi, shawarma, kebabs, and his own bed with a pillow and warm blanket. Not surprisingly, Shaun had a good time and enjoyed himself. Back then, Heval Rezan was still involved with the civil society and was not yet a combat medic. Drinking *chai* all day, Heval Rezan taught Shaun about Mormonism and, bizarrely, the current state of private space travel projects.

During one of those days in March 2016, Shaun was asked to help translate another document into English. The *hevals* were looking for an English native speaker, and Irish was close enough. This time, he had to work in the official Tev Dem offices upstairs. Besides the usual large Öcalan painting, the official office was a bare corridor that connected several equally sparse-looking rooms. The space that served as a kitchen was empty except for a long table, fridge, and cooker. Being true spartan *hevals*, for lunch (very much to Shaun's disappointment) they would eat cold spaghetti mixed with cold tomato paste.

After *chai*, the *hevals* continued with their work. Shaun knew the office held some importance, and when several intellectual and political key figures of the movement appeared, he sensed something big was going on but did not grasp any of the details. Just like Baz and John, his

Kurmanci was good enough to maneuver the battlefield. His vocabulary, however, did not include anything relevant to diplomacy and international relations. The *hevals*, for their part, spoke very little English. After all, that's why Shaun was there in the first place.

Shaun was installed in a small room with a desk, computer, and some swivelly chairs. Next to him sat a Kurdish *heval* from Rojava in front of a laptop with an Arabic keyboard. From a paper bearing Kurmanci writing, the *heval* typed his impromptu translation into Arabic. Then the *heval* emailed the document to himself and opened it on the computer with a Latin keyboard that was sitting on the desk. Next, he copied-and-pasted the Arabic text into Google Translate. The English translation Google offered was copied-and-pasted into a Word document. During all of this, the *heval* explained to Shaun that Google Translate did not understand Kurmanci Kurdish yet. The outcome of the ad hoc translation from Kurmanci into Arabic and the workover by Google's algorithm was technically English, yet some of it made little sense.

Shaun asked what the document was about. In broken English, the *heval* explained there would be a declaration by the Constituent Assembly for the establishment of a Federal Democratic Rojava/Northern, which meant little to Shaun at the time. Acknowledging the newly liberated Arab areas that had joined Rojava, the autonomy from Damascus was reissued and a federal system declared that they would write their own constitution. The councils had just legitimized the political vision of Rojava, with democratic confederalism as its political theory. Acknowledging that Rojava as a political theory had outgrown the Kurdish areas, the name of the autonomous region changed from Rojava to the temporary compromise: Democratic Federation of Rojava—Northern Syria. Therefore, this translation of the draft version of their constitution was extremely important and would be released "all over the world. It had to be perfect."

Drafting their autonomous constitution was furthermore an important diplomatic move. Representatives from Rojava were not present at the brief Syrian peace talks hosted by the UN in Geneva in February 2016 for complex reasons. The vote for autonomy as well as this declaration would thus communicate Rojava's position to the international community.

It was supposed to be a strong political signal. The English version would be read by the UN as well as Washington. Having utter trust in the power of Google, the *hevals* did not wanted the document to be edited. Shaun was only supposed to double-check spelling and grammar. After some debate, the two agreed on minor, absolutely necessary edits.

"We commemorate with respect the martyrs of our people, who wrote with their blood the heroic resistance that has brought our people to the important historical moment of significance they are at today." Shaun suggested at least changing "important historical moment of significance" to "milestone." The *heval* googled milestone, and the first Arabic translation was "a stone set up beside a road to mark the distance in miles to a particular place." "No no no," the *heval* argued, until he found the alternative meaning: "a significant stage or event in the development of something," further down below. And on it went.

The Social Contract continued to speak of the territorial integrity of Syria, and outlined details of the federal structure, the uncompromising equality and political representation of women and any minority as well as organizing councils. Contrary to common belief, it also spoke of private property and the protection of entrepreneurs as long as they abided by progressive environmental laws.[7]

Suddenly, shots were fired outside. Shaun and the *heval* left the small office to see what was going on. People were shouting and running around in the corridors. As it turned out, somebody had posted the Arabic version of the declaration by mistake. The official announcement had been made too early. The *Asayîş* guarding the Tev Dem outside had seen the post and were celebrating with fully automatic bursts into the sky. Out of the Tev Dem's control, the happy news about Rojava's new autonomy spread like wildfire, and soon, shooting and honking spread across Qamishlo.

Originally, the plan had been to release the document simultaneously in all languages. Now, somebody had messed it up, and the English version had to be uploaded online as soon as possible. "Okay, *heval*, we have to work fast now; this needs to go quickly." With Rojava's officials continuously sticking their heads into the small office, inquiring about progress, Shaun and the *heval* finally got it done, and it was dispatched right away. The *hevals* thanked Shaun unceremoniously, and he went back downstairs.

What Shaun had just participated in was arguably the most important moment during his time in Rojava, yet he had absolutely no idea what was going on. Not realizing the gravity of what just happened really epitomizes Rojava. Here, everyone has a voice, and everyone is listened to. Even Shaun, a random Irish guy who was only there temporarily, had been given the opportunity to contribute a small detail to this historic document in a century-old battle for Kurdish freedom. Unlike many warriors throughout the centuries, Shaun had the exceptional opportunity to contribute to the very constitution/Social Contract he pulled the trigger for. His war had not been for oil or economic interests, but freedom. Yet the special nature of the moment was lost on those involved. To them, it was just democracy.

A few months later, in December 2016, a version of the constitution was ratified.[8] With the emergence of the new official name, Rojava disappeared entirely. It simply did not describe the growing Democratic Federation of North-Eastern Syria anymore.

It was March 17, 2016, St. Patrick's Day, and naturally, Shaun wanted a beer. While Heval Rezan passed on the offer, together with another volunteer, Shaun bought a few cans of Tuborg from some Arab guys down the road, and they drank them near the last remains of the old Berlin-Baghdad railway. As they knocked back the warm beer, enjoying the night breeze, two *Asayîş* appeared behind them with their rifles at the ready.

The *Asayîş'* HQ had moved fighters to the Tev Dem building's rooftop because of rising tensions with the Regime. They feared the office might be attacked because the declaration of autonomy had been drafted there. From the rooftop, the *Asayîş* had spotted two guys and suspected Shaun and the other volunteer were intruders trying to gain access to the compound. The PKM gunner on the roof was ready to kill them while the other two lads were creeping up with their fingers on the trigger. The *Asayîş* began to laugh when they recognized the two. "*Hevals*, we almost shot you." Shaun and the other volunteer laughed too. What wonderful chaos in a young democracy.

This episode also shows how democratic confederalism had become a lived political theory. Öcalan's initial ideas or broad theories had evolved way beyond the reach of Imrali Island or the Qandil Mountains. Those ideas inspired the people of Rojava to write their own freedoms and equalities based on their daily struggles. For more than a decade, thousands of people had worked on the implementation of this democracy, debating practical details. Somewhere during this process, between Imrali Island and the Sunni Arab villagers who organized their own defense militia on a day-to-day basis, democratic confederalism slowly changed ownership. At this point, it belongs to the people who live it. It belongs to the hundreds of volunteers who traveled to Rojava to literally keep this political theory alive. To claim it is about the PKK and terrorism is preposterously uninformed.

CHAPTER 16

Operation *Wrath of Euphrates*: March–October 2017

President Donald Trump taking office in 2017 introduced the fourth phase of America's war against the Islamic State. As Trump had promised during his election campaign, he increased the support for America's allies, including the SDF. By March 2017, 400 Marines from the 1st Battalion, 4th Marines, who were part of the 11th Marine Expeditionary Unit, deployed with their artillery in support of the Raqqa front.[1] That same month, about 100 U.S. Army Rangers with Stryker armored personnel carriers deployed on more diplomatic, noncombat-related missions around Manbij. Turkey's invasion forces in Syria increasingly attacked positions of the MMC that secured the Manbij pocket west of the Euphrates.

From the south of Manbij, the Regime and Russia were creeping closer. From the north and west, the Turkish Operation *Euphrates Shield* had become ever more aggressive. In joint patrols with the MMC and the Rangers, America held their hands over their allies and stopped the aggression. Together with the 500 special forces already in the country, the 400 Marines and the 100 Rangers brought the total number of American forces in Syria up to 1,000.[2]

On the ground, SDF forces were increasingly trained by the U.S. Special Forces. In particular, YAT, YPG/YPJ's Anti-Terror Units, was formed into a serious American-style special forces team, the most significant difference being the female operators. During the battle for Manbij in 2016, YAT had been a good, but not exceptional, *tabur* armed with regular AKs and some advanced training and different uniforms from the regular units. By the beginning of Operation *Wrath of Euphrates*,

YAT had become smooth operators who were equipped with gear very similar to that of their American counterparts.

American arms kept arriving directly; M16s, enough ammo to actually train, and good scopes began appearing on the battlefield. As the enemy had shown many times, in a war mainly fought with AKs, an M16 with a scope could make a real difference. Suddenly, several marksmen and women were able to provide effective overwatch in the cities.

On July 6, 2017, Canadian Brigadier-General D. J. Anderson provided rare details on the Train and Equip program. Officially, the CJTF-OIR provided the SDF with 400 vehicles, weapons, and ammunition as well as personal equipment for more than 40,000 SDF troops. Some 8,500 SDF fighters have been trained by CJTF-OIR[3] (meaning by American, French, or British special forces or other highly specialized units). As would become clear during Operation *Wrath of Euphrates*, those 400 vehicles included Humvees as well as advanced APCs. The only weapons system the United States did not supply was ATGMs. Finally, the superiority of firepower on the ground changed in favor of the SDF. Now, the challenge would be to utilize this firepower most effectively in the two narrow cities of Tabqa and Raqqa.

When it came to numbers, equipment, experience, and training, Operation *Wrath of Euphrates*, the campaign to liberate Raqqa, was the "overwhelming force" the Prussian military strategist General Carl von Clausewitz spoke of in his respected 1832 work *On War*.[4] The campaign was divided into five phases. During phases one, two, and three (which started back in November 2016) the countryside north, west, and east around Raqqa was liberated. Since Daesh's tactic was to give up the open countryside relatively easy, these operations were rather unspectacular. By March 2017, the SDF had put their forces into place around Tabqa city and the strategic water dam to begin the actual fighting in phase four.

★

Since the city of Tabqa, the target of phase four, was on the western side of the Euphrates, the battle began spectacularly with 500 predominantly Arab fighters and U.S. Special Forces being airlifted across the river behind enemy lines on March 22, 2017. Establishing a bridgehead south of Tabqa and the dam, the SDF ferried in reinforcements across the impressive Lake Assad. While SDF forces were attacking the eastern end of the dam, the main assault came from fighters south of the river, cut off from the SDF-controlled territory. Carefully, the coalition advanced on their targets, and soon after, the air base south of the city was liberated.

On March 27, 2017, the SDF held their offensive on the dam to let Syrian engineers inspect the already liberated parts. By then, the SDF controlled the northern spillways they could use to control the water pressure.[5] So far, the dam was safe. Still cut off from any support south of the Euphrates, in early April 2017, the SDF surrounded Tabqa and began fighting their way into the city. Operations around the heavily booby-trapped dam continued. Eventually, the pressure of the assault was too much for the enemy, and some kind of deal was struck with the remaining Daesh fighters. It is fair to assume that some of those fighters had their families in Raqqa, a city that had the potential to suffer horribly from the flood wave. In order to prevent heavy losses during vicious street fighting and the water dam from blowing up, the SDF allowed the enemy to retreat.[6]

On May 12, 2017, Hevala Rojda Felat, who commandeered the liberation of Raqqa, announced that Tabqa city and the dam were free. She continued with a warning to the Islamists: "2017 will be the year of freedom for all women, including the Yazidi women who were kidnapped by Daesh."[7] The SDF continued using the momentum and geared up for phase five: the assault on Raqqa city—Daesh's Syrian capital.

★

The battle for Raqqa began on June 6, 2017, when the SDF attacked villages that would eventually morph into the city. At this stage in the war, it was clear that the SDF would eventually liberate Raqqa. The Caliphate as a state-like entity had broken down and was operating in life-preserving mode. What this battle was essentially about was the price Daesh made the SDF pay for their eventual victory. The more SDF fighters and civilians who died, the stronger the bargaining position

Daesh had for the deal that would inevitably be made. Consequently, the SDF advanced very carefully.

Daesh used similar tactics to the ones utilized successfully in the past, including IEDs, small teams or guerilla tactics, and urban snipers. This meant it was again a challenge for the SDF to breach the city and, later, particular barricaded neighborhoods. Throughout the SDF's advance, the alliance was harassed by sporadic mortar fire. Whenever the SDF established a foothold in the city, they were attacked with SVBIEDs, more snipers, and small teams that moved around the advancing SDF *takems* through a web of sophisticated tunnels they had built over the years.[8] Against CJTF-OIR's air strikes, Daesh used a network of bunkers that was connected through more tunnels as well as larger numbers of human shields than they had in the past.[9] According to Amnesty International, 1,600 civilians were killed during the battle by American air strikes and artillery.[10]

By late June 2017, the city of Raqqa was fully encircled and heavy urban combat ensued. By mid-October, a Daesh convoy had left Raqqa as part of the expected deal in return for their surrender.[11] About 400 Daeshis armed with rifles and PKMs withdrew, shielded by an equal number of civilians. On October 20th, the SDF declared victory.[12] Deep in the Sunni Arab desert, the SDF had liberated a city that used to be home to more than 200,000 inhabitants. Operation *Wrath of Euphrates* was finally over, and the Caliphate had de facto ceased to exist. The remaining fanatics and their hostages were on the run in the Deir Ezzor desert with no place to go and no powerful sympathizer on the horizon to save them.

Following the example of Manbij, Tabqa, and Raqqa, eventually, Deir Ezzor would become its own *canton*, governed by an assembly representing all local groups and women. Underlining their commitment to federalism, in September 2018, the official name of the autonomous region changed again to Autonomous Administration of North and East Syria (AANES).[13] Instead of Rojava's original three Kurdish regions, the new autonomous administration included seven *cantons*. Five of those *cantons* are either very heterogenous or predominantly Arab. While Afrin was now under Turkish occupation and Kobane had expanded to the Arab Ain Issa and

Tel Abiat (including the Balikh River region), this was by no means a Kurdish project anymore. Similarly, in the SDC—an alliance of different political parties that forms the governing body for the autonomous region and the SDF—the institutional influence of Arabs increased, reflecting the growth of the autonomous region in Arab homeland.

Regarding the monopoly of violence, the SDF was not in charge of internal security. Instead, the Raqqa Internal Security Forces (RISF), a police force made up of locals, including women, provided security. This force would be the key element in the internal security landscape and was, as Brigadier-General Anderson of the CJTF-OIR acknowledged, an effective idea originating from the SDF[14]—i.e. democratic confederalism.

CHAPTER 17

Al-Jazeera Storm and the American Exit Strategy: September 2017–September 2019

On September 8, 2016, while the battle for Raqqa was still going on, Operation *Al-Jazeera Storm* began to end the Caliphate's last remaining influence in the desert around Deir Ezzor. The operation was spearheaded by the Deir Ezzor Military Council, which included many members of the al-Sheitaat tribe. Their tribe had resisted Daesh in 2014, whereupon to send a message to all other tribes in the region, Daesh executed several hundred al-Sheitaat tribesmen. While many other members of the coalition were getting tired of the war, the Deir Ezzor Military Council and the al-Sheitaat fighters were eager to liberate their homes and eventually finish the gang who had tried to wipe out their people.

On the other side of the border in Iraq, Iraqi security forces and Shia militias had started to clear the remaining ISIS pockets in the Anbar Province. Coordinating Operation *Al-Jazeera Storm* with the Iraqi security forces left no direction for the Islamists to run to anymore. The noose around Daesh's last territory in the desert continued to tighten.

With the support of Russia and Iran, the Syrian Regime had also begun a large offensive to retake the desert west of the Euphrates from Daesh fighters. What followed on the ground became a race south along the Euphrates between the SDF and the Regime. With Daesh finished, those operations were about carving up the remains of the Caliphate in Syria. On the eastern side of the river were the American-supported SDF. On the western side was the Syrian Arab Army supported by Iran and Russia. Soon, tensions between the SDF and the Regime flared up.

By March 2019, Daesh was cut off from the Iraqi border and caught in a pocket between the Regime on the opposite side of the Euphrates and the advancing SDF. Desperate and isolated, between February and March 2019, a couple thousand of the most fanatic Daesh fighters and their families formed a depressing last stand around the city of Baghuz. Amongst trenches and car wrecks, they lived in tents they had built out of blankets and fought like the cornered, wounded beast they were. Eventually, somewhere in the desert, the long war against ISIS ended.

By April 2018, in northeastern Syria, in a region also known as Rojava, the war was over. As expected, there were signs of a Daesh insurgency by sleeper cells, but the Caliphate had ceased to exist, and its territory had been divided up by the Regime; the SDF; and, to a lesser degree, militias backed by Turkey. During the entire operation, only six deployed American servicemen died in Syria, none in active combat.[1] Given the close cooperation on the ground, there were very few friendly fire incidents during which jets bombed the SDF by accident.

No SDF fighter killed American, British, or French soldiers. Instead, all Western forces were warmly welcomed. The allied Western troops had a solid win and was widely viewed as the good guy. Although there were issues, compared to the rest of the Middle East, democracy in Rojava was developing. The Trump administration was praising the SDF for good reasons.[2]

America supported the regional concept of democracy instead of forcing its own ideas onto a foreign place. Supporting, instead of enforcing, meant American soldiers liberated and were cheered instead of being hated and fought. By playing a humbler and more supportive role, America's Middle Eastern policy was suddenly working; it was accepted by the people in the region.

Democratic confederalism was also America's exit strategy, although the term "exit" is confusing as it suggests American troops should withdraw from Syria. Instead, the exit strategy should be understood as the shift by the American military from a combat-oriented mission to a diplomatic one. By physically being there, America was protecting Rojava from any external aggressors, including Russia, Turkey, and Iran. The geopolitical and military power America projected was enough to deter attacks on their allies. America had become Rojava's hegemon or protector,[3] the superpower that held its protective hands over the revolution. The U.S. Army Rangers who conducted joint patrols with Turkey and the Manbij Military Council were an excellent example of exercising this hegemony; the American military controlled the Turkish aggressions whilst taking their security concerns seriously.

Another incident that exemplified America's role as Rojava's hegemon occurred in February 2017 during the battle of Khasham at the Euphrates near the city of Deir Ezzor. A pro-Assad force that included 100 Russian mercenaries had crossed onto the eastern side of the Euphrates, probing American-protected areas. (Probing refers to small attacks with the aim of testing the opponent's strength, determination, and readiness for a possible decisive attack in the future.) When American jets killed all of the intruders, including the Russian mercenaries, President Putin and Iran—Assad's hegemons—understood that America was very determined.

Then, out of the blue, on December 19, 2018, Trump tweeted that the United States would withdraw from Syria:

> We have defeated ISIS in Syria, my only reason for being there during the Trump Presidency. After historic victories against ISIS, it's time to bring our great young people home! Getting out of Syria was no surprise. I've been campaigning on it for years, and six months ago, when I very publicly wanted to do it, I agreed to stay longer. Russia, Iran, Syria & others are the local enemy of ISIS. We were doing there [*sic*] work. Time to come home & rebuild. #MAGA.[4]

When General James Mattis and Brett McGurk resigned over this idea and Trump received pushback from all sides, in January and February 2019, he began backpedaling. Now, the United States administration decided to leave some American troops in the country. Seemingly, everything went back to normal. The idea of America withdrawing did not make any sense and many hoped that Trump had understood the insanity of this step.

Given Turkish aggressions, the SDF knew that a complete American withdrawal would inevitably end with a Turkish invasion. Thus, the SDF began looking for a possible new hegemon to shield them from the Turks. In the days after Trump's initial tweet, they began talks with the Regime but more importantly, with Russia. When America came to its senses and the whole retreat was put on hold, the alliance with the SDF seemingly continued.[5]

Yet the official discourse by the United States administration was growing increasingly erratic and pro-Turkish. After years of denying it, in March 2019, James Jeffrey, Special Representative for Syria Engagement and Special Envoy to the Global Coalition to Defeat ISIS, talked about the YPG having ties to the PKK.[6] Later, in June 2019, he continued the argument in a worryingly uninformed and confusing briefing on Syria.[7] As the doubly special envoy explained, the YPG and their affiliated political parties in Rojava are the Syrian branches of the PKK. Fortunately for the United States, however, the "SDF grew out of the YPG"—a statement that is actually true-ish.

Meanwhile, the SDF continued their decentralization of power and violence. Several military councils were introduced in June 2019 in most major cities along the border with Turkey as well as Raqqa and Tabqa. With the military councils in place, the YPG/YPJ began the deconstruction of some of their border posts and withdrew 3 miles from the border in an effort to de-escalate and be reasonable. In October 2019, Trump tweeted on the subject again.

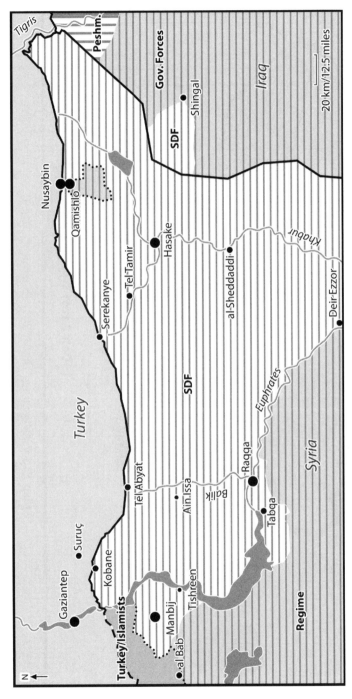

Map 7: Front lines in September 2019 around the Kobane and Cizire *cantons*.

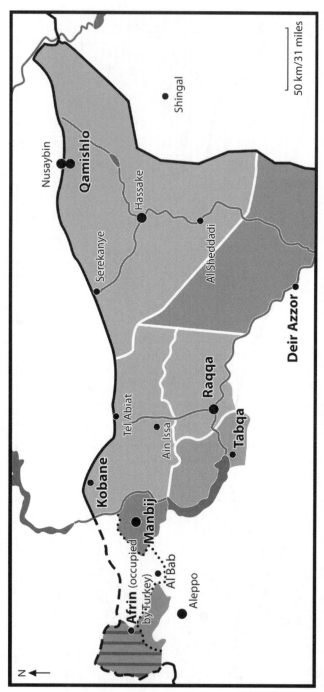

Map 8: Seven *cantons* in October 2021 (compare to Map 1).

PART IV

MADNESS: OCTOBER 2019–NOVEMBER 2020

CHAPTER 18

"America Has Blood on Its Hands": October 2019

On October 6, 2019, a statement by the White House announced America's withdrawal from Syria.

> Today, President Donald J. Trump spoke with President Recep Tayyip Erdogan of Turkey by telephone. Turkey will soon be moving forward with its long-planned operation into Northern Syria. The United States Armed Forces will not support or be involved in the operation, and United States forces ... will no longer be in the immediate area.[1]

This statement set a whole series of unbelievable events in motion and marked the beginning of the fourth phase in America's war against the Islamic State in Syria. As the commander in chief explained to the world a little later, from now on, "Turkey, Europe, Syria, Iran, Iraq, Russia and the Kurds will now have to figure the situation out themselves."[2] America did not want to continue fighting wars abroad. The problem with the argument? The war was already over. For the first time in decades, America had militarily, politically, and morally won, while not a single American soldier had died in direct combat with ISIS (instead, fatalities were due to IEDs and car crashes).

In October 2019, America had transformed into Rojava's hegemon and was supporting the democratic success story by holding its enemies at bay with simple joint patrols. With an extremely light military footprint of just a few hundred U.S. Army Rangers, America enabled a regional democracy. In return, this democratic project was America's ally that kept the United States relevant in the Middle East. All it needed was patience, because a sustainable foreign policy takes time and nurturing. In a bizarre twist of history, U.S. Special Forces were protecting a leftist utopia the Kurds had set in motion.

This short summer of justice, democracy, and hope was destroyed by those tweets and the following statements by Trump and his administration. With the departure of the hegemon, the inevitable started happening. Turkey came with American jets and German tanks and killed Kurds for being Kurds while the world remained silent.

With the Turkish invasion going on and an organized ISIS insurgency picking up in Raqqa while Daesh supporters rioted in the refugee camps, John began feeling physically sick. "This is the most un-American thing I think I have ever seen." Just talking about the subject hurt him. It did not make sense on any level. "We don't betray our allies." John's idol General James Mattis had warned Trump not to do just this, and eventually resigned over the issue. As a Marine veteran, John felt stabbed in the back by America's commander in chief.

Images of human rights violations surfaced. While the usual looting quickly became a side issue, Turkish soldiers and their Islamist allies were humiliating captured YPJ. Just like they had done to Şehîd Barin Kobani in Afrin, they mutilated the bodies of the women they captured. Hevala Hevrin Khalaf was murdered on social media. The Turks killed a female politician who was a symbol of Rojava's equality and boasted about it on social media, mocking her slain body. That was too much. For the first time in John's life, he faced an identity crisis. This entire time, he had been proud to be an American. Fighting for America's values had given him meaning. Now he was ashamed of his president's decision. "Right now, what does America stand for?"

Together, we were trying to piece together a picture of the Turkish invasion, knowing that all of this could have been prevented by some U.S. Ranger joint patrols and a clear American foreign policy. No big troop deployment, no occupation, just some dudes relaxing in the sun and thus deterring Turkey from invading. So easy, so cheap, so doable. We were speechless when we watched the U.S. Special Forces being basically chased out of Rojava by the pro-Turkish Islamists on YouTube. When presidents Trump and Erdoğan talked about a security zone that would stabilize the region, they knew it was a lie.

The Kurds lived along the Syrian-Turkish border for various historical reasons.[3] The security zone that was discussed would be a form of de facto genocide. What Trump and Erdoğan talked about was the systematic displacement that would eventually force 300,000 Kurds and their close allies from their homeland into the desert.

Saddam Hussein and Hafez al-Assad once called this strategy "Arabization." It is the reason for the mess around Kirkuk in Iraq, yet another problem America did not solve before leaving. Trump and Erdoğan talked about peace when it sems that the so-called Turkish-backed Free Syrian Army, or TFSA, had Islamists amongst their ranks.[4] Truly democratic structures were thus replaced by councils of angry, bearded men.

What the Kurds needed to do next was sound out other alliances to hold Turkey at bay. The only one who could do that was President Vladimir Putin. Consequently Mazloum Abdi, SDF's commander in chief, published a comment in *Foreign Policy*[5] in which he justified the decision to strike a deal with the Regime and Russia. Soon after, Regime forces closed in on Manbij to fill the security vacuum America had left overnight.

★

On the ground, the SDF had to fight a NATO force that was trying to take their homes. In particular, the *hevals* in Serekanye put up an incredible resistance against all odds. Unlike America, the Kurds learned from history and prepared for this event. To Turkey's surprise, the YPG/YPJ began combining the PKK's own guerilla warfare with some of ISIS's urban guerilla tactics. Instead of defending the open terrain against armor and an air force, the defenders retreated into the city, where the battlefield was shrunk down, cover was available, and the enemy came within AK range. In the narrow streets and alleys, the NATO force could not utilize its superior firepower. Instead, infantry had to assault the fortified Serekanye.

The resistance used snipers who moved around through tunnels and broken walls between different ambush positions. After firing off each shot, the snipers would move; Turkish F16s were bombing empty positions while the *hevals* already had the next pro-Turkey Islamist in their crosshairs. Completely surrounded, the resistance continued, inflicting unexpected casualties against the invaders, who had overwhelming force on their side. Eventually, and just as Daesh had done, the resistance was in a position to negotiate their organized withdrawal as part of a deal that was stuck.

★

Then came October 22, 2019 in Sochi, Russia, when a very strange yet iconic scene took place. In a rather unspectacular room with two very bizarre lamps in the corners, presidents Putin and Erdoğan, and two very scared interpreters looked at a Syrian map, debating different, new lines in the desert sand. While the interpreters ran back and forth with the maps, the Czar and Caliph drank from their pimp cups. Obviously, there were no refreshments for the two underlings.[6]

The result of this fascinating conversation held in Russian and Turkish was an important part of the future of Syria and essential to the survival of democratic confederalism. Missing from the meeting was the American president, because when it comes to Syria, America does not matter anymore. In their Sochi deal, Putin agreed to Erdoğan's buffer zone 19 miles deep into Syria, running from the Euphrates to the border with Iraq, excluding Qamishlo. This buffer zone would be occupied by Turkey indefinitely.

Including the Turkish invasion in Afrin, since January 2018, half a million Kurds have been displaced. Arabs were put in the Kurds' homes. What Erdoğan referred to as a "buffer" was not just about border posts but having loyal Arabs live between the Kurds and the Turkish border. The Kurds, people from the mountains, were forced to find refuge somewhere in the desert.

Interestingly, the Sochi Agreement also brought up the Adana Agreement, a deal made between Turkey and Syria in 1998. Back then, both countries had been at the brink of war, Syria negotiating from the position of weakness. The Adana Agreement was an anti-PKK deal. Syria not only agreed to stop its support for the PKK, but Assad also declared the *hevals* terrorists and allowed Turkey to fight the PKK 3 miles deep into Syrian territory.[7] The very direct consequence of the Adana Agreement was Öcalan's deportation from Syria and his subsequent imprisonment by Turkey. Thus Putin (who was, after all, Syria's hegemon) reminding the world that the Adana Agreement was still relevant spelled further bad news for the AANES.

In a pre-emptive response to the Russian-Turkish meeting in Sochi two days earlier, on October 20th, Trump tweeted: "Mark Esperanto [*sic*], Secretary of Defense, 'The ceasefire is holding up very nicely. There are some minor skirmishes that have ended quickly. New areas being resettled with the Kurds.' USA soldiers are not in combat or ceasefire zones. We have secured the Oil. Bringing soldiers home!"[8] Besides being fooled by autocorrect, the tweet indicated yet another shift in America's Syria policy. As it turned out later, America would indeed return to Syria with mechanized forces in order to secure the oil fields south of Hasake,[9] which was way outside Turkey's proposed security zone.

Within weeks of the Sochi Agreement, Russian military police began replacing the U.S. Army Rangers around Manbij and elsewhere. Over the following weeks, Russia and the Regime began to establish themselves as Rojava's new hegemon and filled the security vacuum America had created. While America gets to secure 2½ billion barrels of Syrian oil with fragile export routes in the middle of nowhere (geopolitically speaking), Turkey and Russia control everything else. Since Russia has 80 billion barrels of their own reserves[10] and the United States has 47 billion,[11] it is hard to sell this as a win for America, and the deal should not have been prioritized over staying to help a loyal ally that has lost 10,000 lives in the war they fought together.

★

Whatever the future holds for the AANES, democratic confederalism and the blossoming democracy are in jeopardy. Presidents Putin, Assad, and Erdoğan are already in control of large parts of the Rojava Project. In the long term, gender equality, direct democracy, and direct justice are in danger because these are all things the three men hate.

When Putin reminded the SDF and the Kurds of the Adana Agreement in the Sochi deal, he positioned himself as the strongman in the ongoing negotiations with the Kurds. In layman's terms, Putin told the YPG/YPJ that if he did not agree with their terms, he could always push them out of Syria completely. Different to America and Europe, the Russians are still fluent at geopolitics. Putin thus communicated to the *hevals* that he could always have Assad fight them from the south while Turkey crushed them from the north.

With luck, elements of the SDF will continue to provide security to what will remain of Rojava, but this is no longer up to the Kurds or America, the latter having lost all of its credibility. The areas that remain under SDF-American control continue to hold on in a hostile environment while the constant threat of America's complete withdrawal is ever present.

When it comes ot America's official stance towards SDF and associated civilan organisations, there is no more mention of the YPG/YPJ because the democracy project has outgrown Rojava and the Kurds. With the United States Mission of the SDC de facto endorsing democratic confederalism and the Social Contract,[12] it is officially not about terrorism and the PKK anymore but political theory. It is about people who were inspired by a highly theoretical political utopia and began implementing it through trial and error.

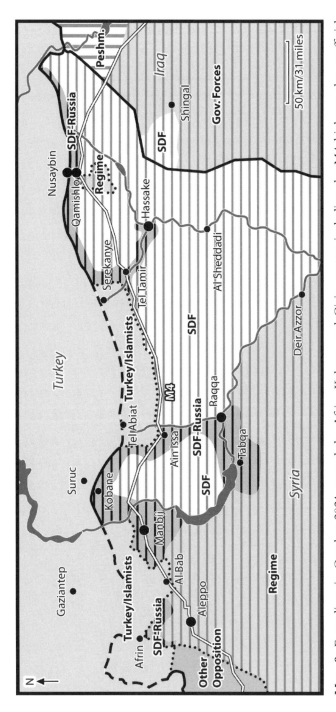

Map 9: Front lines in October 2021 around the Afrin, Kobane, and Cizire *cantons* including the M4 highway, the unofficial southern border of the Turkish "safety-zone" where Kurds are being displaced from (compare to Map 1 that also highlights the predominantly Kurdish areas in Syria).

Conclusion

In June 2014, Daesh fighters took Mosul. In August, the Islamists attacked Shingal and began their genocide against the Yazidi people. In September, President Obama ordered (with a few exceptions) rather symbolic and token air strikes. America's actual war against the Islamic State began around May 2015 at the front lines of Tel Tamir, Hasake and before that, Kobane. While Shaun and Baz watched in awe, America rolled out a decisive campaign that would pave the way for the first large-scale offensives against ISIS. In this first phase of their war on Daesh, CJTF-OIR and Kurdish forces pushed Daesh out of predominantly Kurdish homelands.

The second phase of the war against ISIS was actually introduced by the Kurds, America's closest ally in Syria, when they facilitated the creation of the SDF in October 2015. Enabled by a broad coalition, including several Arab elements, the SDF was able to operate outside of Kurdish areas and attack the Caliphate where it hurt. America needed the SDF to defeat ISIS, and Obama deployed 50 U.S. Special Forces to Rojava in an attempt to consolidate the alliance with the SDF. During the subsequent liberation of al-Hol and the Tishreen Dam between October and December 2015, the SDF and their alliance with the USA were first tested. With both operations at the very end of 2015's fighting season a success, trust between all partners was built. Now Rojava was waiting for the attack on the first major Daesh stronghold, which would begin as soon as the rain cleared in spring 2016.

The al-Hol and Tishreen Dam operations were the first time Western soldiers appeared on the battlefield. Small teams of French special forces collected intelligence and began coordinating air strikes with the SDF front-line commanders. At the same time, the first American shipments of Soviet-style weapons and 7.62×39mm rounds arrived from the Balkans.

At the beginning of the fighting season, in February 2016, the SDF assaulted al-Shaddadi, a strategic city connecting Mosul and Raqqa. CJTF-OIR supported the operation with close air support and more French forces, coordinating air strikes and securing the advancing SDF *taburs* with anti-tank guided missiles against the constant threat of SVBIEDs. With the liberation of al-Shaddadi also a success, Obama increased the special forces contingent further, bringing the total number up to 300.

In May 2016, the SDF and CJTF-OIR assaulted the first major Daesh stronghold: Manbij. During the bloody battle, special forces from France, Britain, and especially the United States took a more active role. Typically, the SDF front-line commanders were always right behind the fighting units, overlooking the situation from a strategic location. Given the way the SDF fought, it was here where most critical interventions on the battlefield were made. Changes in tactics and coordination between different front lines would happen at these *noctas*, where all front-line commanders and attached special forces conducted the war.

For logistical reasons, the position of the front-line commander becomes the central hub for all operations at the front line. *Taburs* would get their orders and briefings here. Units rotating out would stop at this *nocta* first. Often, the fuel truck would be in the vicinity, so all *tabur* drivers came by on a regular basis. It was thus at these *noctas* that all intelligence would come together. Only when someone was placed at these strategic points could a comprehensive, unfiltered picture of the ongoing battle be formed. Having a special forces team cooperating with each of those command elements along the battlefield enabled CJTF-OIR not only to follow the war in real time, but also to plan its next steps with their allies.

From these command posts, special forces would call in air strikes, provide fire support with their mortars and .50cal, or stabilize combat casualties when needed. Here, the special forces could force multiply most effectively whilst avoiding casualties that could turn the deployment into a political nightmare. (As a reminder, during the entire operation in Rojava, no CJTF-OIR soldier died in active fighting.) With only a few dozen highly trained operators at the front lines, America enabled the liberation of Manbij, a major urban battle. Just before leaving office, in December 2016, President Obama ramped up the special forces contingent to 500.

The third phase of America's war on Daesh began with President Donald Trump taking office. Immediately, America's support for the SDF increased. The training of friendly forces intensified, American military equipment was officially shipped to the SDF, and more American troops poured into Rojava. Four hundred Marines deployed to provide artillery support, and 100 U.S. Army Rangers were shipped in for a more diplomatic mission: securing Rojava's contested borders in joint patrols. During this third phase, on the ground, the superiority of firepower changed from Daesh to the ever-growing SDF. In summer 2017, Raqqa was liberated, and by March 2018, the last remains in Deir Ezzor were cleared out.

During this third phase, the war in Rojava ended. In Syria, the remains of the former Caliphate had been divided up between the Syrian Regime supported by Russia and Iran, and the SDF supported by America. For a long time, America had won a morally and ethically justifiable war. There was peace, and the American military's mission switched from being combat-focused to diplomatic. America had become Rojava's hegemon. All the United States had to do was physically be present and, occasionally, show some teeth when probed. In return, America got a success story in the Middle East and a justified reason to stay in the region. It was a good deal that worked for everyone.

It worked because America supported a regional idea of democracy instead of enforcing their own liberal democracy. America decided to indirectly support democratic confederalism in favor of enforcing their own Western version of democracy. Consequently, American soldiers helped liberate instead of occupying.

★

During the War on Terror, America insisted on its supposedly superior democracy. Being an enforced idea, the American version of democracy was never able to override tribal or religious forms of governance and subsequently initiated an insurgency that would cost many lives on all sides. Possibly without even being aware of it, all those past mistakes were avoided in the alliance with the YPG/YPJ and, later, the SDF.

Contrary to the War on Terror, now America was humble and supportive. Instead of enforcing, the American military offered their assistance in the form of air strikes, special forces, mortars, intelligence (including air surveillance), advice, and CCPs. Whatever the SDF requested from this arsenal they received right away. America fought the kind of war Green Berets were trained for.

As the U.S. Special Forces soon found out, when liberating, war is much easier. At the front lines, the special forces were able to be effective without there being much risk of casualties or attacks by sleeper cells. Facing a generally friendly population enabled them to have a very light military footprint. With this approach, internal security in the liberated territory was of little concern. Instead of deploying a large and expensive occupation force, local *Asayîş* from the coalition members would occupy the checkpoints around their hometowns.

Since most civilians were on their side and able to spot different dialects, these old farmers in the *Asayîş* could do a far more effective job than any foreign soldier ever could. Indeed, General David Petraeus made use of this idea when enabling the Sunni Awakening in the Anbar Province in Iraq around 2010.[1] Instead, American troops could be deployed in a mission-specific fashion, meaning the right unit was called in for specialized jobs. Once they had finished, they would leave Rojava again. The best examples were the U.S. Army Rangers patrolling around Manbij, the temporary deployment of the 621st Contingency Response Group that modernized airfields,[2] or the Marines with their howitzers.

Yet American politicians failed to recognize what held the alliance together, what legitimized their operation ethically and morally, and their exit strategy: democratic confederalism and the Kurds. Without the YPG/YPJ, America would lose everything they'd built: an alliance based on trust and democracy, not bundles of dirty dollars.

A just war is not only a war fought for the right and necessary reasons, but for an idea that will improve the lives of the affected people once the fighting is over. Of course, Rojava and all that followed had its flaws and we have written about many of them. Yet, the project should be seen in the context of the wider region. No representative of Rojava we have ever talked to claimed their idea of implementation to be perfect. Yet they are the only ones in Syria and the surrounding area who are actually trying. Democratic confederalism made this war just. Seeing this young democracy project in Rojava suffocate slowly is an unbearable injustice.

The fourth phase began with the announcement of America's withdrawal from Rojava. This phase exposed America's hypocrisy. On the one hand, its politicians feel comfortable enough to impose their democracy on countries they do not understand (i.e. Iraq and Afghanistan); on the other hand, its own democratic structures are incredibly vulnerable to uninformed decisions that bring death and suffering to the Middle East and elsewhere for no apparent reason. America had just stabilized its battle buddy, now it took the tourniquet back off and watched her bleed out slowly. Erratic American foreign policy turned a just war into the usual disaster.

★

The war impacted John, Shaun, and Baz on several levels. Since John got back from Rojava, he hates to sweat or be hungry. Out of principle, his AC unit is always 1 degree Fahrenheit below the outside temperature. Deeply disappointed by America's betrayals of the Kurds and the SDF, John accepted that, right now, America cannot be relied on. Having come to this realization, John had two options. He could either move back into depression or he could learn a personal lesson from those sobering insights into American geopolitics. John decided on the latter because that would mean finishing a story that had begun in December 2014 in the safe house in Sulaymaniyah when he'd met Kosta, Şehîd Kemal, for the first time.

The two Marines had bonded immediately. There was much that united them. They were both warriors drawn toward this war. Yet they were opposites at the same time. Where John wanted to fight against Daesh, Kosta wanted to fight for the Kurds. Where John was driven by a void caused by the missing combat deployment, Kosta wanted to fill the void of feeling useless while others suffered. He was a good soldier and wanted to fight for what was right. To John, it was no surprise that Kosta risked his life to save the *hevals* around him. As Kosta said himself before leaving for Rojava, "Life is not measured in years but by the deeds of men."[3] When he died, the people he'd fought for chanted "Şehîd namirin—Martyrs never die" because to them, his deeds had made him immortal. In Rojava, Kosta told John, "If I fall şehîd, bury me beneath an olive tree so my body will bring life." Today, a little olive tree grows on his grave, and John has not forgotten his vision of there being a humanitarian organization in the front lines.

Bonding with Kosta during the endless days and nights on the berm and in fighting positions changed John's personality. While Kosta was still the baddest, most disciplined warrior he had ever met, he had also been about balance. As a warrior, you need love in your life; otherwise, you become like Daesh: evil. As John explains, Kosta was "strong enough to be gentle" in every sense of the phrase.

★

Shaun developed a craving for eggs. Before the war, he hated even the sight of eggs, but after some young *heval* in the academy fixed him some hard-boiled ones one time, he became hooked. During operations in the heat, when everyone was losing pounds by the week, eggs became a synonym for protein and the short-lived feeling of being full. Shaun and Baz would therefore fantasize about eggs during operations and when each *tabur* received a couple of hundred of them once in a while, they would literally be gone in seconds. Nowadays, Shaun enjoys regular hard-boiled eggs *gundi*-style with a little salt and naan.

Partially inspired by the long debates with Baz during guard duty or when waiting in the staging areas, Shaun cultivated an academic fascination for the war against Daesh. Having gotten to know Rojava a little, he is shocked and disturbed by the limited understanding decision-makers have about the conflict. He, too, is still trying to understand the war he fought in. With Syria a possible burning glass for Western, Israeli, Russian, and Iranian geopolitical ambitions, he now studies international relations, and still follows the conflict live on Twitter.

★

Since his time in Rojava, Baz hates being cold and going to bed hungry—it reminds his body of those miserable muddy nights at the front. As a result of his biography and time in Rojava, Baz also realized that he had very little in common with mainstream society and its value system anymore. In Rojava and elsewhere, people keep dying as a result of disastrous foreign policy, but the vast majority of people in the West simply do not care. Having seen the outfall of wars that get barely any airtime in the news, the former medic is inconsolably disappointed by this disrespect of human life and the planet in general. With our societies being distinctly urban, Baz has left the city with its hectic and passive-aggressive demeanor. He now lives in a forest, where he enjoys the peace and tries to make sense of everything he saw during his time in war and revolution.

Glossary

A-10 "Warthog"—A jet built around a 30mm Gatling gun to provide air support for ground forces

AC-130 gunship—Based on the C-130 Hercules transport, the gunship has different weapons systems added to its side, including a 105mm cannon or 40mm Gatling guns

Abdel Aziz mountains—Strategic mountain range near Hasake and Tel Tamir in Syria

Afrin—one of Rojava's three *cantons*

Alawis—Sect of Shia Islam

Al-Nusra—Al-Qaida offshoot

Americani—The term Kurdish fighters used for all Western volunteers

Ardens—Cigarette brand that fueled the YPG/YPJ and the SDF

Asayîş—Kurdish police/intelligence hybrid

Asayîş Jin—Female police force enforcing the rights of women

Askari doctor—Soldier doctor/combat medic

ATGM—Anti-tank guided missile

Autonomous Administration of North and East Syria (AANES)—Current name of autonomous areas that used to be called Rojava

Ba'ath—In this context, Saddam Hussein's former political party

Barrel bomb—Improvised bombs the Syrian Regime deploys out of helicopters

Barzani—Clan that leads the KDP in Iraq

BMP—Russian armored personal carrier

Caliphate—Territorial unit/state structure of the Islamic State

Canton—Rojava's administrative unit

CCP—casualty collection point, located just behind the fighting, to which all casualties are taken. This is where most injuries are initially assessed and stabilized

Chai—Sweet tea

Civîn—Pre-operation briefing

Cizire—One of Rojava's three *cantons*

Combat lifesaving classes—Class that teaches a basic knowledge of how to provide first aid for common battle injuries

CJTF-OIR—Combined Joint Task Force—Operation *Inherent Resolve*. When talking about the "Americans," this is actually what is meant. This task force fights the war for America by commanding air strikes etc.

Daesh—Derogatory term for the Islamic State

Democratic confederalism—Kurdish democracy project and political theory

Democratic Federation of Rojava—Northern Syria—Temporary official name replacing Rojava

"Dushka"—Russian-made 12.7mm machine gun

Earth berm—Line of defense put up by front-loaders

FOB—Forward operating base

Free Syrian Army—Syrian anti-Regime forces

Fusiliers—In this context, French soldiers with shoulder-held surface-to-surface missiles

GAP—Geopolitically relevant water dam project on the Euphrates and Tigris by Turkey

GPS—Global positioning system

Gund—Village

Gundi—Villager/simpleton

Heval/hevala—Member of the YPG/YPJ and the democracy movement they represent

Hezbollah—Shia militia fighting Daesh on behalf of the Syrian Regime

Imam—Religious leader

IED—Improvised explosive device

Individual First Aid Kit—Essential tools to provide first aid for common battle injuries for one person

IS—See Islamic State

ISIS—See Islamic State

Islamic State—Radical islamists that declared an extremeist version of Caliphate between June 2014 and late 2017. Members of the Islamic State ruled through brutality and fear, and commited genocide and ethnic cleansing against several ethnic and religious groups.

Keffiyeh—Black/red-and-white scarf worn by Kurds and Arabs

Kobane—One of Rojava's three *cantons*

KDP—Kurdistan Democratic Party—One of two main Kurdish parties in Iraq

KRG—Kurdistan Regional Government, autonomous Kurdish Areas in Iraq

Military council—Alliance of local and regional forces in their hometown and cities. The idea forms part of democratic confederalism

MLKP—Marksist Leninist Komünist Parti—Communist party fighting with the SDF

MRAPs—American armored personnel carriers

Murder hole—Small hole in the wall to shoot out of

Nocta—Base

Operator—Alternative term for a special forces soldier

Peshmerga—Kurdish forces in Iraq

PKK—Kurdistan Workers' Party—Turkish Kurdish underground organization

PKM—Belt-fed machine gun

PUK—Patriotic Union of Kurdistan—One of two main Kurdish parties in Iraq

PYD—Democratic Union Party—Main Kurdish party in Syria

Raqqa Internal Security Forces (RISF)—Police force made up of locals

Regime—Syrian government around the Assad clan

Ribat—Military service at quiet front lines undertaken by young ISIS fighters

Rojava—Autonomous Kurdish areas in Syria

Şehîd—Martyr

Serkeftin—"Until victory," Kurdish goodbye

Sharia law—Legal system in Islam

Shia—One of two dominating sects within Islam

Shingal—Homeland of Yazidis and strategic mountain range in Iraq near the Syrian border

SVBIED—Suicide vehicle-borne improvised explosive device

Sunni—One of two dominating sects within Islam

Syrian Democratic Council (SDC)—Political arm of the SDF

Syrian Democratic Forces (SDF)—Kurdish-dominated force fighting ISIS

Tabur—Largest fighting unit in the YPG/YPJ and the SDF

Tabur Şehîd Arges—Specific *tabur*

Tabur Şehîd Gelhat—Specific *tabur*

Tabur Şehîd Karaman—Specific *tabur*

Tabur Silah Grand—Heavy weapons unit. They are in charge of "Dushka" trucks, old tanks etc.

Takem—Sub-unit of a *tabur*

Talabani—Clan that leads the KDP in Iraq

Tell—Hill

Tev Dem—Political organization that communicated democratic confederalism to the people

TOW—Shoulder-held surface-to-surface missile

YAT—The SDF's Anti-Terror Units

Yazidis—Religious group that was targeted by ISIS

YBS—Yazidi militia that is part of the SDF alliance

YPG—Kurdish People's Protection units

YPJ—Kurdish Women's Protection units

Endnotes

Introduction

1   Parts of this scene have been captured on camera starting at 1:21:22 in the following documentary (trigger warning), https://www.youtube.com/watch?v=UJ1290087Yk&t=82s&has_verified=1&bpctr=1613330444.

2   "Meet the American Vigilantes Who Are Fighting ISIS," *The New York Times Magazine* (Sepember 30, 2015), https://www.nytimes.com/2015/10/04/magazine/meet-the-american-vigilantes-who-are-fighting-isis.html.

Chapter 1

1   Elsewhere, Baz outlines the geostrategic importance of the Kurdish oil in the Iraqi mountains. Till Paasche and Howri Mansurbeg, "Kurdistan Regional Government–Turkish energy relations: a complex partnership," *Eurasian Geography and Economics* 55, 2 (2014): 111–132.

2   Article 140 of the Iraqi Constitution was supposed to clarify the legal status of Kirkuk and the surrounding disputed territories. Article 140 foresees a referendum in which the people of Kirkuk decide if they want to stay with Baghdad and Iraq or join the Kurdish autonomy project, which might lead to independence. However, before the referendum can be held, the Arabs that have settled in Kirkuk as part of Saddam's Arabization campaign have to be resettled. Once that is done, the Kurds would hold the majority again and would likely side with Kurdistan. Consequently, Baghdad has no intention of implementing Article 140. Losing Kirkuk would not only mean losing a dusty, mid-size city, but also one of the world's largest oilfields—Kirkuk Field—with an estimated 13.5 billion barrels of reserves. "Why is oil-rich Kirkuk so poor?," Al Jazeer (last modified October 24, 2018). https://www.aljazeera.com/indepth/features/oil-rich-kirkuk-poor-181023230125504.html.

In comparison, Syria only has 2.5 billion barrels in reserves. "Country Analysis Briefs – Syria," EIA (last modified August 1, 2011), https://www.eia.gov/beta/international/analysis_includes/countries_long/Syria/archive/pdf/syria_2011.pdf.

3 SVBIED describes suicide bombers in a truck packed full of explosives, one of Daesh's most effective weapons systems. A detailed account of Daesh SVBIEDs was published by Hugo Kaaman. Besides dissecting the technicalities and use of this fast-evolving weapons system, he introduces comprehensive terminology to analyze different versions of this weapon. Having encountered several Daesh SVBIEDs and treated its casualties, we can confirm Kaaman's open-source research. It is worth understanding the technological genius of these weapons in terms of camouflage, direction, choice of payload, reliability when picking their bombers, and so forth. Hugo Kaaman, "Car Bombs as Weapons of War," (last modified April 1, 2019), https://www.mei.edu/sites/default/files/2019-04/Car_Bombs_as_Weapons_of_War_0.pdf.

Chapter 2

1 "US Carries Out More Airstrikes Against ISIS in Iraq," ABC News (August 8, 2014), https://abcnews.go.com/International/us-carries-air strikes-isis-iraq/story?id=24897334.
2 "U.S. jet fighters, drones strike ISIS fighters, convoys in Iraq," CNN (August 9, 2014), https://www.cnn.com/2014/08/08/world/iraq-options/index.html?hpt=hp_t1.
3 We want to emphasize that we have no formal or informal links to the PKK. We were never member of the PKK or planned to join the PKK. None of us received military training, orders, or weapons from the PKK. We never fought for the PKK's aims and objectives. During out entire time fighting in Syria, we were YPG (later the YPG as part of the SDF). In Shingal and other places, we fought alongside the PKK in a broad alliance. So did American, British, and French special forces.

Chapter 3

1 Christopher Phillips, *The Battle for Syria* (New Haven, London: Yale University Press, 2016).
2 In a belt-fed machine gun that lacks sophisticated optics at night, usually every fifth round is a so-called "tracer" that shoots a red flare that allows a machine gunner to see where he or she is firing in the dark.

Chapter 4

1 In his book published in 1992, Francis Fukuyama famously predicted *The End of History and the Last Man*. The Soviet Union had just collapsed, and liberal democracy and capitalism had won. Supposedly, liberal democracy is proven the superior concept and will now bring peace to the world. Later, the argument was used to justify military interventions, such as the invasion of Iraq in 2003. Similar

to Christian missionaries, the Bush Jr. administration in particular thought liberal democracy would be the general solution for all problems, and those who disagreed with this idea needed to be forced to their luck. Francis Fukuyama, *The End of History and the Last Man* (New York: Free Press, 1992).

2 "The Continuing Saga of Aisha–and the Women of Afghanistan," *Time* (June 25, 2012), https://world.time.com/2012/06/25/the-continuing-saga-of-aisha-and-the-women-of-afghanistan/.

Chapter 5

1 For more information on the PKK-Turkey conflict see Paul White, *The PKK: coming down from the mountains* (London: Zed Books, 2015).

2 "(…) anti-ISIL forces, of which Kurdish forces are a part, but it's a much broader group of people."
"Daily Press Briefing," U.S. Department of State (July 30, 2015), https://2009-2017.state.gov/r/pa/prs/dpb/2015/07/245537.htm.
"(…) is not just the YPG, the Kurds there, but there's Turkoman, there's Syrian Arabs as well, and these have been effective fighting forces as well against ISIL." "Daily Press Briefing," U.S. Department of State (August 11, 2015), https://2009-2017.state.gov/r/pa/prs/dpb/2015/08/245937.htm.
"What we've spoken to before is once these areas are liberated by, as you mentioned, YPG, there's other forces who are effective in going after ISIL." "Daily Press Briefing," U.S. Department of State (September 3, 2015),
https://2009-2017.state.gov/r/pa/prs/dpb/2015/09/246614.htm.

3 The AC-130 is a large Hercules transport plane that the U.S. Air Force equipped with various machine guns and cannons that stick out of its side, and has the most sophisticated night vision and thermal cameras.

Chapter 7

1 After Amnesty International conducted a study in Rojava in July and August 2015, the human rights organization "has documented a range of abuses perpetrated by the autonomous Administration security forces in areas of northern Syria under their control. These abuses include forced displacement, demolition of homes, and the seizure and destruction of property. In some cases, entire villages have been demolished, apparently in retaliation for the perceived support of their Arab or Turkmen residents for the group that calls itself the Islamic State (IS) or other non-state armed groups." According to the report, this occurred in "the town of Suluk and its surrounding villages, including al-Ghbein, Raneen, Hammam al-Turkman, al-Maghat, Mela Berho, and Asaylem, as well as the villages of Abdi

Koy and Tel Fweida in the Tel Abyad and Tel Tamr countryside, respectively, and Husseiniya in Tel Hamees countryside." "We had nowhere else to go," Amnesty International (October 1, 2015), https://www.amnesty.org/download/Documents/MDE2425032015ENGLISH.PDF.

2   When the Middle East was still occupied by the colonial powers, Syria was a French protectorate. Thus, France has a complicated history in Syria and does indeed hold some of the responsibility for the current mess. Whilst acknowledging this complexity, for practical reasons we only focus on the escalating war between ISIS and France we witnessed during our time in Syria.

Chapter 9

1   "A total of 13 organisations have announced the joint establishment of the Democratic Syria Forces.

The 13 organizations include; YPG/YPJ, Al-Sanadid Forces, Syriac Military Council, Burkan Al-Fırat Operations Center, Suwar al-Raqqa, Shams al-Shamal, Lîwa Al-Selcuki, Brigade Groups of Al Jazeera, Jabhat Al-Akrad, Jaysh Al-Thuwar (Revolutionaries' Army involving Jabhat Al-Akrad, Lîwai 99, Special Operations Center 455, Lîwa Al-Selcuki, Ahrar Al-Zawiya, Lîwa Sultan Selîm, Lîwa Şuheda Al-Atarib), Lîwai Al-Tehrîr and Lîwai 99 Muşat."

"Declaration of establishment," Syrian Democratic Forces (October 15, 2015), https://web.archive.org/web/20160224085811/http://kurdishquestion.com/index.php/kurdistan/west-kurdistan/declaration-of-establishment-by-democratic-syria-forces/1179-declaration-of-establishment-by-democratic-syria-forces.html.

2   "The PKK is a foreign terrorist organization. That hasn't changed. And as I've said before, those Kurdish fighters who are effective against Daesh in Syria – while we're not providing direct arms (…)" "Daily Press Briefing," U.S. Department of State (April 28, 2016), https://2009-2017.state.gov/r/pa/prs/dpb/2016/04/256700.htm.

"In terms of the YPG, I'm not aware of any supply drops that we've done for them. We do continue to assist them (…) through air strikes." "Daily Press Briefing," U.S. Department of State (November 10, 2015), https://2009-2017.state.gov/r/pa/prs/dpb/2015/11/249394.htm.

"Certainly, we have provided air support, considerable air support, for a lot of these groups, including the YPG, as they take the fight to ISIL in northern Syria. And we'll continue to do that. But in terms of actual provision of ammunition and small arms ammunition, I can't speak to whether that'll happen or not." "Daily Press Briefing," U.S. Department of State (October 16, 2015) https://2009–2017.state.gov/r/pa/prs/dpb/2015/10/248295.htm.

"With respect to Turkey's comments about these photos, we've been very clear from this podium and elsewhere, our belief that the YPG is not connected to the PKK, which we have designated as a foreign terrorist organization. On the contrary, we believe the YPG, as well as other forces in Syria, in northern Syria, are effectively taking the fight to ISIL and we're going to continue to support them with our advise and assist operations there." "Daily Press Briefing," U.S. Department of State (May 27, 2016), https://2009–2017.state.gov/r/pa/prs/dpb/2016/05/257787.htm.

3 "The SDF, as it's called, has transformed from a primarily Kurdish force to a group that is 40 percent Arab, Assyrian, Christian, and others. Operations around Shaddadi have been a good example of how the SDF continues to operate effectively while absorbing these new diverse volunteers into the organization. I think it's also a testament to the kind of progress that is now tangible on the ground; that as other fighting forces recognize the progress that's being made by Syrian Democratic Forces that are benefitting from the advice and assistance of U.S. forces, that more are joining them." "Press Briefing," White House Press Secretary (March 8, 2016), https://obamawhitehouse.archives.gov/the-press-office/2016/03/08/press-briefing-press-secretary-Shaun-earnest-382016.

"As a reminder, the SDF, which I'll mention maybe again, is an umbrella group which consists of groups of Syrian Kurds, of the Syrian Arab coalition, Assyrians, and other ethnic groups in northern Syria that are all collectively focused on defeating ISIL." "Special briefing," Operation *Inherent Resolve* spokesman Colonel Steve Warren (January 14, 2016), https://2009–2017.state.gov/r/pa/prs/ps/2016/01/251261.htm.

4 "The first delivery, which included 50 tons of ammunition and rocket-propelled grenades, arrived in October 2015, just a month after the shift in policy. The munitions were airdropped to the Kurdish-dominated coalition within the Syrian Democratic Forces (…) SOCOM would purchase $238.5 million in weapons and ammunition from Bulgaria, Bosnia and Herzegovina, the Czech Republic, Kazakhstan, Poland, Romania, Serbia and Ukraine (…) SOCOM will buy an additional $172 million in arms this fiscal year. The shopping list includes tens of thousands of AK-47s and RPGs and hundreds of millions of pieces of ammunition." "Revealed: The Pentagon Is Spending Up To $2.2 Billion on Soviet-Style Arms for Syrian Rebels," OCCRP (September 12, 2017), https://www.occrp.org/en/makingakilling/the-pentagon-is-spending-2-billion-on-soviet-style-arms-for-syrian-rebels.

5 The fighting season describes the time war is possible due to geographical conditions. In Syria, the fighting season refers to the time during the summer when the desert is dry enough to move troops, logistics and heavy armor. Especially during the winter rains, the desert is too muddy for any large operation to succeed.

6 For details on this particular episode of American foreign policy, we recommend John Bulloch and Harvey Morris, *No Friends but the Mountains: The Tragic History of the Kurds* (London: Oxford University Press, 1992).

7 Anja Flach, Ercan Ayboga and Michael Knapp, *Revolution in Rojava, Frauenbewegung und Kommunalismus zwischen Krieg und Embargo* (Hamburg: VSA, 2015).

228 • AMERICA'S WAR IN SYRIA

Chapter 10

1   While the Kurdish *jineology* might be a form of feminism, it should not be mistaken with Western feminist discourse. Both discourses developed in parallel but in very different contexts. To us, it feels like *jineology* is Western feminism's big, strong sister. She does not protest against fascists but goes out at night and beats them up.

2   In her highly controversial series "Eichmann in Jerusalem" in *The New Yorker*, published in 1963, Hannah Arendt explained in essence how fascism worked and how the Holocaust could have happened in a supposedly cultured civilised country like Germany. Hannah Arendt, "Eichmann in Jerusalem," *The New Yorker* (February 16, 1963), https://www.newyorker.com/magazine/1963/02/16/eichmann-in-jerusalem-i.

3   Throughout his trial in Jerusalem, Eichmann insisted that he was not evil but just a normal man who followed orders like millions of others in the German Reich. Emphasis on his own banality was his defense. Hannah Arendt agreed with him; he was average and banal, and yet he was guilty.

4   To understand fascism, according to Hannah Arendt, we need to accept that it is not just a system of psychopathic murderers or evil people. Instead, fascism created a structure whereby regular people do their jobs and follow orders but are a tiny, seemingly innocent part of a murderous system.

5   For details on the recruiting of European teenagers and young adults into Daesh, see Anna Erelle, *In the Skin of a Jihadist: A Young Journalist Enters the ISIS Recruitment Network* (New York: Harper, 2015).

Chapter 11

1   U.S. Department of Defense, *Tactical Combat Casualty Care and Wound Treatment,* Edition 200, United States Army Medical Centre and School (Fort Sam Houston, Texas).

2   "Obama announces an additional 250 special operations forces to Syria," CNN (April 25th, 2016), https://edition.cnn.com/2016/04/24/politics/obama-special-operations-syria/.

Chapter 13

1   In the context of war, the term "casualty" usually refers to any person injured and/or dead. However, over time, the medic team used the term only for injured but living people. Dead SDF fighters or civilians would be referred to as "*şehîd*."

2   U.S. Department of Defense, *Tactical Combat Casualty Care and Wound Treatment.*

Chapter 14

1   "Force multiplication" is one of the tasks of U.S. Special Forces. Here it refers to a small team of American operators who train and equip local forces, coordinate air strikes directly from the ground, and so forth. Thus, the small special forces team multiplies the effectiveness of their local ally exponentially.

2   "Timeline: Attacks in France," BBC (July 26, 2016), https://www.bbc.com/news/world-europe-33288542.

3   "We've never provided weapons to the YPG. And we have provided equipment to vetted Arab elements of the Syrian Democratic Forces. This equipment has (…) included ammunition and other tactical equipment to assist the coalition's counter-ISIL operations." "Daily Press Briefing," U.S. Department of State (December 27, 2016), https://2009–2017.state.gov/r/pa/prs/dpb/2016/12/266077.htm.
"And we're obviously pleased to see this coalition of forces that includes Arabs and Kurds and Turkmen fighters beginning to focus on what's necessary to retake the city in Syria that ISIL has designated as their capital. (…) Those Syrian Democratic forces also benefit from the equipment that the United States and our coalition partners have provided them." "Press Gaggle," White House Press Secretary (November 7, 2016), https://obamawhitehouse.archives.gov/the-press-office/2016/11/07/press-gaggle-press-secretary-Shaun-earnest-en-route-ann-arbor-michigan.

4   "We do not associate [with] the YPG. What we have made clear about the YPG is that they are, among others, local forces who are combating very effectively Daesh in northern Syria. PKK is another matter." "Daily Press Briefing," U.S. Department of State (November 7, 2016), https://2009–2017.state.gov/r/pa/prs/dpb/2016/11/264175.htm.

5   "Syria conflict: US to send troops to help seize Raqqa from IS," BBC (December 10, 2016), https://www.bbc.com/news/world-middle-east-38274191.

Chapter 15

1   Joost Jongerden published a short and accessible paper on the complexity of Turkish water geopolitics.
Joost Jongerden, "Dams and Politics in Turkey: Utilizing Water, Developing Conflict," *Middle East Policy* 17, 1 (2010): 137–143.

2   Till Paasche, "Syrian and Iraqi Kurds: conflict and cooperation," *Middle East Policy* 22, 1 (2015): 77–88.

3   Murray Bookchin, *The Ecology of Freedom - The Emergence and Dissolution of Hierarchy* (Cheshire Books, 1982).

4   "Revolution ist nicht ein kurzer Akt, wo mal irgendwas geschieht und dann ist alles anders. Revolution ist ein langer komplizierter Prozess, wo der Mensch anders werden muss." Rudi Dutschke. Unreferenced video of a speech by Dutschke, https://www.youtube.com/watch?v=ON_uqhAkPnI. [last accessed December 9, 2019].

5   Phillips, *The Battle for Syria*.

6   Paasche, "Syrian and Iraqi Kurds: conflict and cooperation."

7   "Final Declaration of the Rojava – Northern Syria Democratic Federal System Constituent Assembly announcing the establishment of a federal democratic Rojava/Northern Syria," Rojava Information Centre (March 17, 2016), https://rojavainformationcenter.com/background/political-system-documents/.

8   "The Social Contract for the Democratic Federation of Northern Syria," Rojava Information Centre (December 29, 2016), https://rojavainformationcenter.com/background/political-system-documents/.

Chapter 16

1   "Marines have arrived in Syria to fire artillery in the fight for Raqqa," *The Washington Post* (March 8, 2017), https://www.washingtonpost.com/news/checkpoint/wp/2017/03/08/marines-have-arrived-in-syria-to-fire-artillery-in-the-fight-for-raqqa/.

2   "U.S. Is Sending 400 More Troops to Syria," *The New York Times* (March 9, 2017), https://www.nytimes.com/2017/03/09/world/middleeast/us-troops-syria.html.

3   "In Syria, we have trained over 8,500 members of the SDF. And just this year have delivered weapons and ammunition and over 400 vehicles and personal equipment for over 40,000 troops" "Department of Defense Press Briefing," Brigadier-General D. J. Anderson (July 6, 2017), https://www.inherentresolve.mil/Media-Library/Article/1249035/department-of-defense-press-briefing-by-brigadier-general-anderson-via-teleconf/ [accessed December 9th, 2019].

4   Carl von Clausewitz, *Vom Kriege. Hinterlassenes Werk des Generals Carl von Clausewitz* (Dümmler, Berlin, 1952).

5   "US-backed forces 'capture' Tabqa airbase from ISIL," Al Jazeera (March 27, 2017), https://www.aljazeera.com/news/2017/03/backed-forces-capture-tabqa-air-base-isil-170327033050002.html.

6   "Isis gives up Tabqa Dam in exchange for fighters' lives in deal with US-backed forces advancing on Raqqa," *Independent* (May 13, 2017), https://www.independent.co.uk/news/world/middle-east/isis-syria-raqqa-offensive-advance-tabqa-dam-deal-sdf-kurds-ypg-us-led-coalition-deal-deserted-a7733101.html. [accessed December 9, 2019]

7   "We avenged Yazidi women with the liberation of Tabqa," Rojda Felat (May 12, 2017), https://www.ypgrojava.org/Rojda-Felat%3A-We-avenged-Yazidi-women-with-the-liberation-of-Tabqa.

8   "Department of Defense Press Briefing," Colonel Ryan Dillon (September 7, 2017), https://www.defense.gov/Newsroom/Transcripts/Transcript/Article/1302517/department-of-defense-press-briefing-by-colonel-dillon-via-teleconference-from/.

9   "A Guide to the Islamic State's way of Urban Warfare," Modern War Institute at West Point (July 9, 2018), https://mwi.usma.edu/guide-islamic-states-way-urban-warfare/.

10 "Syria: Unprecedented investigation reveals US-led Coalition killed more than 1,600 civilians in Raqqa 'death trap'," Amnesty International (April 25, 2019), https://www.amnesty.org/en/latest/news/2019/04/syria-unprecedented-investigation-reveals-us-led-coalition-killed-more-than-1600-civilians-in-raqqa-death-trap/.

11 "Last Isis fighters in Raqqa broker deal to leave Syrian city – local official," *Guardian* (October 14, 2017), https://www.theguardian.com/world/2017/oct/14/last-isis-fighters-in-raqqa-seek-deal-to-leave-former-capital-in-syria.

12 "Syrian Democratic Forces declare total elimination of so-called caliphate and 100% territorial defeat of ISIS. On this unique day, we commemorate thousands of martyrs whose efforts made the victory possible. #SDFDefeatedISIS," Mustafa Bali (March 22, 2019), https://twitter.com/mustefabali/status/1109338396256813056?ref_src=twsrc%5Etfw%7Ctwcamp%5Etweetembed&ref_url=https%3A%2F%2Fwww.foxnews.com%2Fworld%2Fus-backed-syrian-force-declares-victory-over-islamic-state-end-of-caliphate.

13 "Final declaration of the founding congress of the Autonomous Administration of North and East Syria," Rojava Information Centre (September 6, 2018), https://rojavainformationcenter.com/background/political-system-documents/.

14 "[T]he SDF is (…) the clearance force and (…) the hold force; it's not the police force at all. But we (…) have anticipated the requirement [for a police force], and so have the SDF. (…) for instance in the Raqqa area, we're already starting to work on something that's called the Raqqa Internal Security Force. And this will be locals that will work for the Raqqa Council. So it'll work for local governance (sic), and they'll be ready to establish that policing function, (…) that safety and security element. (…) So that's a pretty good job of prediction. (…) But this is a great idea that the SDF has come up with, and we'll assist them in the training and preparation work for what's known as the RISF, or the Raqqa Internal Security Force." "Department of Defense Press Briefing," Brigadier-General D. J. Anderson (July 6, 2017), https://www.inherentresolve.mil/Media-Library/Article/1249035/department-of-defense-press-briefing-by-brigadier-general-anderson-via-teleconf/.

Chapter 17

1   One American soldier died from an IED on November 24, 2016. "Carter Offers Condolences for Fallen U.S. Service Member in Syria," Department of Defense (November 24, 2016), https://www.defense.gov/Explore/News/Article/Article/1012963/carter-offers-condolences-for-fallen-us-service-member-in-syria/. One American soldier died in a car accident on May 26, 2017. "US service member killed in Syria identified as 22-year-old from Georgia," ABC News (May 27, 2017), https://abcnews.go.com/International/us-service-member-killed-accident-syria/story?id=47658836.

One American and one British soldier were killed by an IED. "US and British troops killed in Syria blast," CNN (March 30, 2018), https://www.cnn.com/2018/03/30/politics/syria-coalition-ied/index.html.

Two American soldiers and two more Americans died in a SVBIED attack on January 16, 2019. "4 Americans among those killed in Syria attack claimed by ISIS," CNN (January 17, 2019), https://www.cnn.com/2019/01/16/politics/syria-attack-us-patrolled-city/index.html.

One American soldiers died of unknown reasons on April 22, 2019. "US service member dies in noncombat incident in Syria," *Military Times* (April 29, 2019), https://www.militarytimes.com/news/your-military/2019/04/29/us-service-member-dies-in-non-combat-incident-in-syria/.

2 "We support the Syrian Democratic Forces, and they've done a tremendous job in liberating Raqqa."
"Press Briefing," U.S. Department of State (November 9, 2017), https://www.state.gov/briefings/department-press-briefing-november-9-2017/.
"I also want to recognize our partner, the Syrian Democratic Forces (SDF), for their sacrifices in liberating approximately 50,000 square kilometers from ISIS, including what had been its de-facto capital of Raqqa. At the start of this year, ISIS was planning major external attacks from Raqqa; today, Raqqa is no longer an ISIS sanctuary, thanks to the SDF, which suffered over 1,000 casualties in an extremely difficult five-month battle." "Letter to D-ISIS Coalition Partners on the Progress of the Past Year," Brett McGurk (December 29, 2017), https://www.state.gov/letter-to-d-isis-coalition-partners-on-the-progress-of-the-past-year/
"We commend the bravery and sacrifice of the Syrian Democratic Forces." "Statement on the Continued Success of Operations To Defeat ISIS in Syria," Michael Pompeo (July 22, 2018), https://www.state.gov/statement-on-the-continued-success-of-operations-to-defeat-isis-in-syria/.

3 In this context, a hegemon, the senior partner in the relationship, guarantees its smaller, junior partner's protection in exchange for military, strategic, geographic, political, or economical benefits that the junior partner has to offer.

4 "We have defeated ISIS in Syria, my only reason for being there during the Trump Presidency," President Donald Trump (December 19, 2018), https://twitter.com/realdonaldtrump/status/1075397797929775105?lang=de.

5 "How Trump betrayed the General who defeated ISIS," Robin Wright (April 4, 2019), https://www.newyorker.com/news/dispatch/how-trump-betrayed-the-general-who-defeated-isis.

6 "In terms of the Kurds, what we're working with is with Turkey to have a safe zone of some length along the Turkish border where there would be no YPG forces, because Turkey feels very nervous about the YPG and their ties to the PKK." "Briefing With Special Representative for Syria Engagement and Special Envoy for the Global Coalition To Defeat ISIS Ambassador," James Jeffrey (March 25, 2019), https://www.state.gov/briefing-with-special-representative-for-syria-

engagement-and-special-envoy-for-the-global-coalition-to-defeat-isis-ambassador-james-jeffrey/.

7   "The YPG, again, the SDF is the military force which officially we deal with. But that SDF grew out of the YPG which is the military army of the PYD which is essentially the Syrian branch of the PKK. And it has various civilian operations. The SDC and the autonomous administration, and they've got new names. There's a whole group of names but it basically refers to the military and political local forces who are not predominantly but largely Kurdish." "Press Briefing," James Jeffrey (June 27, 2019), https://www.state.gov/press-briefing-with-ambassador-james-jeffrey/.

Chapter 18

1   "Statement from the Press Secretary," (October 6, 2019), https://www.whitehouse.gov/briefings-statements/statement-press-secretary-85/.

2   "…again said 'NO,' thinking, as usual, that the U.S. is always the 'sucker,' on NATO, on Trade, on everything. The Kurds fought with us, but were paid massive amounts of money and equipment to do so. They have been fighting Turkey for decades. I held off this fight fo…," President Donald Trump (October 7, 2019), https://twitter.com/realDonaldTrump/status/1181172465772482563.
    "…almost 3 years, but it is time for us to get out of these ridiculous Endless Wars, many of them tribal, and bring our soldiers home. WE WILL FIGHT WHERE IT IS TO OUR BENEFIT, AND ONLY FIGHT TO WIN. Turkey, Europe, Syria, Iran, Iraq, Russia and the Kurds will now have to…," President Donald Trump (October 7, 2019), https://twitter.com/realDonaldTrump/status/1181172467676565505.

3   Michael Gunter, *Out of Nowhere: The Kurds of Syria in Peace and War* (Oxford University Press, 2014).

4   "Turkey accused of recruiting ex-Isis fighters in their thousands to attack Kurds in Syria," *Independent* (February 7, 2018), https://www.independent.co.uk/news/world/middle-east/turkey-isis-afrin-syria-kurds-free-syrian-army-jihadi-video-fighters-recruits-a8199166.html.

5   "If We Have to Choose Between Compromise and Genocide, We Will Choose Our People," Mazloum Abadi (October 13, 2019), https://foreignpolicy.com/2019/10/13/kurds-assad-syria-russia-putin-turkey-genocide/.

6   "Putin, Erdogan hold tete-a-tete in Sochi," Ruptly, Russia (October 22, 2019), https://www.youtube.com/watch?v=Jy7ipV7Upbc.

7   "Analysis: What does the Adana deal mean for Turkey and Syria?," Al Jazeera (October 23, 2019), https://www.aljazeera.com/news/2019/10/analysis-adana-deal-turkey-syria-191022194719603.html.

8   "Trump: 'We have secured the Oil. Bringing soldiers home!'," *The Hill* (October 20, 2019), https://thehill.com/homenews/administration/466623-trump-we-have-secured-the-oil-bringing-soldiers-home.

9   "US to send 'mechanised forces' to Syrian oilfields," *Guardian* (October 25, 2019), https://www.theguardian.com/world/2019/oct/24/us-military-syria-tanks-oil-fields. "'Secure the oil': Trump's Syria strategy leaves Pentagon perplexed," *Guardian* (November 8, 2019), https://www.theguardian.com/us-news/2019/nov/08/secure-the-oil-trumps-syria-strategy-leaves-pentagon-perplexed.

10 "Russia," EIA, https://www.eia.gov/international/analysis/country/RUS [last accessed September 1, 2015].

11 "U.S. Crude Oil and Natural Gas Proved Reserves, Year-end 2019," EIA (January 11, 2021), https://www.eia.gov/naturalgas/crudeoilreserves/.

12 The U.S. Mission to the Syrian Democratic Council is Amercia's diplomatic link to the civilian councils and SDF
    "Together toward a democratic Syria," Syrian Democratic Council, U.S. Mission, https://www.syriandemocraticcouncil.us/ [last accessed September 26, 2021].

Conclusion

1   Martha Cottam, Joe Huseby, and Bruno Baltodano, *Confronting al Qaeda: The Sunni Awakening and American Strategy in al Anbar* (Lanham, Rowman and Littlefield, 2016).

2   "US expands air base in northern Syria for use in battle for Raqqa," *Stars and Stripes* (April 3, 2017), https://www.stripes.com/news/us-expands-air-base-in-northern-syria-for-use-in-battle-for-raqqa-1.461874.

3   To learn more about our fallen brother Kosta/Şehîd Kemal, please watch "Our Last Conversation – Erik Kostandinos Scurfield | Heval Kemal" on https://www.youtube.com/watch?v=nncW5B6Z_F0. Şehîd Namerin.

Index

9/11 attacks, 21, 36

AANES (Autonomous Administration of North and East Syria), 192–3, 207
Abdel Aziz, 4, 56, 57–60
Abdi, Mazloum, 205
Abu Layla, 89–90
Adana Agreement, 179, 206–7, 208
Afghanistan, 36–7, 38, 48
Afrin, *15*, 23–4, 182, 183
aircraft, Turkish: F16s, 85, 86
aircraft, U.S.:
    A-10 "Warthog," 109, 110, 111, 150
    AC-130, 3, 4, 52–3
Akif, Heval, 72, 76
Alawis, 64, 74
Ali, Heval, 137, 142, 147, 148
Amnesty International, 65–6, 192
Anderson, Brig-Gen D. J., 190, 193
Arab fighters, 56–7, 91–2, 190–1
    and SDC, 80, 82
    and SDF, 134, 135
Arab lands, 63–7
Arab Spring, 38, 181
Arendt, Hannah, 117, 118
Armanc, Heval, 74–5, 161
arms supplies, 90–1, 190, 212
Asayîş (police/security forces), 49–50, 112, 124–5, 126, 187, 214
    and Manbij, 158–9, 160
al-Assad, Bashar, 180, 182, 206–7

al-Assad, Hafez, 178–9, 180, 181, 205
Assad, Lake, 191
ATGMs (anti-tank guided missiles), 48
Azadi, Hevala, 39–40, 72

al-Bab, 133, 135, 170, 172
Balikh River, 63–6, 73, 82–3
Barzani tribe, 10
Bawer, Heval, 74–5, 98, 161
Baz, *see* Paasche, Till "Baz"
berms, 2, 26–8, 30, 51, 59
Bin Laden, Osama, 17
Bookchin, Murray, 180
Britain, *see* Great Britain
British Special Forces, 37–8, 168, 169, 170

Caliphate, *see* Daesh
casualties, *see* medics
Chechens, 95
child soldiers, 41, 59–60
Christians, 50–1, 101, 102
CIA (Central Intelligence Agency), 48
civilians, 1, 75–6, 119, 192
    and Arab lands, 63–4, 65
    and Manbij, 157, 158–60, 170–1
    and al-Shaddadi, 107–8, 112, 116
Cizire, 23–4, 60, 182, 183
    and maps, *15*, *33*, *120*
CJTF-OIR (Combined Task Force—Operation Inherent Resolve), 86,

93, 106, 147, 153–4, 157, 190, 192, 212–13; *see also* operations: *Inherent Resolve*
clothing, 84–5
communication, 32

Daesh, 2, 3, 4, 5–6, 9, 11–12, 211–13
  and Arab lands, 63–4
  and ATGMs, 48
  and Christian communities, 50–1
  and Euphrates crossing, 139–40
  and first offensive, 57–8
  and Hasake, 73–4, 75
  and Iraq, 195–6
  and Manbij, 148, 149, 150–7, 161–3, 171–2
  and Mosul, 11–12, 13–14
  and Nice attack, 170
  and Paris attacks, 67, 92, 93
  and Raqqa, 191–2
  and Rojava, 23–4, 26–8
  and al-Shaddadi, 99, 103, 109–17
  and Shingal, 29–31, 86, 87
  and Sunnis, 82
  and system, 117–19
  and Tel Abiat, 71–3
  and Tishreen Dam, 93–5
  and Turkey, 133
  and U.S. air strikes, 52–3
  and USA, 203
  and Yazidis, 17–18, 19, 25–6
  and YPG/YPJ, 182
Deir Ezzor, 192, 195
democratic confederalism, 81–3, 121, 135, 183–8
  and PKK, 180–2, 183–4
  and USA, 196, 214–15
Dohuk, 124–5
Dutschke, Rudi, 181

embargos, 65
Erbil, 10, 11, 18, 69–70, 124–6

Erdoğan, Recep Tayyip, 203, 204–5, 206, 207
Euphrates River, 133, 134–40, 177–8

fascism, 25–6
Felat, Hevala Rojda, 191
Foxx, John, 1–2, 4–5, 21–2, 26–9, 215–16
  and Euphrates crossing, 135–7, 138–40, 142–4
  and Manbij, 146–9, 152–7, 159–60, 165
  and Northern Sun Battalion, 89–90
  and PKK, 19
  and al-Shaddadi, 103, 105, 106, 107–8, 115–16, 117
  and Shingal, 29–31, 32, 86
  and transit base, 121, 122, 123
  and Trump, 204
France, 4–5, 67, 92–3
French special forces, 4, 67, 92–3, 115, 212
  and Manbij, 165, 170
FSA (Free Syrian Army), 22, 205

GAP (Southeastern Anatolia Project), 177–8
genocide, 9, 17–18, 47, 123
Germany, 25–6
Great Britain, 4–5, 24, 126; *see also* British Special Forces

Hasake, 73–6, 182
Hezbollah, 48, 68, 74, 75
Hisbah, 14
al-Hol offensive, 87–8, *120*, 211–12

IEDs (improvised explosive devices), 1, 6, 71, 163
Iran, 9, 10, 48, 195
Iraq, 9, 10–11, 178, 182, 195–6, 214; *see also* KDP; Mosul; Shingal

Iraq War, 21, 36–7
Iraqi Army, 3, 11, 13, 18–19
ISIS (Islamic State), *see* Daesh
Islamists, *see* Daesh
Ištar, 107

Jaza, *33*
Jefferson, 39, 40–2, 71–2, 73–5
    and front line, 49–50, 51–2, 58
Jeffrey, James, 198
Jihadi John, 95
John, *see* Foxx, John

KDP (Kurdistan Democratic Party), 10,
    22, 123–6
Khalaf, Hevala Hevrin, 204
Khasham, battle of, 197
Kirkuk, 11, 13, 205
Kobane, *15*, 23–4, 30, *33*, 45, 60, *120*
    and autonomy, 182, 183
Kosta, *see* Scurfield, Erik Kostandinos
    "Kosta"
Kurdistan Region in Iraq, 9, 10
Kurds, 3–4, 9–11, 173
    and SDF, 81–3, 84
    and Turkey, 177, 204–5
    see also Peshmerga; PKK; YPG; YPJ

Lebanon, 178
Lenny, 136, 138–9
    and Manbij, 146, 148, 149, 152–5,
    156–7
Libya, 22

Manbij, 1, 4–5, 133, 134, 135, 212–13
    and campaign, 145–65, 167–72
Maoists, 68
maps:
    and 2014 front lines, *15*, *33*
    and 2015 front lines, *43*, *61*
    and 2016 front lines, *120*, *174*
    and 2019 front lines, *199*

and 2021 *cantons*, *200*, *209*
martyrdom, 41, 45–6
Matson, Jordan, 22
Mattis, Gen James, 197, 204
Mazlum, Heval, 68–9, 71–2
McGurk, Brett, 197
medics, 31–2, 76, 121–3, 141–2
    and Manbij, 145–6, 150, 158–60,
    162–5, 167–72
    and TMU, 127–32
Mirkan, Şehîd Arin, 45–6
MLKP (Marxist Leninist Komünist
    Parti), 86
MMC (Manbij Military Council),
    172, 189
mortars, 167
Mosul, 3, 9, 11–14, 45
Murray, Shaun, 2–3, 19, 35–8, 88–9,
    216–17
    and Arab fighters, 56–7
    and front line, 49–50, 51–2, 53, 58
    and Peshmerga, 69–70
    and prison, 124–6
    and Rojava constitution, 184–5,
    186–7
    and al-Shaddadi, 102–3, 105, 106,
    115–16
    and Shingal, 85–7
    and Tel Erfan, 40–2, 46
    and Tev Dem, 121–2
    and Tishreen Dam, 93–5
    and transit camp, 38–9, 40
    and weaponry, 90–1

Northern Ireland, 35–6
Northern Sun Battalion, 89–90
al-Nusra, 56, 182

Obama, Barack, 3, 4, 11, 86, 172
    and air strikes, 31, 47
    and SDF, 80, 96, 173
    and special forces, 211, 212, 213
    and Yazidis, 17, 18

Öcalan, Abdullah, 22–3, 91, 107, 178,
180–1
and imprisonment, 179–80
oil, 10, 207
operations:
Euphrates Shield (2016), 172, 189
Inherent Resolve (2015), 2–3, 4, 68
Al-Jazeera Storm (2016), 195–6
Sandstorm (Chammal) (2015), 67, 93
Sheddad (2016), 4–5
Wrath of Euphrates (2017), 189–93
Wrath of Khabur (2016), 101–6,
107–17

Paasche, Till "Baz," 1–3, 5, 6, 9, 25–6,
217
and Arab fighters, 56–7
and Erbil, 18
and Euphrates crossing, 138
and front line, 49–50, 51–2, 53, 58
and Hasake, 73–6
and Manbij, 145–6, 158–60, 163,
164–5, 167, 168–9, 171
and Mosul, 11–12
and PKK, 183
and Rojava, 20, 81, 83
and al-Shaddadi, 102–3, 104–5,
109–12, 113, 114–15
and al-Shaddadi, 99
and taburs, 97–8
and Tel Abiat, 64, 65–6, 67, 72
and Tel Erfan, 40–2, 46
and Tev Dem, 122–3, 126–7
and TMU, 127–8, 129–31
and transit camp, 38–40
Peshmerga, 3, 10, 11–13, 18, 69–70
and Shingal, 31, 86
and USA, 47–8
and Yazidis, 19
Petraeus, Gen David, 214
PKK (Kurdistan Workers' Party), 3,
22–4, 177, 178–82

and Adana Agreement, 206–7
and democratic confederalism, 183–4
and Shingal, 31, 86
and Turkey, 47
and women, 106–7
and Yazidis, 19–20
and YPG/YPJ, 79–80, 83–4
see also Öcalan, Abdullah
PUK (Patriotic Union of Kurdistan),
10, 22
Putin, Vladimir, 205, 206, 207–8
PYD (Democratic Union Party), 47

al-Qaida, 56, 57
Qamishlo, 26, 90, 98, 122, 126–7,
181, 184

Ramadan, 73–4
Raqqa, 83, 96, 190, 191–3, 213
reports, 121–3
Rezan, Heval, 128–9, 162–3, 184
RISF (Raqqa Internal Security Forces),
193
Rojava, 20, 23–4, 26–9, 79–80
and constitution, 183–8
and SDF, 81–4, 87–9
and USA, 46–7, 196–7, 203–4
see also AANES
Rojin, Hevala, 142–3, 148
Royal Marines, 24
Roza, Hevala, 141–2, 146, 164, 167–8
Russia, 74, 98, 195, 206–8
Rustem, Heval, 99–100, 103, 105
and al-Shaddadi, 109, 110, 111, 112,
113, 116

SAA (Syrian Arab Army), 172
Saddam Hussein, 13, 17, 18, 36, 205
schools, 74, 75–6
Scurfield, Erik Kostandinos "Kosta,"
24–5, 26–7, 29, 31–2, 122, 215–16
SDC (Syrian Democratic Council),
80, 193

SDF (Syrian Democratic Forces), 4–5,
79, 80–5, 211–12
and arms, 90–1
and Iraq, 195–6
and Manbij, 147, 151–2, 155–7,
160–2, 163, 169, 170–1, 171–2
and PKK, 177
and Raqqa, 191–3
and Rojava, 87–9
and Russia, 98
and al-Shaddadi, 100, 101, 102, 103,
109–17
and SVBIEDs, 140–1
and Tabqa, 190–1
and Tishreen Dam, 93–4, 95–6
and Turkey, 133–4
and USA, 173, 189, 197–8, 208
and YPG/YPJ, 134–5
see also Northern Sun Battalion
al-Shaddadi, 98–9, 100, 101–6, 107–19,
212
map, 120
Shaun, see Murray, Shaun
al-Sheitaat tribe, 195
Shia militias, 48; see also Hezbollah
Shingal (Sinjar), 10, 17–20, 25, 29–31,
85–7
and map, 33
smuggling, 22, 38, 85, 90, 118–19, 122,
123–4
Sochi Agreement, 206–8
Şoreş, Heval, 109, 110–12, 113, 114, 131
Sulaymaniyah, 10
Sunni Islam, 9, 10, 64, 82
SVBIEDs (suicide vehicle-borne
improvised explosive devices), 13–14,
48, 59, 72
and Euphrates crossing, 140–1
and Hasake, 75
and Manbij, 156, 161–2
and Raqqa, 192
and al-Shaddadi, 103–4

Syria, 9, 10, 22, 178–80
and civil war, 181–2
and Iraq, 195–6
and Sochi Agreement, 206–8
see also Deir Ezzor; Hasake; Manbij;
maps; Raqqa; Rojava; SDF; al-
Shaddadi; Tabqa; Tel Abiat; Tel
Erfan; Tel Tamir; Tishreen Dam

Tabqa, 190–1
taburs (assault units), 58–60, 97–8,
212–13
and Arab fighters, 91–2
and al-Shaddadi, 105–6
takems (assault units), 58–9
Talabani family, 10
Tekoşer, Heval, 129
Tel Abiat, 4, 60, 63–9, 71–3, 82–3
Tel Erfan, 40–2, 46
Tel Hamis, 32
Tel Tamir, 2–3, 40, 43, 49–52, 55–6
Tev Dem, 121–3, 183, 184–7
Tigris River, 177–8
Tishreen Dam, 90, 93–6, 211–12
map, 120
TMU (Tactical Medical Unit), 127–32
TOW (tube-launched, optically-tracked,
wire-guided) missiles, 48
Trump, Donald, 189, 197, 198, 207, 213
and Turkey, 203, 204–5
Tuaregs, 56
Turkey, 3, 5, 9, 10
and Adana Agreement, 206–7
and al-Bab, 170, 172–3
and border, 133–4
and commanders, 84
and GAP water dam, 177–8
and invasion, 203–6
and Maoists, 68
and Nusaybin, 123
and PKK, 23, 47, 178–9
and SDF, 94, 96, 134–5, 197

and Shingal, 86
and USA, 49, 60, 79

UK, see Great Britain
United Nations (UN), 86–7, 185–6
United States of America (USA), 3–5,
   9–11, 36–7, 48–9
   and arms supplies, 90–1, 190
   and SDF, 98
   and withdrawal, 196–8, 203–4, 207,
      208, 215
   and YPG/YPJ, 60, 67–8, 79
   see also Obama, Barack
U.S. Air Force (USAF), 18, 46–7, 52–3,
   59; see also aircraft, U.S.
U.S. Army Rangers, 189, 197, 203, 207,
   213, 214
U.S. Marine Corps, 2, 21–2, 106
U.S. Special Forces, 10, 36, 49, 58,
   96, 131
   and Euphrates crossing, 136, 138
   and liberation, 214
   and Manbij, 165, 167–9, 170, 172–3
   and Tabqa, 190–1
   and training, 189, 190
Uzbeks, 95

war crimes, 65–6
weaponry, 40, 47; see also arms supplies
women, see YPJ

YAT (SDF Anti-Terror Units), 156,
   189–90
Yazidis, 17–20, 25, 29, 47, 86, 87
YBS (Yazidi militia), 86
YJA STAR, 106–7
YPG (Kurdish People's Defense Units),
   2, 3, 4, 5, 58–60, 182

and child soldiers, 41
and Manbij, 146–50, 152–60
and PKK, 79–80, 83–4
and Putin, 208
and Rojava, 27–9, 81
and SDF, 84–5, 95–6, 134–5
and al-Shaddadi, 101
and Tel Abiat, 63–9
and Turkey, 205–6
and USA, 49
and withdrawal, 198
and Yazidis, 20
and YPJ, 55–6
see also Mazlum, Heval
YPJ (Kurdish Women's Protection
   units), 2, 3, 4, 5, 143–4
and Daesh, 182
and Manbij, 146–9, 163
and martyrs, 45–6
and PKK, 79–80, 83–4
and Putin, 208
and Rojava, 27–9, 81
and SDF, 84–5, 95–6, 134–5
and al-Shaddadi, 101, 103–4, 106,
   107–8, 109–10, 113–15
and taburs, 58–60
and Tel Abiat, 63–4, 65–9
and Turkey, 204, 205–6
and USA, 49
and withdrawal, 198
and Yazidis, 20
and YPG, 55–6

Zagros, Heval, 97, 98–9, 127–8,
   129, 138
and Manbij, 145–6, 167, 168
and al-Shaddadi, 103, 105, 115–16
and transit base, 121, 122, 123, 126–7